TEACHER'S

EVERY DAY COUNTS™

CALENDAR MATH

Andy Clark

•

Janet G. Gillespie

•

Patsy F. Kanter

GRADE
6

GREAT SOURCE
EDUCATION GROUP

A Houghton Mifflin Company
Wilmington, Massachusetts

Acknowledgments

Special thanks to

- **my colleagues and mentors:** Allyn Snider, who introduced me to materials by Robert Wirtz and Marilyn Burns when I needed it; Jan Gillespie, for inviting me into a select group of 3rd grade teachers trying out a *Math Their Way* curriculum; Millie Johnson, whose workshops made all of us realize how much fun math can be; Martin Gardner, whose books taught me more mathematics than I ever learned in school.
- **my co-authors:** Jan Gillespie and Patsy Kanter, for envisioning the idea for a calendar program.
- **my family:** Joseph, Daniel, and Aaron, who always insisted that I be their papa, not their teacher; and most of all to my partner, friend, and wife Cheryl, who always inspires and supports me in every endeavor, and without whom none of this could be written.
- **the Great Source team:** Rick Duthe, Sandra Easton, Susan Rogalski, and Richard Spencer, for making this book a reality.

Credits

Cover Design: Dinardo Design
Cover Illustration: Rob Dunlavey
Electronic Art: PC&F, Inc.

Copyright © 1998 by Great Source Education Group, Inc. All rights reserved.

Permission to reproduce the Teaching Resources pages is granted to the users of *Every Day Counts Calendar Math*. No other part of this work may be reproduced or transmitted in any form or by any means, electronic or mechanical, including photocopying and recording, or by any information storage or retrieval system without the prior written permission of Great Source Education Group, Inc., unless such copying is expressly permitted by federal copyright law. Address inquiries to Permissions, Great Source Education Group, Inc., 181 Ballardvale Street, Wilmington, MA 01887.

Printed in the United States of America

Every Day Counts is a trademark of Houghton Mifflin Company

International Standard Book Number: 0-669-44056-6

1 2 3 4 5 6 7 8 9 0 VCG 02 01 00 99 98 97

URL address: http://www.greatsource.com/

EVERY DAY COUNTS

CALENDAR MATH

 WHAT IS *EVERY DAY COUNTS™ CALENDAR MATH*?

 AN INTERACTIVE MATH BULLETIN BOARD

Every Day Counts *Calendar Math* provides 10 to 15 minutes of supplementary math instruction each day. It revolves around a simple bulletin board containing a Calendar, a Counting Tape to count the days of school, and other elements that change throughout the year, such as Clocks, Coin Counters, and Graphs. Each day students and their teachers use current data from the various elements on the bulletin board to get a new angle on mathematical relationships. It's almost like looking through a kaleidoscope, with every turn bringing a new array of relationships to examine. While discussing the data from the bulletin board for a few minutes a day, students at every grade level get the opportunity to analyze data, perceive patterns, explore mathematical relationships, and communicate their thinking.

Calendar Math was strongly influenced by the ideas of Donna Burk, Allyn Snider, Paula Symonds, the late Mary Baratta-Lorton, and the late Robert Wirtz. The Calendar ideas, gathered from the work of Baratta-Lorton, Burk, Snider, and Symonds, convinced us that daily examination of mathematical relationships could help children of all grade levels build mathematical

competence and confidence. Robert Wirtz's strong belief that children could learn from sharing their discoveries encouraged us to make students' observations and thinking the driving force behind our activities.

We began developing different activities involving a high level of student interaction that could be incorporated daily. Therefore, *Calendar Math* provides different elements for each grade level, during each month of the school year. These elements focus on mathematical relationships central to the curriculum at each grade. As a result, kindergartners to sixth graders are offered daily exposure to place value, measurement, time, money, mental math, geometry, estimation, patterns and functions, graphing, and statistics. This exposure is visual, hands-on, and interactive.

 WHY USE *EVERY DAY COUNTS CALENDAR MATH*?

 A LITTLE TIME = A LOT OF MATH

Our experience with elementary students has taught us that constructing mathematical understandings takes time—often more than a unit of study can provide. With *Calendar Math*, students have the entire year to explore critical concepts at their grade level through multiple experiences. For example, in the primary grades, developing an understanding of how our base ten system works is critical. To support this, the Daily Depositor and Counting Tape provide concrete experiences with grouping, counting, and recording hundreds, tens, and ones. In grade 5, students are guided through a difficult transition by investigating increments with the Fraction A Day and Daily Decimal elements. These important concepts are presented over an extended time rather than in one unit, providing the opportunity to preview as well as review them throughout the year.

Q > HOW IS *EVERY DAY COUNTS CALENDAR MATH* SPECIAL?

A > CLASSROOM DISCUSSION: THE HEART OF *EVERY DAY COUNTS CALENDAR MATH*

Calendar Math gives students the opportunity to talk about what they see and to understand and learn from one another. Many sample questions provide a springboard for classroom discussion. The purpose of asking so many questions is to encourage children's thinking. Asking students to share the various ways they arrived at answers helps them see that there are many ways to work with numbers and to approach problems. They also see that the same way of working out a problem may be explained in several different ways. Class discussions are rich in communication and language when students share their thinking and learn from one another.

Q > HOW IS *EVERY DAY COUNTS CALENDAR MATH* ORGANIZED?

A > BY GRADE LEVEL, BY MONTHS

Each grade level book is organized by month. On the opening page for each month, there is a picture of what the elements on the Every Day Bulletin Board might look like at some point during the month. A brief overview of suggested elements and activities for the month follows. When each element is introduced, you will find the **FOCUS** for that activity, a list of **MATERIALS**, an explanation of how to conduct an **UPDATE PROCEDURE** daily, and suggestions for encouraging **DISCUSSION** throughout the month. These discussions invite students to analyze the accumulating data, make predictions, and justify their thinking. Sometimes there are **HELPFUL HINTS** for preparing or enhancing an activity. These have often originated from teachers using the elements of *Calendar Math* in their classrooms.

Q > *EVERY DAY COUNTS CALENDAR MATH* HAS SO MANY ACTIVITIES. HOW CAN I CHOOSE?

A > START SMALL AND ADD ON LATER

Skim the introduction to each month and thumb through the book to see the range of elements that make up *Calendar Math* at your grade level. The first year we suggest you start small and limit the number of elements you share with the class. Your preparation can be minimized, and your primary focus can be on facilitating students' discussion. We have found that less is often more when getting started with these new activities.

You might begin with the yearlong elements—the Counting Tape and Calendar. Or you might choose an element that provides experience with a topic students have had difficulty with in the past. Or you might simply pick elements that are most interesting to you. Your interest will most likely have a positive effect on your students' involvement.

HOW DO I GET THE MATERIALS FOR *EVERY DAY COUNTS CALENDAR MATH?*

 ## PURCHASE THE KIT

Materials for *Calendar Math* are available in a kit. There is a section in the back of the Teacher's Guide with Teaching Resources copymasters to be used to accompany the elements. Photocopying and using clear pockets or lamination on these copymasters will allow for daily updating by using colored markers. Small vinyl pockets or photo album pockets can function as clear pockets, to hold money or objects. Keeping a small supply box with pushpins and markers near your Calendar is very handy. The elements used throughout *Calendar Math* are the Calendar and the Counting Tape. Elements featured throughout the year in Grade 6 include the Daily Pattern and the Daily Variable. Below are explanations for using each of these elements:

CALENDAR: Use the Every Day Calendar and Month Strips provided in the kit. Make a $\frac{3}{4}$-inch horizontal cut at the top of each square on the Calendar. This way the Calendar Pieces can be attached to the Calendar with paper clips. When placing patterns on the calendar, use the numbered Calendar Pieces provided in the kit or create Calendar Pieces with the Teaching Resources copymasters in the back of the book. Feel free to use your own cutouts to form a different pattern each month.

COUNTING TAPE AND PERCENT CIRCLE: Use the adding machine tape provided in the kit and the Percent Circle copymaster in the back of the Teacher's Guide. This element is designed to allow students to see equivalent decimals, fractions, and percents for each day they are in school. Two-inch squares of construction paper or self-stick removable notes will also be needed. By using various colors, the Counting Tape can be made more visually attractive for the students.

DAILY PATTERN: The patterns are derived from displays of geometrical shapes created by the teacher for this purpose. Students can easily assist in this task. It is helpful for the students if the shapes can be posted on pieces of construction paper and displayed around the classroom. So that the pattern is easily visible to all students, large sheets of newsprint should be used to create charts outlining the pattern for each month.

DAILY VARIABLE: Students are given a different expression each month using the date as a variable. They are also given the opportunity to graph many of these expressions. Large sheets of newsprint and graph paper will be needed to make the daily changes in the value of the expressions visible to the students.

 ## HOW DO I GET STARTED WITH *EVERY DAY COUNTS CALENDAR MATH?*

 ## CREATE THE *EVERY DAY COUNTS CALENDAR MATH* BULLETIN BOARD IN A HIGHLY VISIBLE AREA OF YOUR ROOM

First, you will need to choose a place in your room where you can create a bulletin board that is easily accessible to you and your students. Many teachers who use *Calendar Math* do not hang everything in one location. Sometimes graphs are placed across the room or the Counting Tape is hung under the chalkboard. What really counts is that you and your students can see and interact easily at the bulletin board. Then, decide which elements you want to begin with and have those pieces ready for the first day of school or as soon thereafter as possible. Students in 6th grade can update many elements of *Calendar Math* by themselves. They can also help create some of the special materials needed throughout the year.

EVERY DAY COUNTS

CALENDAR MATH

TABLE OF CONTENTS

GRADE 6

AUGUST/SEPTEMBER

GETTING STARTED

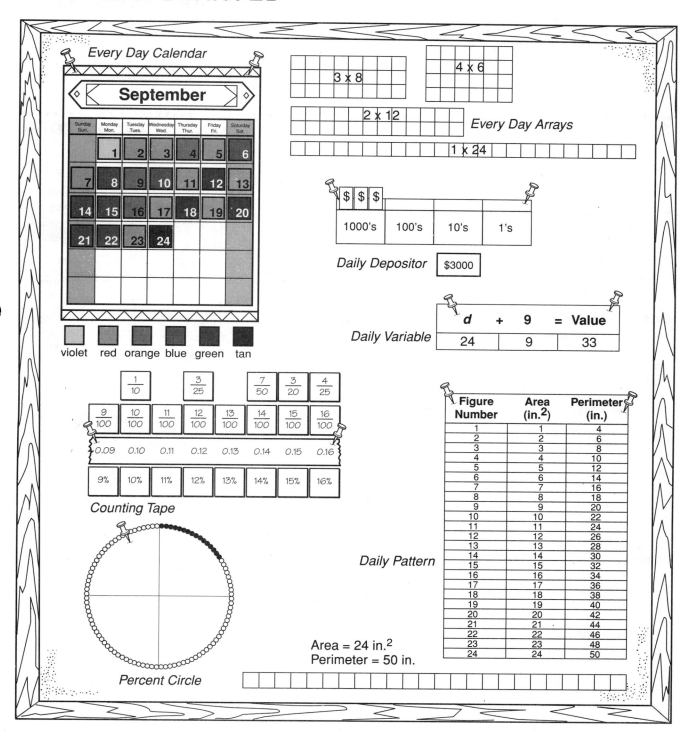

Every Day Calendar

September

Sunday Sun.	Monday Mon.	Tuesday Tues.	Wednesday Wed.	Thursday Thur.	Friday Fri.	Saturday Sat.
	1	2	3	4	5	6
7	8	9	10	11	12	13
14	15	16	17	18	19	20
21	22	23	24			

violet red orange blue green tan

3 x 8

4 x 6

2 x 12

Every Day Arrays

1 x 24

1000's	100's	10's	1's
$ $ $			

Daily Depositor $3000

Daily Variable

d	+ 9	= Value
24	9	33

Counting Tape

$\frac{1}{10}$	$\frac{3}{25}$		$\frac{7}{50}$	$\frac{3}{20}$	$\frac{4}{25}$

$\frac{9}{100}$	$\frac{10}{100}$	$\frac{11}{100}$	$\frac{12}{100}$	$\frac{13}{100}$	$\frac{14}{100}$	$\frac{15}{100}$	$\frac{16}{100}$

0.09 0.10 0.11 0.12 0.13 0.14 0.15 0.16

9%	10%	11%	12%	13%	14%	15%	16%

Percent Circle

Daily Pattern

Figure Number	Area (in.^{2})	Perimeter (in.)
1	1	4
2	2	6
3	3	8
4	4	10
5	5	12
6	6	14
7	7	16
8	8	18
9	9	20
10	10	22
11	11	24
12	12	26
13	13	28
14	14	30
15	15	32
16	16	34
17	17	36
18	18	38
19	19	40
20	20	42
21	21	44
22	22	46
23	23	48
24	24	50

Area = 24 in.^{2}
Perimeter = 50 in.

Only a few elements of Every Day Counts Calendar Math are used in the first month of school so that students can become aware of the procedures that will be used all year. These elements will focus on a few key topics, including a review of factors, an introduction to percent, and the concept of variable. The Every Day Calendar, Every Day Array, Counting Tape and Percent Circle, Daily Pattern, Daily Variable, and Daily Depositor will be introduced in September. Begin the Counting Tape and Percent Circle on the first day of school, whenever that is for your school.

> You may choose to begin with only three or four elements and add other elements next month. Three elements that are especially useful to begin with are the Every Day Calendar, the Daily Arrays, and the Counting Tape and Percent Circle. The Daily Pattern can be added in the second or third week of school.

EVERY DAY ELEMENT

CALENDAR

violet red orange blue green

FOCUS
▶ Analyzing and predicting patterns
▶ Mastering factors and multiples
▶ Analyzing prime, composite, and square numbers
▶ Recognizing factors for numbers to 30

MATERIALS
Every Day Calendar, September Month Strip, September Calendar Pieces, or Square Cutouts (TR1) and colored markers

SUGGESTED PATTERN FOR SEPTEMBER
The September Calendar Pieces show the number of factors for each date. The number 1, being a unique number, is indicated with a violet square. Prime numbers are red squares. Numbers having four factors are blue squares, those with six factors are green squares, and those with eight factors are tan squares. Square numbers except for 1 are orange squares.

OVERVIEW
Throughout the year, the Every Day Calendar will be used to investigate number theory, particularly issues surrounding factors and divisibility. The Calendar will also be used to present investigations into attributes of geometric figures.

In September, students will attempt to discover the reason for the pattern of Calendar Pieces. The color of each piece depends on the number of factors for the date. As students recognize this relationship, they will be asked to predict the color for subsequent days. Eventually, students will be responsible for discovering the color for the day on their own.

FREQUENCY
Update daily. Once a week allow extended discussion. By the third week, students should be able to predict the color for the day accurately.

UPDATE PROCEDURE

Display the Every Day Calendar with the September Month Strip attached. Each day, add the September Calendar Piece for the date. If you choose to use the Square Cutouts (TR1), simply write the date with the appropriate colored marker. Post the Calendar Pieces for the weekend dates on Monday. The color scheme for September appears below.

1 = violet
2, 3, 5, 7, 11, 13, 17, 19, 23, 29 (prime numbers) = red
6, 8, 10, 14, 15, 21, 22, 26, 27 (4 factors) = blue
4, 9, 16, 25 (odd number of factors, square numbers) = orange
12, 18, 20, 28 (6 factors) = green
24, 30 (8 factors) = tan

DISCUSSION FOR THE BEGINNING OF THE MONTH

On the first day of school, put up the September Calendar Pieces through the current date, or use the Square Cutouts (TR1) and write the dates with the appropriate colored marker. For example, if school begins on September 5, put up the pieces for the first five days. Explain that you will use the Calendar to demonstrate a special math topic or pattern. Ask students to offer explanations for the color arrangement of the first few days. Write these student explanations next to the Calendar. Ask students to check for reasonableness. Invite them to continue to investigate the reason behind the pattern as the days continue. Don't indicate whether an explanation is accurate yet. Before the twelfth day, ask students if they think more than four colors will be required for the month. As students discover the reason for the pattern, let them determine the color for the day before posting the new Calendar Piece.

SAMPLE DISCUSSION FOR THE EIGHTEENTH DAY OF THE MONTH

Teacher: Today is the eighteenth day of the month. Can you tell me what colors we can't use today?
Student: Red.
Teacher: Why?
Student: Because 18 is divisible by other numbers.
Teacher: What does that mean?
Student: It can be divided into 3 piles of 6.
Teacher: Who can explain why that is important?
Student: 18 has lots of factors, like 6 & 3 and 9 & 2.
Teacher: So why can't we use red?
Student: All of the red numbers have only two factors.
Teacher: Does anyone know what these numbers are called?
Student: Prime numbers.

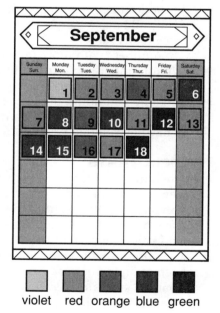

Here are some additional questions that can be used for discussion.

▶ Which color is most common?
▶ Which color is least common?
▶ What do we call the numbers in the red squares? (Prime numbers.) How can we define what a prime number is? (It has only two factors, the number 1 and itself.)
▶ How do the numbers in blue squares differ from the numbers in red squares? (They have more than two factors, and can be divided into equal piles of other numbers.)
▶ Which numbers are in orange squares? (4, 9, 16) What do you notice about these numbers? (They are square numbers.)
▶ Why do you think the number 1 is in a square that is a different color from all the others? (It is a unique number because it isn't prime or composite. It is a square number.)

DISCUSSION FOR THE END OF THE MONTH

These questions can be used to encourage discussion.

▶ How many numbers between 1 and 10 are in red squares? (4) How many between 11 and 20? (4) How about between 21 and 30? (2) Is there any pattern to the frequency of the prime numbers? (No, but there are fewer of them as the numbers get larger.)
▶ What will the next prime number be? (31)
▶ Are there any consecutive prime numbers? (2 and 3 are the only ones.)
▶ What do the numbers 12, 18, 20, and 28 have in common? (They all have 6 factors.)
▶ How many factors do 24 and 30 have? (8) Do you think there are numbers with more factors?
▶ What number between 1 and 100 do you think has the greatest number of factors?
▶ What do you notice about the number of factors of square numbers that is different from other composite numbers? (They have an odd number of factors.)

HELPFUL HINTS

▶ Encourage students to make conjectures. Don't worry if student predictions are not always correct. Instead, look for reasonableness. Point out to the students that mathematicians have been investigating prime numbers for thousands of years and still can't predict their order.
▶ Questions about which numbers have the same number of factors and which factors two numbers have in common will sharpen student understanding of factors. Create additional questions like these to encourage further discussion.
▶ Invite students to find efficient ways to discover all the factors of a particular number.
▶ Allow students sufficient time to make discoveries on their own, rather than giving out information too quickly.

EVERY DAY ELEMENT

FOCUS
▶ Visualizing numbers as rectangular arrays
▶ Mastering factors and multiples
▶ Analyzing prime, composite, and square numbers to 30

MATERIALS
10 by 10 Squared Paper (TR2), scissors, tape

OVERVIEW
Use this element in conjunction with the Every Day Calendar pattern to review prime and composite numbers and factors with students. This element enables students to visualize factors by having them construct rectangular arrays for quantities. Students use the date to discover all the rectangles that can be made from that quantity. For example, on the twelfth of the month, students cut out rectangles that are 1×12, 2×6, and 3×4. A rectangle that is congruent, or that can be rotated to look the same as another, is not considered to be a different rectangle. A 1×12 rectangle is considered the same as a 12×1 rectangle. Students will recognize that 1, 2, 3, 4, 6, and 12 are all factors of 12. Another way to visualize this is to think of 12 objects arranged into equal rows. We can make 1 row of 12, 2 rows of 6, and 3 rows of 4. Therefore these are all factors of 12.

FREQUENCY
Assign this to a different student each day. Discuss once a week. Be sure to link the Arrays with the Calendar pattern each day.

UPDATE PROCEDURE
Each day, a different student will be responsible for determining all possible rectangular Arrays for the date and creating the Array(s) from 10 by 10 Squared Paper (TR2). The factors should be written on each Array. On Mondays, three students will be responsible for the weekend and Monday. You may choose to display the Arrays on a background of construction paper. Use additional copies of the 10 by 10 Squared Paper and tape to construct rectangles having more than 10 squares on one side.

The Array(s) should be displayed on the bulletin board near the Calendar each day. As new Arrays are posted, move the old ones to a larger display area where they can be visible to the students. If there is not space to do this, the Arrays can be stored and displayed in a notebook. They should be available for student reference for the next few months.

DISCUSSION FOR THE BEGINNING AND MIDDLE OF THE MONTH
On the first day of school, ask students to consider the quantity represented by the date. If it is the 4th, ask students to imagine 4 square tiles. Ask them how many ways these 4 tiles can be arranged to make a rectangular floor. How many different rectangles can be made? (Two, a 2×2 and a 1×4.) What is the area of this floor? (4 tiles.) Ask students to consider a 4×1 rectangle.

1 · 1 x 1

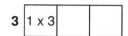
2 · 1 x 2

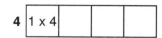
3 · 1 x 3

4 · 1 x 4

4 · 2 x 2

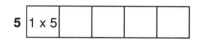
5 · 1 x 5

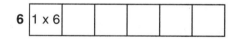
6 · 1 x 6

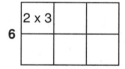
6 · 2 x 3

Is this different from a 1 × 4 rectangle? How is it different? Explain that if a rectangle is congruent, or can be rotated to look the same as another, we will not consider it to be different.

Ask the students to determine how many different rectangular Arrays can be made for the quantity represented by the date. If the date is the 7th, only one rectangle can be made. If it is the 8th, there are two. Explain that on the 8th, you can make one rectangle that is 1 row of 8 and another that is 2 rows of 4. Ask if there are any others. Students may mention a rectangle with 4 rows of 2. Remind them that if a rectangle can be rotated to look like another, we will not consider it to be different. Select one or two students to create the Array(s) for the day and to write the factors on each one. Then display them on the bulletin board.

These questions can be used to stimulate class discussion about the Arrays.
▶ Which numbers this month will have the largest number of factors or rectangles? (24 and 30.)
▶ Which number will have the smallest number of factors? (1 is the only number with only one factor. It is unique.)
▶ What do we call a number with only one possible rectangular Array, with factors 1 and itself? (A prime number.)
▶ What do we call numbers with more than two factors? (Composite numbers.)
▶ What do you notice about all even numbers other than 2? (They are composite numbers.)
▶ Are all odd numbers prime? (No.)
▶ Which numbers make squares? (1, 4, 9, 16, 25)

These arrays are the same.

SAMPLE DISCUSSION FOR THE END OF THE MONTH

Teacher: When you examine the Arrays for the numbers from 1 to 30, do you notice any pattern to the prime and composite numbers?
Student: All the even numbers have 2 for a factor.
Teacher: That's true. Are they all composite numbers?
Student: Yes, except for 2.
Teacher: Do you see any other patterns?
Student: Numbers that you can double over and over have more rectangles.
Teacher: Can you explain what you mean by that?
Student: Well, 24 is 12 doubled, and 12 is 6 doubled, and 6 is 3 doubled. So you can make lots of rectangles.
Teacher: That's a really important idea. We will talk about that again when we discuss prime factors. Does anyone see any pattern to the prime numbers?

QUESTIONS FOR FURTHER DISCUSSION
▶ What are the factors for 12? (1, 2, 3, 4, 6, 12)
▶ What are the factors for 24? (1, 2, 3, 4, 6, 8, 12, 24)
▶ Which numbers have the same number of factors?
▶ What factor(s) do 15 and 12 have in common? (3)
▶ What factors do 16 and 24 have in common? (2, 4, 8) What is the largest factor they have in common? (8)
▶ Which numbers can be divided into the most rectangles? (24, 30)

EVERY DAY ELEMENT

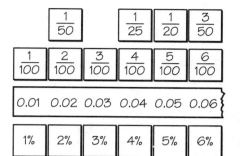

FOCUS

▶ Counting with decimals, fractions, and percents
▶ Visualizing percent with a circular model
▶ Understanding percent as a fraction
▶ Comparing decimals, fractions, and percents; recognizing equivalencies
▶ Developing understanding with commonly used decimals, fractions, and percents

MATERIALS

3" × 200" adding machine tape, self-stick removable notes or 2-in. squares of construction paper, Percent Circle (TR3)

OVERVIEW

The Counting Tape is used to give students daily exposure to counting by hundredths, or 1% each day. Students use the Tape to represent the first one hundred days of school. Each day of school, then, represents one hundredth of the Tape. The Tape should be two hundred inches long, giving two inches for each day. Indicate these sections using small marks at two-inch intervals along the top and bottom edges of the adding machine tape. The marks will identify how much space to allow when recording the decimal on the Counting Tape. You may also choose to write the decimal on a self-stick removable note and post it on the Tape. A self-stick removable note with the corresponding fraction form is posted above each decimal, and another with the equivalent percent is posted below it. One of the small circles around the Percent Circle is colored each day to mark off another one hundredth, enabling students to form a visual image of the relationship between hundredths and percents.

FREQUENCY

Update daily. Discuss once or twice a week.

UPDATE PROCEDURE FOR THE COUNTING TAPE

On the first day of school, show students the length of the Counting Tape. Explain that it will represent the first one hundred days of school. Each day will be recorded as 0.01, to represent one hundredth of this time. Write *0.01* on the Counting Tape. Explain that 0.01 looks like "zero point zero one," but it means one hundredth. Write $\frac{1}{100}$ on a self-stick removable note and post it above the decimal.

Ask students to mention percents with which they are familiar. Discuss 100%, 50%, and any other common percents the students mention. Explain that percent is a special proportion that relates to the number of hundredths. The decimal 0.01 equals 1%. Write *1%* on a self-stick removable note and post it below the decimal.

Each day add one hundredth, recording the decimal, the fraction, and the percent in the same way. The daily repetition allows students to recognize the relationship between decimals, fractions, and percents. In addition, if a fraction can be written in a simpler form, add a self-stick removable note with the simpler fraction above the hundredths fraction. For example, $\frac{15}{100}$ can be written as $\frac{3}{20}$.

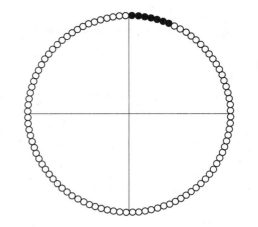

UPDATE PROCEDURE FOR THE PERCENT CIRCLE

Ask students to examine the one hundred small circles on the Percent Circle (TR3), and explain that one of these circles will be colored for each day of school. Each circle, then, will also represent one out of the first one hundred days of school. Another way of saying this is 1%, or one out of one hundred.

SAMPLE DISCUSSION FOR THE FIRST DAY

Teacher: This Tape will represent the first one hundred days of school. Each day is one hundredth of the whole one hundred days. We'll record it on the Counting Tape each day, first in decimal form, then as a fraction, and finally as a percent. Can anyone show us how to write $\frac{1}{100}$ as a decimal?

Student: Like this. (Writes *0.01* on chalkboard.)

Teacher: (Writes *0.01* on Counting Tape.) How do we write this as a fraction?

Student: (Writes $\frac{1}{100}$ on chalkboard.)

Teacher: Good. Now look at the Percent Circle. Notice that there are one hundred circles spaced evenly around it. Each day, we'll color one of the small circles. On the first day, what fraction of the circles will be colored?

Student: $\frac{1}{100}$.

Teacher: If all the circles are colored, what percent is that?

Student: 100%.

Teacher: If fifty of the circles are colored, what percent would that be?

Student: 50%.

Teacher: Then what percent is it if one of the circles is colored?

Student: 1%? I'm not sure.

Teacher: What do the rest of you think?

DISCUSSION FOR THE MIDDLE OF THE MONTH

► Questions should help students develop insights that will enable them to move comfortably from decimal form to fractional form and to percent.

► On the 5th day of school, ask students to write the decimal 0.05, the fraction $\frac{5}{100}$, and 5%. Ask students to write other equivalent fractions. (Accept answers such as $\frac{10}{200}$ and $\frac{1}{20}$.) Ask students how they recognize that $\frac{5}{100}$ is the same as $\frac{1}{20}$. (Accept answers such as there are 20 nickels in a dollar, there are 20 fives in every one hundred, and $\frac{5}{100}$ can be simplified to $\frac{1}{20}$.) Lead students to recognize that $\frac{1}{20}$ is the same as 5%.

► On the 10th day of school, repeat this discussion using $\frac{10}{100}$, $\frac{1}{10}$, 0.1, and 10%. Be sure to refer to the visual model of the Percent Circle often, focusing on the ten colored circles out of one hundred circles.

DISCUSSION FOR THE END OF THE MONTH

Use the following questions to encourage discussion.

► How do we write 20% as a decimal? (0.20 or 0.2)

► Why can 0.2 and 0.20 both represent 20%? (They are equivalent decimals.)

► What are some other ways we can write 20% as a fraction? ($\frac{1}{5}$, $\frac{2}{10}$, $\frac{20}{100}$, and so on.)

► If 20 is 20% of 100, what is 20% of 200? (40)

► How about 20% of 1000? (200)

HELPFUL HINTS

▶ Notice that the questions are designed to help students focus on reasoning with percents and decimals. To determine 20% of 200, students first find 20% of 100 and then double that amount. To find 5% of a number, students might find $\frac{1}{20}$ of the number, or perhaps find 0.1 of the number and than take half of that. The Counting Tape and Percent Circle questions will help students move comfortably between percents, decimals, and fractions and increase their ability to reason with these numbers.

▶ Avoid teaching procedures for converting fractions into percents or decimals too quickly. These procedures are often taught without meaning, context, or explanation, with the result that students learn what works but not why it works.

▶ Try to encourage understanding of commonly used decimals, fractions, and percents so that students are at ease with them. These should include decimal and percent representations for $\frac{1}{2}, \frac{1}{3}, \frac{1}{4}, \frac{3}{4}, \frac{1}{6}, \frac{1}{8}, \frac{1}{10}, \frac{1}{20}$, and $\frac{1}{16}$.

▶ Although you may choose to discuss this element only once a week, be sure to maintain the Counting Tape and Percent Circle every day. The repetition enables students to make easy connections between decimals, fractions, and percents.

EVERY DAY ELEMENT

FOCUS
▶ Recognizing frequently used patterns
▶ Discovering relationships between area and perimeter
▶ Describing and analyzing mathematical relationships

MATERIALS
Inch Squared Paper (TR4), scissors, tape, paper for a chart

OVERVIEW
Mathematics is both the art of discovering and the science of defining patterns. Each month, a different pattern resulting from a geometric or numerical relationship will be presented. Students will be encouraged to examine these relationships to discover the underlying pattern. By using number tables, visual images, and mathematical symbols, students will be encouraged to understand these patterns from a variety of approaches. Students will offer conjectures for a rule describing the pattern and will make predictions for continuing it. Using this process each day will allow students to discover the pattern. Concepts of variables and formulas will be introduced to extend each pattern.

FREQUENCY
Students can update the pattern daily, including weekend days on Monday. Discuss and make predictions each week.

UPDATE PROCEDURE
The pattern for this month will be to add one square inch of area each day. Students will use a simple relationship between the perimeter and area of a rectangle to discover and describe a pattern, maintain a number table, and record the relationship with mathematical symbols.

DAILY PATTERN

Area = 1 in.²
Perimeter = 4 in.

Area = 2 in.²
Perimeter = 6 in.

Area = 3 in.²
Perimeter = 8 in.

Area = 4 in.²
Perimeter = 10 in.

Area = 5 in.²
Perimeter = 12 in.

The square inches are added in a row, so that on the thirtieth day students are using a 1 in. × 30 in. rectangle. The figures can be displayed on a piece of construction paper to make them more visible. Each new figure should be added to the display so that all thirty rectangles are visible at the end of the month. If there is not room to do this, the figures can be displayed somewhere else in the classroom or in a notebook.

Make a chart with three columns labeled *Figure Number*, *Area (in.²)*, and *Perimeter (in.)*. Record the numbers for each figure on the chart daily. On the first day, use one square from the Inch Squared Paper (TR4) to begin the discussion.

SAMPLE DISCUSSION FOR THE FIRST DAY OF THE MONTH

Teacher: Here is one square. How much space is in this square?

Student: You have to measure it.

Teacher: How do you measure it? Is there an instrument for measuring the space inside the square?

Student: No, but you can measure the sides and then multiply it.

Teacher: Multiply what?

Student: The sides.

Teacher: All of them?

Student: No. You know what I mean.

Teacher: I think I do. One of the things I would like to show you is why mathematicians like to be as clear and precise as possible when they use language. That's why definitions, words, and symbols are important, so we can try to understand each other, whether we are in Asia, Africa, Europe, or the Americas. What is the mathematical word for the space inside this figure?

Student: Area.

Teacher: What units do we use to measure this square?

Student: Inches or centimeters.

Teacher: But won't that tell us how long or wide it is, not how much space is in it?

Student: That's why you multiply the two sides, because that will tell you how many little squares fit inside.

Teacher: What do you mean by little squares?

Student: Like square inches.

Teacher: Yes. The area is the number of squares that will fit inside this space. I'll make this problem easier. I will tell you that each side of this square is 1 inch long, so the area is 1 square inch. One square inch will fit into this square.

Student: Of course.

Teacher: So the area is one square inch. If my pet ant lived here, it would have one square inch of room to play in. Suppose I want to keep my ant inside this square. How much fence will I need? How far is it around the square?

Student: Four.

Teacher: Four what?

Student: Four inches.

Teacher: Yes, and what is the distance around this figure called?

Student: Perimeter.

Teacher: So let's write down on this chart that the area of figure number 1 is 1 square inch and the perimeter is 4 inches. Tomorrow, I will put up the next figure, and I want you to notice the area and perimeter of the new figure.

Notice that in the discussion, the teacher encourages the students to clarify any confusion on their own, instead of offering answers.

If you have already covered the subject of area and perimeter, you may choose to skip the beginning of this discussion.

DISCUSSION FOR THE MIDDLE OF THE MONTH

For the next few days, post figures whose area increases daily by one square inch. Discuss to determine the area and perimeter of each figure, but don't record anything on the chart. After four or five days of adding figures, work with the students to fill in the numbers on the chart, and then resume the discussion.

Some possible questions might include:
▶ How much does the area of the figure increase each day? (By one square inch.)
▶ Who can explain how to determine the perimeter for today's figure? Who has another way to figure it out? Does anyone see still another way to figure it out?

Some possible student responses about the perimeter of the seventh figure might include:
▶ I know that the first and last squares have three inches along the outside of the rectangle and all the rest have two.
▶ I added two more to yesterday's perimeter.
▶ I can figure out the perimeter because I know there are seven inches on the top, seven on the bottom, and two on the ends.
▶ Since it's the seventh figure, you can double that number and add two. (Be sure students recognize that these last two responses are two ways of saying the same thing.)

DISCUSSION FOR THE END OF THE MONTH

Continue posting new figures and updating the chart. At the end of the month, refer to the chart and use these questions to stimulate discussion of the pattern.
▶ Can anyone predict what the perimeter of the next figure will be? What are some strategies for figuring it out? (One student expressed it this way: "The squares on both ends of the figure always have three sides, so that is 2×3, or 6. The rest of the squares always have two sides, and there are always two less of these squares than the number of the date. So the perimeter is always $(2 \times 3) + 2(n - 2)$.")
▶ Can you predict what the perimeter of the thirtieth figure will be? (62 inches.) The one hundredth figure? (202 inches.)
▶ How would you explain the relationship between the area and the perimeter of all of these figures? (The perimeter is twice the area and 2 more.)
▶ Can you try to explain why the perimeter of each figure is twice the area plus two more? (Each square inch in the figure has a top and a bottom length. The two squares at either end of the figure each have a side of one inch.)
▶ What other patterns do you see between the area and the perimeter?

Figure Number	Area (in.^{2})	Perimeter (in.)
1	1	4
2	2	6
3	3	8
4	4	10
5	5	12
6	6	14
7	7	16
8	8	18
9	9	20
10	10	22
11	11	24
12	12	26
13	13	28
14	14	30
15	15	32
16	16	34
17	17	36
18	18	38
19	19	40
20	20	42
21	21	44
22	22	46
23	23	48
24	24	50
25	25	52
26	26	54
27	27	56
28	28	58
29	29	60
30	30	62

HELPFUL HINTS

▶ In the classroom discussions, encourage students to find multiple strategies for predicting the perimeter and area.

▶ As frequently as possible, help students see the connection between the number table and the visual model of the figures.

▶ Toward the end of the month, you can begin to use symbols for variables, such as perimeter = 2 squares + 2 , or $p = 2n + 2$. Be sure to explain that n means the number of squares in the figure and that $2n$ means two times the number of squares. This may be confusing at first, but repetition will help to make it clear.

EVERY DAY ELEMENT

FOCUS

▶ Understanding the concept of a variable
▶ Using mathematical symbols to record variables
▶ Evaluating mathematical expressions

MATERIALS

Paper for a chart

OVERVIEW

Algebra is the study of systems in which we generalize rules and procedures. For example, even young children know that adding two things to three things is the same as adding three things to two things. In algebra, we generalize this to say that when dealing with real numbers, $a + b = b + a$, where a and b are real numbers. Helping students generalize and recording their generalizations is an important aspect of the sixth grade curriculum. Many students think that algebra is just arithmetic with letters. To begin to prepare students for algebraic thinking, it is helpful to provide many experiences with the concept, use, and recording of variables.

In this element, we will use the date and the month to write expressions and then evaluate them. In the first month, we will simply add the date to the number of the month. In subsequent months we will multiply the date by 10, 100, or 0.1 and add it to the number of the month. The goal of this exercise is to encourage students to use expressions containing variables and to find the value for these expressions.

FREQUENCY

Update two times a week, including the weekend days. Discuss once a week.

DAILY VARIABLE

Date	+	Number of the Month	=	Value

d	+	9	=	Value

x	+	9	=	Value

1	9	10
2	9	11
3	9	12
4	9	13
5	9	14
6	9	15
7	9	16
8	9	17
9	9	18
10	9	19
11	9	20
12	9	21
13	9	22
14	9	23
15	9	24
16	9	25
17	9	26
18	9	27
19	9	28
20	9	29
21	9	30
22	9	31
23	9	32
24	9	33
25	9	34
26	9	35
27	9	36
28	9	37
29	9	38
30	9	39

UPDATE PROCEDURE

On a piece of paper, create a chart with three columns labeled *Date*, *Number of the Month*, and *Value*. Put "+" over the line separating the "Date" and "Number of the Month" columns. Place "=" over the line separating the "Number of the Month" and "Value" columns. Ask students for the date and the number of the month. They may reply that today is the 7th and that September is the 9th month. Record this on the chart as $7 + 9$. Ask students to evaluate this, to determine the total value. When they respond with 16, explain that this is the value for the 7th day of the 9th month. Explain that the expression we use will be different each month, but during September we will use the expression "Date plus 9 (Number of the Month) equals Value." Ask students to predict what the value will be for the 10th day of the month. (19)

In the second week of school, conduct a second brief discussion on the value for the date and month. Ask students to predict the value for the 20th day.

In the third week of school, make new labels for the columns of the chart. Replace "Date" with d and "Number of the Month" with 9. Explain that this is just a different way of writing the same expression we have used during September. The expression just looks different when we write it as "$d + 9$ = Value." Ask students to predict the value for the last day of the month.

In the last week of the month, change the column labels to the expression "$x + 9$ = Value." Explain that you have chosen the letter x instead of d to represent the date. It is important to tell the students that this x does not mean to multiply. It is simply another way of writing the same expression we have been using all month. We could use any letter or symbol such as a box or a circle, but x, y, and n are often used to represent a number or quantity.

HELPFUL HINTS

► Try to encourage student's natural enthusiasm for studying algebra by appealing to their sense of growing up and being ready to learn something new and advanced.

► Use this element as a means to entice all students into the world of abstract mathematical thinking.

► You may want students to begin to evaluate additional expressions, such as twice the date plus the month, or $2d + m$.

► Allow students to write expressions of their own, and ask other students to evaluate them.

► In future months, students will make graphs of the Daily Variable expressions. Since the expression used in September is a simple one, it is a good idea to begin by graphing it if time allows. Near the end of the month, have the students graph the expression, with the x-axis representing the date and the y-axis representing the value of the expression $x + 9$.

EVERY DAY ELEMENT

FOCUS
▶ Developing an understanding of common percents
▶ Using and calculating percents

MATERIALS
Four 3 × 6 clear pockets for Depositor, Play Money on colored cardstock or copies of Play Money (TR 5 and TR6), 3 × 5 cards for recording sheet, 3 × 6 clear pocket to hold recording sheet

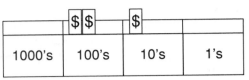

	$ $	$	
1000's	100's	10's	1's

$210

OVERVIEW
This element will be used to enable students to understand and apply the concept of percent. In the first half of the year, students will work with easily computed percents. They will calculate values mentally, rather than on paper, using place value reasoning. They will discover benchmarks for commonly used percents such as 10%, 5%, and 1% and use these benchmarks to calculate other percentages. In the second half of the year, students will continue to use percents but with an emphasis on the effect of compounding interest and how interest adds value to principle.

In September, students calculate 10% of the date times $100. This will help them recognize 10% as $\frac{1}{10}$, or 0.1 of a quantity. As students share their strategies with each other, they learn efficient ways to do this computation mentally.

FREQUENCY
Update daily. Include the weekend days on Monday. Discuss once or twice a week.

UPDATE PROCEDURE
Each day, the date will be multiplied by $100. In September, students will mentally calculate 10% of this amount and deposit it in the Daily Depositor. For example, on the 7th of September, students will deposit 10% of $700, or $70. Students will calculate this mentally by using $\frac{10}{100}$, or $\frac{1}{10}$, of $700. On Mondays, three students will update the weekend, depositing money for Saturday, Sunday, and Monday. Record the new total every day.

Ask students to guess how much money the class will collect by the end of the month. Accept all estimates and post them on a piece of paper. After two weeks, ask students to revise their guesses by making new estimates. Discuss these estimates in terms of their reasonableness.

Since students will be asked to compare the monthly totals for each of the first four months of school, make a small chart next to the Depositor showing the month, the mathematical operation, and the total amount deposited for each month of the school year, from September to December only. Update the chart at the end of each of those months.

SAMPLE DISCUSSION FOR THE BEGINNING OF THE MONTH

Teacher: Today is the 7th of September. Each day, a student will be responsible for depositing some money in our Daily Depositor. To determine the amount to deposit, we will find 10% of the date times $100. Since today is the 7th, we will find 10% of $700. What does 100% mean?

Student: The whole thing.

Teacher: Yes, the entire quantity. So what is 100% of $700?

Student: $700?

Teacher: Yes. What would 50% of $700 be, and how do you figure that?

Student: Well 50% is half, and half of $700 is $350.

Teacher: How did you do that?

Student: I'm smart.

Teacher: Can you explain it to me so that I can use the same strategy that you use?

Student: I know if you double 35 you get 70, so if you double 350 you get 700. So I took half of $700 to get $350.

Teacher: Does everyone understand that? Now comes the difficult question. What does 10% mean? If 100% means the whole amount, and 50% means $\frac{1}{2}$, or $\frac{5}{10}$, what does 10% mean?

Student: $\frac{1}{100}$?

Teacher: Why do you think that?

Student: Well, it means out of one hundred.

Teacher: Yes. What does 1% mean then?

Student: Well, 1 out of 100.

Teacher: So what does 10% mean?

Student: Oh, 10 out of 100.

Teacher: Yes, and what is another way of saying $\frac{10}{100}$, a simpler fraction?

Student: $\frac{1}{10}$.

Teacher: So $\frac{10}{100}$ is the same as $\frac{1}{10}$, which is the same as 0.1, which equals 10%. How can we figure 10% of $700 then?

Student: Well if 100% of $700 is $700, then $\frac{1}{10}$ of that is $70. You just divide by 10.

Teacher: Any other strategies?

Ask, How much will be deposited tomorrow, the 8th? ($80)

Explain that each day a different student will be responsible for determining the value of 10% of $100 times the date and depositing that amount in the Depositor.

DISCUSSION FOR THE MIDDLE AND END OF THE MONTH

These questions can be used to continue the discussion of common percentages throughout the month.

▶ Today is the 15th, so what is 10% of $1500? ($150)

▶ How did you figure that out?

▶ What pattern do you notice when you find 10% of a number? (The amount is divided by 10, so you move the decimal point one place to the left.)

▶ Who can describe a fast way to figure out 10% of any number?

▶ What is 10% of $100? ($10) Of $1000? ($100) Of $10,000? ($1000, and so on.)

▶ What is 10% of $2200? ($220)

- ► How much money do you estimate we will have by the end of the month?
- ► How much will we deposit on the last day of September? ($300)
- ► What is 10% of $30? ($3.00)
- ► What is 10% of $3.00? ($0.30)
- ► Do you see a pattern in finding 10% of a number?

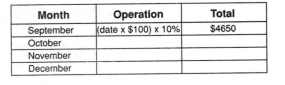

Month	Operation	Total
September	(date x $100) x 10%	$4650
October		
November		
December		

HELPFUL HINTS

- ► Avoid showing students that finding 10% of a number involves multiplying by 0.10 with paper and pencil.
- ► Encourage students to find different strategies for finding $\frac{1}{10}$, or 0.1 of a number.
- ► Toward the end of the month, be sure to show both $\frac{1}{10}$ and 0.10 as ways of recording 10%.
- ► Encourage students to refer often to the Counting Tape and Percent Circle for help.
- ► Ask students to calculate 10% of a number using the calculator. Show them how to use the percent key. Ask them to find the answer on the calculator without using the percent key.
- ► Pick a number such as 1200. Ask half the class to use their calculators to determine 10%. Ask the other half to figure it out mentally. Which was easier? Faster?
- ► At the end of the month, check to see that all students can mentally find 10% of a number.
- ► Give students the following problem:
  A $100 pair of tennis shoes is marked down 10%. How much is taken off? What is the sale price? So many people want those shoes that the store decides to raise the price 10%. What is the price now? Will it be $100? Why not? (10% of $100 is $10 off, so the sale price is $90. Raising the price 10% means raising it $\frac{1}{10}$ of $90, which is $9, so the new price is $99.)
- ► Encourage students to bring in newspaper ads that involve the use of percents.

OCTOBER

MOVING RIGHT ALONG

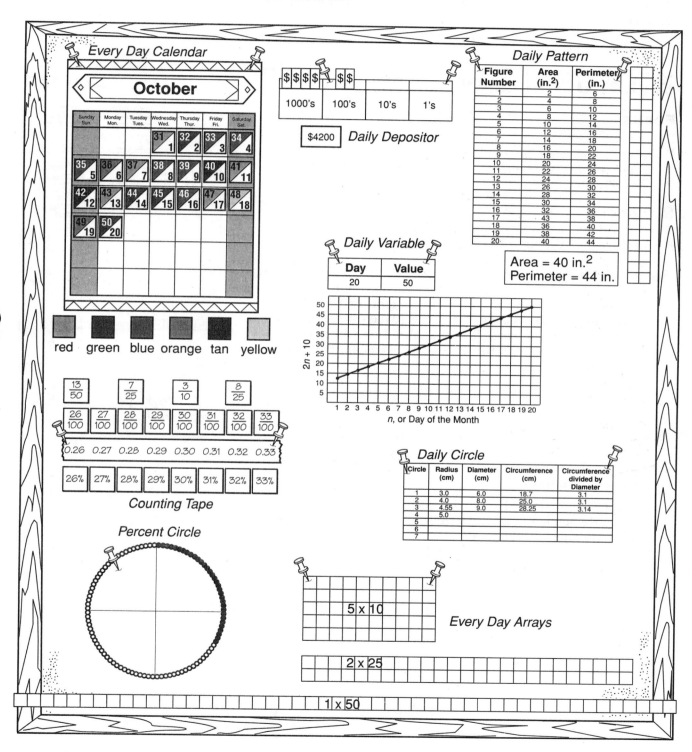

Every Day Calendar

October

Sunday Sun.	Monday Mon.	Tuesday Tues.	Wednesday Wed.	Thursday Thur.	Friday Fri.	Saturday Sat.
			31 / 1	32 / 2	33 / 3	34 / 4
35 / 5	36 / 6	37 / 7	38 / 8	39 / 9	40 / 10	41 / 11
42 / 12	43 / 13	44 / 14	45 / 15	46 / 16	47 / 17	48 / 18
49 / 19	50 / 20					

red green blue orange tan yellow

Counting Tape

$\frac{13}{50}$ $\frac{7}{25}$ $\frac{3}{10}$ $\frac{8}{25}$

$\frac{26}{100}$ $\frac{27}{100}$ $\frac{28}{100}$ $\frac{29}{100}$ $\frac{30}{100}$ $\frac{31}{100}$ $\frac{32}{100}$ $\frac{33}{100}$

0.26 0.27 0.28 0.29 0.30 0.31 0.32 0.33

26% 27% 28% 29% 30% 31% 32% 33%

Percent Circle

1000's	100's	10's	1's
$ $ $ $	$ $		

$4200 **Daily Depositor**

Daily Variable

Day	Value
20	50

$2n + 10$

n, or Day of the Month

Daily Pattern

Figure Number	Area (in.^{2})	Perimeter (in.)
1	2	6
2	4	8
3	6	10
4	8	12
5	10	14
6	12	16
7	14	18
8	16	20
9	18	22
10	20	24
11	22	26
12	24	28
13	26	30
14	28	32
15	30	34
16	32	36
17	43	38
18	36	40
19	38	42
20	40	44

Area = 40 in.^{2}
Perimeter = 44 in.

Daily Circle

Circle	Radius (cm)	Diameter (cm)	Circumference (cm)	Circumference divided by Diameter
1	3.0	6.0	18.7	3.1
2	4.0	8.0	25.0	3.1
3	4.55	9.0	28.25	3.14
4	5.0			
5				
6				
7				

Every Day Arrays

5 x 10

2 x 25

1 x 50

We will continue to use the Calendar Math elements that were introduced in September. These elements include the Every Day Calendar, Every Day Array, Counting Tape and Percent Circle, Daily Pattern, Daily Variable, and Daily Depositor. Only one new element, the Daily Circle, will be introduced this month, so if you chose not to use an element last month you may begin it in October.

EVERY DAY ELEMENT

CALENDAR

FOCUS

- ► Analyzing and predicting patterns
- ► Mastering factors and multiples
- ► Analyzing prime, composite, and square numbers
- ► Recognizing factors for numbers to 61

MATERIALS

Every Day Calendar, October Month Strip, October Calendar Pieces, or Square Cutouts (TR1) and colored markers

SUGGESTED PATTERN FOR OCTOBER

As in September, the October Calendar Pieces show the number of factors for each date. However, to enable students to use factors for larger numbers, we will add 30 (for the 30 days in September) to the October date. For example, on October 1 we will consider the number 31, a prime number. The color scheme for October appears below.

31, 37, 41, 43, 47, 53, 59, 61 (prime numbers) = red
33, 34, 35, 38, 39, 46, 51, 55, 57, 58 (4 factors) = blue
32, 44, 45, 50, 52 (6 factors) = green
36, 49 (odd number of factors, square numbers) = orange
40, 42, 54, 56 (8 factors) = tan
48 (10 factors) = yellow
60 (12 factors) = purple

The FREQUENCY for the Every Day Calendar continues from September. Remember to add 30 to the date during October. See page 2 for a detailed description.

October

Sunday Sun.	Monday Mon.	Tuesday Tues.	Wednesday Wed.	Thursday Thur.	Friday Fri.	Saturday Sat.
			31 / 1	32 / 2	33 / 3	34 / 4
35 / 5	36 / 6	37 / 7	38 / 8	39 / 9	40 / 10	

red   green   blue   orange   tan

UPDATE PROCEDURE

If you are using the October Calendar Pieces, the UPDATE PRO-CEDURE continues from September. See page 2 for a detailed description. If you choose to use the Square Cutouts (TR1), you will need to write two numbers on each square during October. The date, written with a black marker, should appear in the lower right corner. A diagonal extending from the lower left to the upper right corner should be added. Colored markers can then be used to write the date plus 30 in the upper left corner. In either case, continue to let the students determine the color for the day before posting the new Calendar Piece. Post the Calendar Pieces for the weekend dates on Monday.

SAMPLE DISCUSSION FOR THE BEGINNING OF THE MONTH

Teacher: We could repeat the pattern we used last month, but I think that's too simple for you. So I'm going to make October's pattern more challenging. Let's continue the idea we used last month, but we will add the 30 days of September to the date during October. Then we will decide the number of factors and pick the right color.

Student: Who says we don't want simple?

Teacher: Well, today is the 1st of October, so today we will need to determine the number of factors for 31. What color would you suggest?

Student: Violet?

Teacher: Why?

Student: Because 1 is neither prime nor composite?

Teacher: That's true, but we have added the 1 to the 30 days of September, so we would like to consider the number 31.

Student: Oh, I see. Then it would be red.

Teacher: Why?

Student: Because I can't think of any numbers you can divide 31 into.

Teacher: Can anyone explain this in another way?

Student: 31 has no factors other than 1 and 31, so it is a prime number, and prime numbers are red.

DISCUSSION THROUGHOUT THE MONTH

Continue the pattern for the rest of the month. Have extended discussions weekly, especially on interesting numbers such as square numbers 36 and 49; 48, which has ten factors; 51, which looks prime but isn't; and 60, which has the most factors.

EVERY DAY ELEMENT

FOCUS
► Visualizing numbers as rectangular arrays
► Mastering factors and multiples
► Analyzing prime, composite, and square numbers to 61

The MATERIALS, FREQUENCY, and UPDATE PROCEDURE are the same as for September, except that we will add 30 to the date. This means that the number the students are working with each day will be the same for the Calendar and the Arrays. For example, the first rectangle will be a 1 x 31 rectangle. See page 5 for a detailed description.

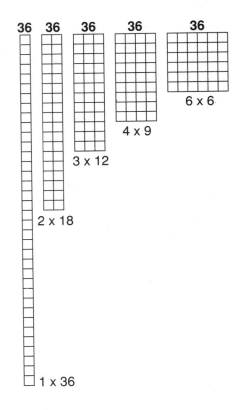

36 36 36 36 36

6 x 6
4 x 9
3 x 12
2 x 18
1 x 36

DISCUSSION THROUGHOUT THE MONTH
The following questions may be used to initiate discussion during October.
► As numbers get larger, do they have more factors? (Some do, others don't.)
► Do you find any pattern to the number of factors for a number? (None discernible.)
► Do you see any pattern to the colors of the numbers on the Calendar? (While there is no pattern, there are interesting observations to be made. For example, between 0 and 10 there are four prime numbers, between 11 and 20 there are four more, but between 21 and 30 and between 31 and 40 there are only two prime numbers. Maybe there will be two prime numbers in each group of ten as we continue up, but between 41 and 50 there are three prime numbers. Observations about which color predominates in each group of ten might also be interesting.)
► Are there any consecutive prime numbers between 31 and 61? (No.) Why not? (Because every even number is divisible by 2, and every consecutive pair of whole numbers must contain one even number.)
► Do you see any prime numbers that are close, one number apart? (Yes, such as 29 and 31, or 41 and 43.) These are called twin primes.
► Do you think there will be more prime numbers between 40 and 50, or between 50 and 60? Why? (There seem to be fewer prime numbers as number size increases.)
► What makes 49 so interesting? (Other than itself and 1, it is only divisible by 7, and it is a square number.)
► When you are figuring out the factors for a number, what strategies do you use? (Encourage students to share strategies, such as looking for factors such as 2, 4, and 8, or for systematically dividing a number by 2, 3, 4, and so on.)
► Which of the numbers through 61 has the most factors? (60)

Helpful Hints

▶ Display all the Arrays for the numbers from 1 to 61 for several months. Refer to them when students are looking for factors.

▶ Suggest that students write short paragraphs describing a favorite number. Encourage them to describe that number as completely as possible. In one class, a girl wrote:

> I love the number 24. Not only is it the number on my soccer jersey, but it has the most factors of any number below 30. So if you had 24 cookies you could share them equally with 2 kids, 3 kids, 4 kids, 6 kids, 8 kids, 12 kids, and 24 kids. Of course, if you didn't have anybody to share them with, you could eat all 24 cookies yourself. Now, not only that but if you start with 3 and double that, then double that, then double that, you will get 24. So with just the numbers 2 and 3 you can get 24. Also 24 is two dozen eggs. Twenty-four inches is two feet and twenty-four ounces is one and a half pounds. I guess you can see why I like the number 24.
>
> P.S. If you turn 24 around and make it 42, it still has 8 factors, but there are some different factors.

▶ Remember that a good understanding of factors and multiples is the key arithmetic knowledge which will enable students to work comfortably and efficiently with ratios, fractions, and algebraic expressions.

EVERY DAY ELEMENT

COUNTING TAPE AND PERCENT CIRCLE

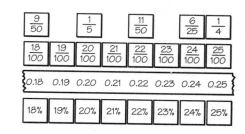

Focus

▶ Counting with decimals, fractions and percents
▶ Visualizing percent with a circular model
▶ Understanding percent as a fraction
▶ Comparing decimals, fractions, and percents; recognizing equivalencies
▶ Developing understanding with commonly used decimals, fractions, and percents

The MATERIALS, FREQUENCY, and UPDATE PROCEDURE are the same as for September. See page 7 for a detailed description.

Discussion Throughout the Month

The following questions and topics can be used to initiate discussion of decimals, fractions, and percents during October.

▶ The 25th day of school probably occurs in this month, and deserves extensive discussion. The decimal 0.25 can be written as a fraction. What is it? Look at the Percent Circle for some clues. (0.25 is the same as $\frac{1}{4}$.)

▶ What percent is equivalent to $\frac{1}{4}$? (25%)

▶ What percent does $\frac{3}{4}$ represent? (75%) What day of school will that be? (The 75th day.)

▶ If 25 is 25% of 100, what is 25% of 200? (50)

▶ What is 25% of 1000? (250)

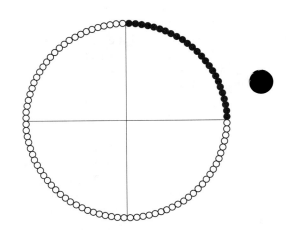

- ▶ If 25%, or 0.25, is $\frac{1}{4}$, what percent or decimal is represented by $\frac{1}{8}$? (Encourage students to think of $\frac{1}{8}$ as half of $\frac{1}{4}$, and therefore half of 25%, or half of 0.25. Reasoning in this way will help students to develop confidence in mental computation and will increase their skill with paper and pencil computation as well.)
- ▶ Is 30, or 30%, the same as $\frac{1}{3}$ of 100? (Encourage students to see that it is close, but not exactly $\frac{1}{3}$.)
- ▶ Notice that many fractions, such as $\frac{1}{4}$ and $\frac{1}{5}$, can easily be converted into percents by counting the number of colored circles out of the one hundred on the Percent Circle. Will every fraction work this way? (No. When we color $\frac{1}{4}$, or 1 out of every 4 circles, we color 25 circles and leave 75 uncolored. We use all one hundred circles. But when we color $\frac{1}{8}$, or 1 out of every 8 circles, we have 4 circles left over. We use only 96 of the circles, so we would have to color $\frac{1}{2}$ of a circle to make it work. Coloring $\frac{1}{7}$ of the circles would be even more challenging.)
- ▶ How about $\frac{1}{3}$? How many circles must we color to show $\frac{1}{3}$ of the first 100 days? (If we color one out of every three circles, we have one circle left over. We would use 99 of the circles, so we would have to color $\frac{1}{3}$ of a circle to make it work. $33\frac{1}{3}$ circles would be colored and $66\frac{2}{3}$ would be uncolored.)
- ▶ On the 33rd day, invite students to speculate if 0.33, or 33%, is equivalent to $\frac{1}{3}$. What decimal equivalent does equal $\frac{1}{3}$? How about $\frac{2}{3}$?

HELPFUL HINTS

- ▶ The combination of a linear model (Counting Tape) and circular model (Percent Circle) helps students recognize commonly used percents and helps them link these percents to decimal and fractional equivalents. Be sure to refer from one model to the other often.
- ▶ Frequently used percents and fractions can be used as "benchmarks" to evaluate other percents and fractions. For example, knowing that 25% is $\frac{1}{4}$ of the circle and that 50% is $\frac{1}{2}$ of a circle will help students recognize that 37% is more than $\frac{1}{4}$ but less than $\frac{1}{2}$, and may even be very close to right in between.

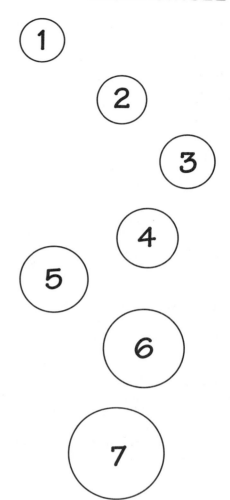

FOCUS

► Using mathematical language to describe circles
► Discovering the relationships between radius, diameter, and circumference
► Measuring using metric units of length
► Recognizing the importance of accurate measurement

MATERIALS

Seven October Circles, a centimeter ruler showing millimeters, string, scissors, paper for a chart, calculators

OVERVIEW

The geometry of the circle is usually a new concept in sixth grade. As adults, we remember memorizing formulas about circles, but rarely were we allowed to investigate and discover circular relationships on our own. Many adults know that $\pi = 3.14$, but do not understand that it is the ratio between the circumference and the diameter of a circle. This month, students will discover the relationships between the radius, diameter and circumference of circles by measuring the October Circles. They will keep a table of their measurements and begin to define the relationships between the elements of the circle. Enough time will be allowed so that all students can discover these relationships.

The process of creating the table this month is an attempt to allow the students to see how mathematicians may have approximated π in the past. The goal is for the students to recognize that π represents both a physical and a mathematical relationship between the elements of a circle. This goal, along with an appreciation of the importance and difficulty of accurate measurement, should be stressed throughout the month.

FREQUENCY

Update daily on each school day. Discuss every three days. Because the teacher will need to be involved in the measurement and calculation activities, do not include the weekend days for the Daily Circle element in October. Measuring three elements of each of the October Circles will fill the twenty or so school days this month.

UPDATE PROCEDURE

Label the October Circles in ascending size from 1 to 7. Set up a chart with five columns and seven horizontal rows. Label the first column *Circle* and list the numbers 1 through 7. Do not label the other columns yet.

The middle three columns of the chart will contain the results of the student's measurements of the circles. When measuring the circles, it will be helpful to have two students take each measurement. Since measuring parts of circles is extremely difficult, their measurements will probably be different. A good solution is to split the difference between the two measurements and record the result on the chart. At best, all measurements will be crude. The measurements and calulations shown here on the charts reflect the inaccuracies that are likely to occur when measuring circles. You may want to point out to the students that even if the teacher took all the measurements, they probably wouldn't all be accurate. That is because our measuring tools are limited in their precision, so our measurements will not be exact no matter how careful we are. Encourage the students to do the best they can. Stress the importance of careful and accurate measurement throughout the month. In most cases, measuring to the nearest millimeter, or tenth of a centimeter, will be sufficient. However, if the students can easily determine the measurement to the half millimeter, the result can be recorded on the chart that way.

Select Circle 1 and ask two students to measure the distance from the center of the circle to a point on the outside of the circle with the centimeter ruler. Remind them to measure as carefully as they can. If their measurements agree, enter the result in the second column of the chart. If the measurements are different, write the two numbers on the chalkboard and reconcile them by splitting the difference between them. Encourage the students to participate in determining the measurement that is recorded. This procedure should be followed for all measurements of the circles throughout the month.

The next day, ask two students to measure the distance across the same circle through the center point and to record the measurement in the third column of the chart. On the third day, ask two students to measure the distance around the same circle by laying a string tightly around its outside edge. Cut the string carefully, measure its length, and record the measurement in the fourth column of the chart. Repeat this three-step procedure 7 times during the month, filling in the entire chart. Another option is to record the three measurements for each circle in one day and repeat the procedure every three days. In either case, delay extended discussion about the information on the chart until measurements for two or three circles are complete. The fifth column of the chart will remain blank for now.

DISCUSSION FOR THE BEGINNING OF THE MONTH

Ask students to tell what they know about circles, including any terms or properties they have learned. Don't comment on them, simply list them. Explain that this month they will be studying the circle. You may want to mention that mathematicians of many different cultures have been fascinated with circles since ancient times. Today, circles are still studied by scientists and mathematicians interested in how planets move in space, or how particles move in atoms.

Ask students to describe a circle. What makes a circle a circle? How does it differ from an ellipse or a polygon? If students have not already provided the terms circumference, radius, and diameter, ask students for the mathematical names for the distance around a circle, the distance across a circle, and the distance from the center of a circle to a point on the circle. Be sure that students understand that the diameter must extend through the center of a circle and is the longest length that can be drawn across a circle. Once these mathematical terms have been discussed, label the three middle columns on the chart *Radius*, *Diameter*, and *Circumference*.

Tell the students that they will be measuring these parts of circles to see if they can discover any special relationships that may exist between them. Some students may already be familiar with these relationships. Encourage students to make hypotheses and explain that they are going to use the empirical data from the chart to test these hypotheses.

Ask students to offer ideas on how the circumference of a circle can be measured, since rulers don't bend. Explain again that it is important for measurements to be as accurate as possible to find precise relationships.

Tell students they will be using centimeter rulers that are divided not only into centimeters but into millimeters as well, each centimeter being divided into 10 divisions called millimeters.

SAMPLE DISCUSSION FOR THE BEGINNING OF THE MONTH

Teacher: How big is a centimeter? Can you show me something that is 1 centimeter long?
Student: The width of my little finger.
Student: My button.
Student: The width of a large paper clip.
Teacher: How many centimeters are there in a meter?
Student: 100.
Teacher: If there are 10 millimeters in a centimeter, then how many millimeters are there in a meter?
Student: 1000.
Teacher: How did you get that answer?

Be sure that the students understand that a millimeter is one tenth of a centimeter. Since they will be measuring distances with a ruler showing both centimeters and millimeters, the students will need to understand that their results need to be expressed in centimeters and tenths of centimeters. Explain that sometimes it will be clear that the measurement can be estimated to one half of a millimeter, or five hundredths of a centimeter.

Circle	Radius (cm)	Diameter (cm)	Circumference (cm)	
1	3.0	6.0	18.7	
2	4.0	8.0	25.0	
3	4.55	9.0	28.25	
4				
5				
6				
7				

SAMPLE DISCUSSION FOR THE MIDDLE OF THE MONTH

Teacher: Let's see how the circumference of a circle compares to its diameter. Looking at our chart, what do you notice about the size of the circumference compared to the size of the diameter?
Student: Do you mean figure out how much bigger the circumference is than the diameter?
Teacher: How would you do that?
Student: We can subtract the diameter from the circumference.
Teacher: If we do that for the first two circles, do we get nearly the same number for an answer?
Student: No.
Teacher: You're right. If we subtract, every result will be different. What I would like to know is how many times bigger the circumference is than the diameter. How can we figure that out?

Student: Can we divide the circumference by the diameter?

Teacher: Yes. The fifth column of our chart will show us how many times bigger the circumference is than the diameter for each circle. Try this with your calculators.

Student: My answer has a lot of numbers after the decimal point.

Teacher: Yes, that will happen when we do the calculations. Because our calculations use measurements we have made to the nearest tenth or hundredth of a centimeter, we'll need to determine how to round the results of our calculations. If the measurements for a circle are made to the tenth of a centimeter, we can only round our calculations to the tenth for those circles. If any measurement for a circle has been estimated to the hundredth of a centimeter, we can round our calculations to the hundredth for that circle. If we had a measuring tool that could measure to the thousandth of a centimeter, then we could round our calculations to the nearest thousandth. In general, we need to limit our results to the same number of decimal places as our measurements. This makes our calculations as accurate as our measurements.

It is very important to discuss the procedure for rounding the calculations when you divide the circumference by the diameter. Students may say that the more digits included in the result, the closer π will be to its actual value. However, scientists argue that all calculations should be rounded to the same number of significant digits as the measurements used in those calculations. For example, if the diameter of one of the circles has been measured as 3.55 centimeters, then the calculations should be rounded to the hundredth. This is important for keeping the mathematical results in line with the scientific data used in an experiment.

FURTHER DISCUSSION FOR THE MIDDLE OF THE MONTH

After discussing the relationship between the circumference and the diameter of a circle and explaining the procedure for rounding the calculations, label the fifth column of the chart *Circumference divided by Diameter*. Explain that this column will contain the results of student calculations for each of the October Circles. Have the students use their calculators, and fill in this column for the circles that have been measured so far. Even with rough measurements and rounding, the results of these calculations should result in a range between 3.0 and 3.4, which are good approximations of π.

Circle	Radius (cm)	Diameter (cm)	Circumference (cm)	Circumference divided by Diameter
1	3.0	6.0	18.7	3.1
2	4.0	8.0	25.0	3.1
3	4.55	9.0	28.25	3.14
4	5.0	10.0	31.3	3.1
5	5.5	11.1	34.45	3.10
6	6.0	12.0	37.7	3.1
7	7.5	15.0	47.0	3.1

DISCUSSION FOR THE END OF THE MONTH

These questions can be used to continue the discussion about circles. Refer to the chart frequently.

▶ How can we describe the relationship between the diameter and the radius of a circle? (The diameter contains two radii, or $d = 2r$.)

► Looking at our chart, we can see that sometimes the diameter is not exactly twice as long as the radius. Why might that be? (The measurements must not be accurate because, by definition, the diameter must be twice the radius.)

► Look at the numbers we have calculated so far for the circumference divided by the diameter. What relationship can we discover between these two parts of a circle? What range of numbers do we have in the fifth column, from smallest to largest? (The range should be between 3.0 and 3.4.) Based on our measurements and calculations, can we say that every circle shows the same relationship? (Probably not, because it is so difficult to measure the parts of a circle accurately.) Do you think it should be same for every circle, or just close? (As mathematicians have accurately calculated the relationships between parts of circles with greater and greater precision, they have discovered that this relationship holds. The relationship between the circumference and the diameter is called pi (π).)

► Are there any circles that we've measured that make it easy to see this relationship? (Perhaps some circle measurements are numbers that are easy to manipulate mentally, so that the relationship between the diameter and the circumference is easy to see.)

► How can we use the string to display this relationship? (We should be able to see a little more than three diameter lengths in a string that is the length of the circumference.)

HELPFUL HINTS

► Emphasize that both our inaccuracy in measuring and the limitations of our measuring tools make these calculations rough approximations for pi. The goal is to let the students see that pi is both a number and the expression of a physical relationship between the circumference and the diameter of a circle.

► Have students stand in a circle. Measure the distance across the circle of students and then the distance around the students. Compare these measurements to those on the chart.

► Have a contest for students to memorize as many digits of pi as they can.

► Using a tennis ball can, cut a length of string that will exactly fit the circumference of the can. Before showing this string to the students, ask them to guess whether the string will be longer than the height of the can. See how quickly they realize that there are three balls in the can and that the circumference of the can will be slightly more than three diameters and extend slightly above the top of the can.

► Students may enjoy using their knowledge of pi to solve the following problems.
—The sun is about 93,000,000 miles from the earth. If we assume that the earth makes a perfect circle around the sun, how far does it travel in a year? (2 times 93,000,000 times pi, or 584,336,234 miles.)
—A bicycle wheel has a radius of 50 centimeters. How far does it travel if it turns one hundred times? (2 times 50 times pi times 100, or 31,416 centimeters.) How many meters is that? (314.16 meters.)

► If there is time, you may choose to discuss the difference between real circles that can be measured, and theoretically perfect circles that can be described. To find pi to the millions of places, mathematicians don't use measurements. They use ideas about the perfect circle. The history of mathematics is full of this tension between applied mathematics, like constructing a round building or measuring the orbits of planets, and pure mathematics, or mathematics that exists only in the world of ideas.

▶ Invite students to study the facts and history of π, especially the contributions of many different cultures to this history. Many interesting facts are presented here.

—The fact that the ratio of the circumference of a circle to its diameter is constant has been known for so long that it is quite untraceable. The earliest values for π were found by measurement. In the Egyptian Rhind Papyrus, which was written about 1650 B.C., there is good evidence for $4(\frac{8}{9})^2 = 3.16$ as a value for π.

—The first theoretical calculation was probably carried out by Archimedes of Syracuse, who lived from about 287 to 212 B.C.

—A Babylonian tablet from about 220 B.C. gives the value 3.125 for π.

—In the sixth century, the Chinese astronomer Ching-Chih used the proportion $\frac{355}{133}$ to calculate pi. This is a much better approximation than previous ones. It is only off by three millionths or so.

—In the sixteenth century, German mathematician Ludolph van Ceulen calculated π to 35 places. The number was carved into his tombstone.

—Pi was first used in its current sense by English mathematician William Jones in 1706.

EVERY DAY ELEMENT

DAILY PATTERN

Area = 2 in.^{2}
Perimeter = 6 in.

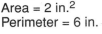

Area = 4 in.^{2}
Perimeter = 8 in.

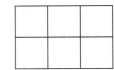

Area = 6 in.^{2}
Perimeter = 10 in.

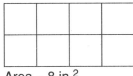

Area = 8 in.^{2}
Perimeter = 12 in.

Area = 10 in.^{2}
Perimeter = 14 in.

FOCUS

▶ Recognizing frequently used patterns
▶ Discovering relationships between area and perimeter
▶ Describing and analyzing mathematical relationships
▶ Creating mathematical expressions

The MATERIALS and FREQUENCY are the same as for September. See page 9 for a detailed description.

UPDATE PROCEDURE

The pattern for this month will be to add two square inches of area each day. On the first day of the month, use two squares from the Inch Squared Paper (TR4) to begin the discussion. The square inches are added in a strip two inches high, so that on the thirty-first day students are using a strip thirty-one inches long and two inches wide. Remember to record the figure number, the area, and the perimeter on the chart each day.

DISCUSSION THROUGHOUT THE MONTH

These questions can be used to encourage discussion during the month.

▶ How many square inches are added each day? (2)
▶ What is the perimeter of the first figure of the month? (6 inches.)
▶ What is the perimeter of the rectangle on October 3rd? (10 inches.) How did you determine that? Some possible student responses might include:
  • There are 3 inches on the top and bottom and 2 on each side.
  • The rectangle has a length of 3 inches and a width of 2 inches, then double that.
  • Add 2 to the previous figure.
  • The perimeter is the number of squares, or two times the date, plus 4. In each case, show how this can be seen from the figure and from the table. For example, you can show that each square has a length of 1 inch, plus the 2 inches on each side.
▶ On the 10th day, what will the area of the rectangle be? (2 times the date, or 20 square inches.)
▶ Can you predict what the area and perimeter of the 20th figure will be? Let's wait and see if our prediction is right.
▶ What will the area be on the last day of the month? (62 square inches, or 2 times 31.)

At the end of the month, ask students to predict the area and perimeter of the 100th figure. Then ask the same question about the 1000th figure.

The end of the month is probably a good time to begin to record the students' thinking with mathematical expressions. For the October rectangle:

area (a) = 2 times the date $(2n)$

perimeter (p) = 2 times the date $(2n)$ + 4

$p = a + 4$

p = 2 times (length (l) + width (w)), or $2 (l + w)$

Explain that when we use mathematical symbols, $2n$ means $2 \times n$. It is also helpful to remind students to perform operations within parentheses first. The use of mathematical symbols may cause some initial confusion, but continued exposure to this notation will bring understanding. For now, we are not expecting full comprehension.

Daily Pattern

Figure Number	Area (in.^{2})	Perimeter (in.)
1	2	6
2	4	8
3	6	10
4	8	12
5	10	14
6	12	16
7	14	18
8	16	20
9	18	22
10	20	24
11	22	26
12	24	28
13	26	30
14	28	32
15	30	34
16	32	36
17	34	38
18	36	40
19	38	42
20	40	44
21	42	46
22	44	48
23	46	50
24	48	52
25	50	54
26	52	56
27	54	58
28	56	60
29	58	62
30	60	64
31	62	66

EVERY DAY ELEMENT

DAILY VARIABLE

FOCUS
▶ Understanding the concept of a variable
▶ Using mathematical symbols to record variables
▶ Evaluating and graphing mathematical expressions

MATERIALS
Paper for a chart, large piece of graph paper

FREQUENCY
Update daily, including the weekend days on Monday. Discuss once each week.

UPDATE PROCEDURE
Students will continue to evaluate an expression tied to the date and the number of the month. In October, students will determine the value for twice the date plus 10, for the 10th month. Repeat the procedure used last month to evaluate the new expression. Keep a table again this month for the Daily Variable. The table should have two columns labeled *Day* and *Value*.

SAMPLE DISCUSSION FOR THE TWENTY-FIFTH DAY OF THE MONTH

Teacher: Today is the 25th of October. We want to find the value of $2n + 10$ where n is the number of the day and 10 represents the tenth month, October. What is the value of the expression $2n + 10$ when n is 25?
Student: 60.
Teacher: How did you do that?
Student: Well, I multiplied 25 by 2 and then added ten.
Teacher: How did you know to multiply by 2?
Student: Because it says $2n$ and that means there are two of them. It's the same as multiplying by 2.

Day	Value
1	12
2	14
3	16
4	18
5	20
6	22
7	24
8	26
9	28
10	30
11	32
12	34
13	36
14	38
15	40
16	42
17	44
18	46
19	48
20	50
21	52
22	54
23	56
24	58
25	60
26	62
27	64
28	66
29	68
30	70
31	72

GRAPHING THE EXPRESSION
On a large piece of graph paper, label the x-axis n, *or Day of the Month*. Label the y-axis $2n + 10$. Explain that in this case n means the number of the date. Show students how to find the coordinates of the first few days. Ask students where the fifth point will be on the graph. Maintain the graph daily.

Students will be asked to make comparisons between this graph and the one they will make in December. At the end of October, either move this graph to a different display area or store it until needed.

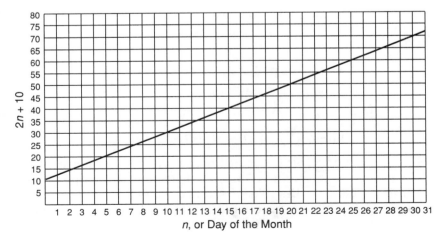

DISCUSSION THROUGHOUT THE MONTH

The following questions will be helpful in stimulating discussion.

▶ How much are we increasing each day? (2)

▶ Before day 1, what would the value of the expression be? In other words, if $n = 0$, what is the value of the expression? (10) Can we locate this point on the graph? (0, 10)

▶ As we increase n by 1 each day, by how much does the expression $2n + 10$ increase? (2)

▶ What will happen if we connect these points on the graph? (We get a straight line.)

▶ Let's examine this line. How much does n increase between each point? (1)

▶ How much does $2n + 10$ increase between each point? (2)

▶ How much does the vertical distance increase for every increase horizontally? (It increases vertically 2 for every 1 it increases horizontally.)

HELPFUL HINT

▶ By helping students graph an expression, we are preparing them for algebra. One key element that will make algebra understandable to all students is the relationship between an expression, or equation, and its graphic and numerical representation. The ability to translate from table to graph and back to symbol is essential. The informal practice provided by the Daily Variable should help students with this skill.

EVERY DAY ELEMENT

DAILY DEPOSITOR

FOCUS

▶ Developing an understanding of common percents
▶ Using and calculating percents

The MATERIALS and FREQUENCY are the same as for September. See page 14 for a detailed description.

UPDATE PROCEDURE

Each day, the date will be multiplied by $100. Students will then mentally calculate 20% of this amount and deposit it in the Daily Depositor. Students should also mentally calculate the daily addition to arrive at the new total. For example, on the 4th day, students should mentally add the $80 to be deposited to the total from the first three days, $120, to get the new total of $200. The new total should be written on the recording sheet each day. See if the students can predict how much money will be deposited this month. Hopefully, they will use the data from September. At the end of the month, be sure to add the total amount deposited in October to the chart showing the total deposited in September.

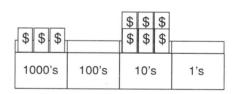

| 1000's | 100's | 10's | 1's |

$3060

Month	Operation	Total
September	(date x $100) x 10%	$4650
October	(date x $100) x 20%	$9920
November		
December		

Teacher: Today is the 18th of October. We have $3060 deposited so far this month. How do we figure out how much we should deposit today?

Student: We multiply the date by $100 and then find 20% of that.

Teacher: Good. Now talk to the person next to you and figure out how much 20% of $1800 is. Be prepared to share your thinking.

Student: It's $360.

Teacher: Why do you think that is the right amount?

Student: Because we know that 10% is $\frac{1}{10}$ of $1800, and $\frac{1}{10}$ of $1800 is $180. Then we doubled that to find 20%, because 20% is 10% plus 10%. So it is $360.

Teacher: Good. How did you know that $180 doubled is $360?

Student: Because 150 plus 150 is 300, and 30 plus 30 is 60.

Teacher: Did anyone figure out the 20% differently?

Student: Well, we knew that 20% is $\frac{1}{5}$ so we divided $1800 by 5.

Teacher: Did you do this in your head?

Student: No, we wrote it down.

Teacher: That's fine. I wonder if there are ways to divide by 5 quickly in your head? Did anyone figure out 20% of $1800 in a different way?

Student: We knew that yesterday we deposited $340 because it was 20% of $1700, so we realized that each day we just increase by $20.

Teacher: That's really observant. Why does that work?

Continue throughout the month to emphasize strategies that enable students to efficiently calculate percentages in their heads. In particular, encourage the use of the 10% benchmark. Avoid paper and pencil solutions for these percentages.

NOVEMBER

KEEPING UP THE MOMENTUM

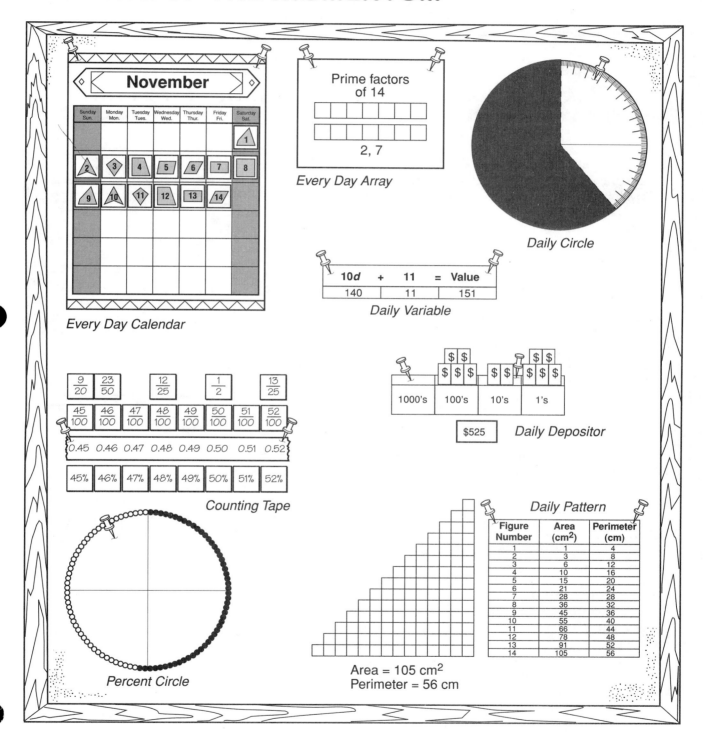

November

Sunday Sun.	Monday Mon.	Tuesday Tues.	Wednesday Wed.	Thursday Thur.	Friday Fri.	Saturday Sat.
						1
2	3	4	5	6	7	8
9	10	11	12	13	14	

Every Day Calendar

Prime factors of 14

2, 7

Every Day Array

Daily Circle

10*d*	+	11	=	Value
140		11		151

Daily Variable

$\frac{9}{20}$	$\frac{23}{50}$		$\frac{12}{25}$		$\frac{1}{2}$		$\frac{13}{25}$

$\frac{45}{100}$	$\frac{46}{100}$	$\frac{47}{100}$	$\frac{48}{100}$	$\frac{49}{100}$	$\frac{50}{100}$	$\frac{51}{100}$	$\frac{52}{100}$

0.45	0.46	0.47	0.48	0.49	0.50	0.51	0.52

45%	46%	47%	48%	49%	50%	51%	52%

Counting Tape

1000's	100's	10's	1's

$525

Daily Depositor

Percent Circle

Daily Pattern

Figure Number	Area (cm²)	Perimeter (cm)
1	1	4
2	3	8
3	6	12
4	10	16
5	15	20
6	21	24
7	28	28
8	36	32
9	45	36
10	55	40
11	66	44
12	78	48
13	91	52
14	105	56

Area = 105 cm²
Perimeter = 56 cm

By now, students should be developing some ease with fractional recording and equivalence. The Every Day Calendar, Every Day Array, Counting Tape and Percent Circle, Daily Circle, Daily Pattern, Daily Variable, and Daily Depositor continue this month with a few modifications. The Calendar this month will focus on properties of quadrilaterals. The Daily Pattern emphasizes triangular numbers. The Daily Circle is used in November to develop an understanding of degrees. Students are introduced to prime factors with the Every Day Array.

EVERY DAY ELEMENT

CALENDAR

FOCUS

► Analyzing and predicting patterns
► Recognizing and analyzing quadrilaterals
► Developing an understanding of the concepts of convex and concave
► Sorting and classifying shapes according to properties

MATERIALS

Every Day Calendar, November Month Strip, November Calendar Pieces, or Quadrilateral Cutouts (TR7) and marker

SUGGESTED PATTERN FOR NOVEMBER

For the next three months, students will explore some of the basic properties of a variety of quadrilaterals. In November, students will examine different quadrilaterals and notice their similarities and differences. While much technical vocabulary is introduced, the emphasis will be on informal logic and reasoning, rather than on mere memorization. The questions we will need to repeat for students are, "What do you notice about this figure?" and "Is this true of all figures with this name?" In November, the Calendar will feature an eight-day pattern of shapes in the following order: quadrilateral, arrowhead, kite, trapezoid, parallelogram, rhombus, rectangle, and square. Every fourth figure will have at least one right angle.

FREQUENCY

Update daily. Include the weekend dates on Monday. Discuss at the end of each week.

UPDATE PROCEDURE

Each day, post the November Calendar Piece for the date. If you choose to use the Quadrilateral Cutouts (TR7), write the date on each Calendar Piece before posting. Ask the students to study the quadrilateral carefully each day, keeping in mind that they may be asked to describe it to a person who can't see it. On Friday of each week discuss all the figures for the week.

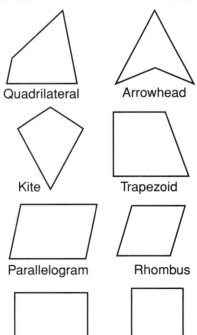

Quadrilateral Arrowhead

Kite Trapezoid

Parallelogram Rhombus

Rectangle Square

Teacher: Triangles are closed figures with three straight lines. Quadrilaterals are closed figures with four straight lines. What are some names for these four-sided figures?

Student: Squares, rectangles, and trapezoids.

Teacher: Some of these have parallel sides. Do all four-sided polygons have parallel sides?

Student: Yes.

Teacher: Can anyone draw a four-sided polygon that does not have any parallel sides?

Student: (Demonstrating) Yes you can.

Teacher: Yes. So not all quadrilaterals have one or more sets of parallel sides. A four-sided figure with at least one set of parallel opposite sides is called a trapezoid. A quadrilateral with both sets of opposite sides parallel is called a parallelogram. We'll list these names here, so you have something to refer to when discussing these figures. Here's another figure (drawing an arrowhead) whose sides are not parallel. Is this a quadrilateral? Why?

Student: No, because it doesn't have four sides.

Student: Yes, it has four sides, but they're different because they go into the shape.

Teacher: Let's see if this figure meets all the requirements to be a quadrilateral. It has four straight sides and it is closed. So yes, it is a quadrilateral. How does it differ from most of the quadrilaterals we have seen before?

Student: Well, it looks more like a bent triangle. But it does have four sides.

Teacher: When a figure has an angle that is more than 180° inside it, we call that a concave shape. I remember that word by thinking that a cave goes in, so a concave shape has some sides that go into it, creating (indicating) this big angle which we will talk about again later on. The other figures are called convex. They don't have these big angles in them. For now, I would like you to keep studying the quadrilaterals that we put up each day. I would like you to be able to describe them in geometric terms, to compare them, and to see if we can find any patterns on the Calendar.

parallel sides

no parallel sides

DISCUSSION FOR THE MIDDLE OF THE MONTH

Use these questions to continue discussion about quadrilaterals.

► What is the order of these quadrilaterals on the Calendar? (Quadrilateral, arrowhead, kite, trapezoid, parallelogram, rhombus, rectangle, and square.)

► What are the similarities between them? (All are four-sided polygons.)

► What are some differences? (Some are concave, some are convex. Some have no parallel sides, some have one set of parallel sides, and some have two sets of parallel sides. Some have right angles, some don't.)

► How many diagonals do all these figures have? (Students will probably answer that some have two and others have one. Point out to students that a diagonal connects one corner, or vertex, to another. So you can draw a diagonal outside the polygon. Every quadrilateral has two diagonals.)

► Which figures have diagonals outside the polygon? (The concave shapes.)

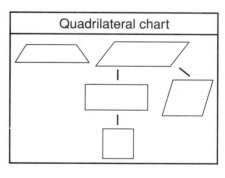

Quadrilateral chart

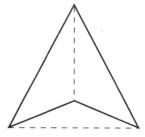

DISCUSSION FOR THE END OF THE MONTH

These questions will encourage discussion about quadrilaterals and their properties.

▶ Which shapes have four equal sides? (Rhombus and square.)

▶ A square is a special kind of rhombus. What makes it a square? (Right angles.)

▶ A square is also a special kind of rectangle. What makes it unique among rectangles? (All four sides are the same.)

▶ Who can explain why a square is both a rhombus and a rectangle? (The opposite sides are parallel and it has four equal sides, like a rhombus. It has four right angles like a rectangle.)

▶ What do you notice about every fourth figure on the Calendar? (They have right angles.)

▶ This trapezoid has a right angle in it. Do all trapezoids have a right angle? (No.)

▶ Can you draw three different kinds of trapezoids? (The upper three boxes in the right column of the Quadrilateral Cutouts (TR7) contain larger versions of the trapezoids illustrated here. They can be used to compare their shapes, special features, and diagonals with the students. You might want to select students to draw in the diagonals of these figures.)

▶ Draw the diagonals for each of these figures. What do you notice about them? (Some have perpendicular diagonals and some do not. Some have diagonals that are equal in length and some do not.)

▶ How often do the arrowheads appear? (On the 2nd, 10th, and the 18th days. In other words, they appear every 8th day, beginning on the 2nd day.)

▶ On the 26th, the figure is an arrowhead. On what dates would the next two arrowheads appear if the month continued? (On the 34th and the 42nd days.)

▶ How did you figure this out? (By adding 8 to the previous number.)

▶ How can you predict the dates for an arrowhead? (Accept a variety of answers, including the general rule that every number that is two more than a multiple of 8 will be an arrowhead. If students say only that it will be a multiple of 8, write the numbers 2, 10, 18, and 26 and ask if these are multiples of 8. Then write the numbers 0, 8, 16, and 24 below these, so students can see that arrowheads appear on the 2nd day of the month and on every date that is 2 more than a multiple of 8.)

▶ If we were to extend the pattern, would the figure on the 80th day be an arrowhead? How about the 81st day? The 82nd day? (Only the 82nd day, because 82 is 2 more than 80, which is a multiple of 8.)

3 different trapezoids.
All have one set of parallel opposite sides.

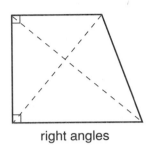

right angles

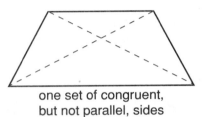

one set of congruent, but not parallel, sides

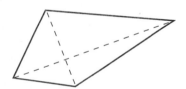

no right angle
no congruent sides

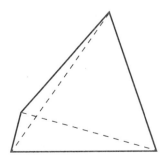

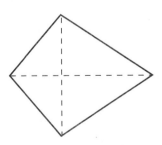

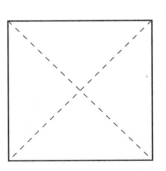

EVERY DAY ELEMENT

FOCUS
▶ Determining prime factors of a number
▶ Understanding that every number has a unique way of being factored into prime factors
▶ Using visual models to explain prime factors

MATERIALS
10 by 10 Squared Paper (TR2), scissors, tape, paper for a chart, construction paper (optional)

FREQUENCY
Update daily. Include the weekend days on Monday. Discuss twice each week.

UPDATE PROCEDURE
In mathematics, we often use a few simple definitions and obvious truths, called postulates, to construct statements called theorems. Theorems are statements that can be proved to be true using these definitions and postulates. A basic theorem in number theory, the Fundamental Theorem of Arithmetic, shows that prime numbers are the building blocks of all positive integers. Every positive integer is a product of prime numbers in one and only one way, except for the order of the factors. In November, we will use the Arrays to display prime factors for the numbers from 1 to 30, corresponding to the day of the month. Prime numbers are, by definition, the result of multiplying one and that number, so it is the composite numbers that require factoring into primes. For example, the number 8 can be made into a 4×2 rectangle, as well as a 1×8 rectangle. The 4×2 rectangle can be broken up into two 2×2 rectangles. So the prime factors for 8 are $2 \times 2 \times 2$, or two groups of 2×2 rectangles. These are the only prime factors for 8.

Each day, ask a student to cut out a rectangle from the 10 by 10 Squared Paper (TR2) to represent the date, and to divide this rectangle into smaller rectangles representing the prime factors of the original number. The student should record the prime factors on a chart. The student should continue to divide the rectangle until only prime numbers are left. For example, twelve squares can be made into a 3×4 rectangle. This can be further cut into two 2×3 rectangles. A student who begins with a 2×6 rectangle will be able to divide this into two 2×3 rectangles. No matter which rectangle is used as the initial representation of the composite, the same prime factors emerge. Use tape to construct rectangles having more than 10 squares. Each Array can be displayed on a piece of construction paper and posted around the room during the month.

Prime factors of 6

2, 3

Prime factors of 8
two 2 x 2, or
2 x 2 x 2

Prime factors of 12

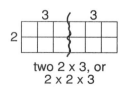

2 x 2 x 3

two 2 x 3, or
2 x 2 x 3

SAMPLE DISCUSSION FOR THE BEGINNING OF THE MONTH

Teacher: This month, we will continue to build rectangular arrays for the days of the month. However, in November we are going to do something different with these Arrays. We are going to look very carefully at the composite numbers, the numbers with more than one possible rectangle. Some mathematicians have said that every number can be broken into prime factors. That means that every composite number is the result of multiplying some prime numbers. We are going to see if this is true for the thirty days in November. What is the date today?

Student: November 4th.

Teacher: So we need the rectangles for 1, 2, 3, and 4. I have the rectangles for the first, second and third here. How many rectangles will there be for each of those days?

Student: One for each day, because they are prime numbers.

Teacher: Is 1 a prime number?

Student: Well you can only make one rectangle for the number 1.

Teacher: That is true. It would be interesting to ask mathematicians why they don't consider 1 to be a prime number. But the definition of a prime number is that it is the product of 1 and itself, implying that it is a number other than 1. So mathematicians have agreed that 1 will not be considered a prime number. (You may also want to mention that the number 1 doesn't have a unique set of prime factors, since 1×1 is the same as $1 \times 1 \times 1$, or $1 \times 1 \times 1 \times 1$, and so on.) What about the number 4? Is it prime or composite, and why?

Student: Composite, because you can make a 1×4 and a 2×2 rectangle.

Teacher: We know that 2 is a prime number, so the prime factors of 4 are 2×2. Is 4 the product of any other prime numbers?

Student: No, only 2×2.

Teacher: Let me show you how to draw a factor tree for 4. I want you to use these factor trees when it is your day to record the prime factors. Tomorrow we'll have another prime number, so we'll wait awhile to decide if all composite numbers can be broken into prime factors in one and only one way.

Number	Prime factors
1	1
2	1, 2
3	1, 3
4	2, 2
5	1, 5
6	2, 3
7	1, 7
8	2, 2, 2
9	3, 3
10	2, 5
11	1, 11
12	2, 2, 3
13	1, 13
14	2, 7
15	3, 5
16	2, 2, 2, 2
17	1, 17
18	2, 3, 3
19	1, 19
20	2, 2, 5
21	3, 7
22	2, 11
23	1, 23
24	2, 2, 2, 3
25	5, 5
26	2, 13
27	3, 3, 3
28	2, 2, 7
29	1, 29
30	2, 3, 5

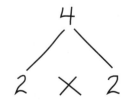

DISCUSSION FOR THE MIDDLE OF THE MONTH

Use these questions to discuss prime factors.

► Today is the 15th of November. What rectangle can we make to find prime factors? (A 3 × 5 rectangle.)

► Are these prime factors? (Yes.)

► Today is the 18th. How many rectangles can you make? (3)

► Which one should we start with to look for prime factors? (Either the 6 × 3 or the 9 × 2 rectangle can be used.)

► If we start with the 6 × 3 rectangle, how can we cut it into equal parts? (Two 3 × 3 rectangles, or 2 × 3 × 3. Note that the 2 × 9 rectangle is a little more complicated, because the 9 must also be factored. If this proves to be confusing, have the students look back to the 9th day to find the prime factors for 9.)

► Today is the 20th of the month. Does anyone want to make a guess about what the prime factors might be, before we divide the rectangles? (2 × 2 × 5)

► Which rectangle should we start with? (Either the 4 × 5 or the 2 × 10 rectangle.)

► If we start with the 4 × 5 rectangle, how can we divide it? (Into two 2 × 5 rectangles.)

► If we start with the 2 × 10 rectangle, how can we divide it? (Into two 2 × 5 rectangles.)

DISCUSSION FOR THE END OF THE MONTH

These questions deal with factoring the numbers that come up later in the month.

► 24 is an interesting number. Which rectangle should we start with? (The 4 × 6, the 3 × 8, or the 2 × 12 rectangle.)

► Draw a sketch of each one of these and see if you can find the prime factors for 24. (2 × 2 × 2 × 3. Point out that there are 4 factors—three 2's and one 3. Also point out that the 4 × 6 rectangle requires you to divide twice.)

► What are the prime factors of 30? (2 × 3 × 5) What rectangle will you use to figure this out? (The 5 × 6, the 2 × 15, or the 3 × 10 rectangle.)

HELPFUL HINTS

► Some students may be able to factor these numbers mentally. Encourage students to draw rectangles or to use graph paper to verify their answers.

► Encourage students to use different strategies for finding the prime factors. Some may always divide a number in half. Others may look for factors that are composite numbers and then factor these.

► This activity helps students develop mastery of factors and to recognize prime numbers. It is probably worth returning to several times throughout the year.

► In future months, you may want to choose a number from the number line and find the prime factors for it.

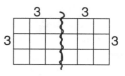

Prime factors of 18

two 3 x 3, or
2 x 3 x 3

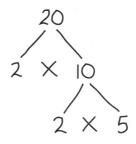

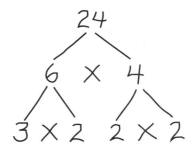

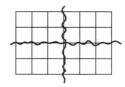

Prime factors of 24

FOCUS

▶ Counting with decimals, fractions, and percents
▶ Visualizing percent with a circular model
▶ Understanding percent as a fraction
▶ Comparing decimals, fractions, and percents; recognizing equivalencies
▶ Developing understanding with commonly used decimals, fractions, and percents

The MATERIALS and FREQUENCY continue from September. See page 7 for a detailed description.

UPDATE PROCEDURE

Students should be responsible for the daily update. Be sure to remind them that the writing must be legible and as neat as possible. Challenge them to find as many equivalent fractions as possible for each decimal. Make sure the Percent Circle is updated with the Counting Tape. The fiftieth day of school will probably occur during November. The sixty-seventh school day may also occur this month. These are excellent opportunities to establish benchmarks for students.

SAMPLE DISCUSSION FOR THE FIFTIETH DAY OF SCHOOL

Teacher: The length of the Counting Tape represents the first one hundred days of school. Each day represents one hundredth of the whole. The length of the Tape is one whole—one hundred days. How many days would $\frac{1}{2}$ of the Counting Tape represent?

Student: 50.

Teacher: How do you know?

Student: Well if the whole is 100, then $\frac{1}{2}$ is 50. If you divide 100 days into 2 equal parts, each part contains 50 days.

Teacher: Other than measuring with a tape measure, how could we determine where the halfway mark is on the Tape?

Student: Take a string and fold it in half.

Student: Have two people start walking from each end of the Tape, and where they meet is the middle if they take the same size steps.

Student: Fold the paper into two equal pieces.

Teacher: These are all good ideas. How can we record the decimal for this 50th day?

Student: (Writes *0.50* on the Counting Tape.)

Teacher: And what is the equivalent fraction?

Student: $\frac{50}{100}$, or $\frac{1}{2}$.

Teacher: What percent of the Counting Tape have we filled in?

Student: 50%.

Teacher: Yes. $\frac{1}{2}$, 0.5, and 0.50 are all equal to 50% of the whole. How much of the Tape will be filled in when we have 100%?

Student: The whole Tape, the whole one hundred days.

Teacher: What if we wanted to know 150% of the Tape? That would be a whole Tape and half a Tape more. On what day of school would we have 150% of the whole?

Student: Day 150.

Teacher: Yes, and how long would the Tape be?

Student: $1\frac{1}{2}$ Tapes long.

Teacher: Good. If we want to know 50% of any number, how can we determine that quantity?

Student: Find $\frac{1}{2}$ of it.

COUNTING TAPE AND PERCENT CIRCLE

$\frac{27}{50}$	$\frac{11}{20}$	$\frac{14}{25}$		$\frac{29}{50}$		$\frac{3}{5}$

$\frac{53}{100}$	$\frac{54}{100}$	$\frac{55}{100}$	$\frac{56}{100}$	$\frac{57}{100}$	$\frac{58}{100}$	$\frac{59}{100}$	$\frac{60}{100}$

0.53	0.54	0.55	0.56	0.57	0.58	0.59	0.60

53%	54%	55%	56%	57%	58%	59%	60%

SAMPLE DISCUSSION FOR SIXTY-THIRD DAY OF SCHOOL

Teacher: What day represented $\frac{1}{4}$, or 25%, of the whole one hundred days?

Student: Day 25.

Teacher: What day represented 50%, or $\frac{1}{2}$?

Student: Day 50.

Teacher: $\frac{1}{8}$ is half of $\frac{1}{4}$, so what day represented $\frac{1}{8}$?

Student: Half of 25?

Teacher: And what is half of 25?

Student: $12\frac{1}{2}$, or 12.5.

Teacher: What day is that?

Student: Halfway between the 12th and the 13th day.

Teacher: Half a day is a really complicated idea. What time is it when half the day is gone?

Student: When does the day begin? At midnight, or in the morning?

Teacher: That's a good question. Does anyone know?

Student: Well I think the day begins at midnight really, even though it's dark. That's when the date changes. If you are born after midnight, it's the next day.

Teacher: So what time will it be when half a day has passed?

Student: Noon.

Teacher: So $\frac{1}{8}$ of one hundred days is $12\frac{1}{2}$ days, which is the same as 12.5% of the days, or noon on the 13th day. What percentage is $\frac{2}{8}$?

Student: 25%.

Teacher: How about $\frac{3}{8}$? Remember that each $\frac{1}{8}$ is 12.5%.

Student: 37.5%.

Teacher: And $\frac{4}{8}$?

Student: Same as $\frac{1}{2}$, 50%.

Teacher: What about $\frac{5}{8}$?

Student: 62.5%.

Teacher: How did you get that answer?

Student: It's 50% and 12.5% more, so it's 62.5 %.

Teacher: Today is the 63rd day of school. What percent of the first one hundred days is that?

Student: 63%.

Teacher: Is that more or less than $\frac{5}{8}$?

Student: It's a little more.

Teacher: Yes, because $\frac{5}{8}$ is 62.5%. So at noon today we will have completed $\frac{5}{8}$ of the first one hundred days of school. Now we have some benchmarks we can use to compare common fractions with equivalent percents. For what fractions do we know some equivalent percents?

Student: $\frac{1}{2}$ is 50%. $\frac{1}{4}$ is 25%. $\frac{5}{8}$ is 62.5%. $\frac{1}{3}$ is $33\frac{1}{3}$%. $\frac{2}{5}$ is 40%.

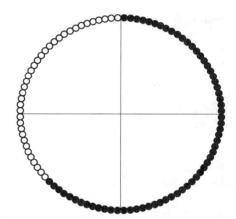

HELPFUL HINTS

▶ Since the students will be primarily responsible for updating this element, it is the teacher's role to make sure that the daily update is correct and to lead the discussion.

▶ Encourage students to find equivalent fractions as often as possible by referring them to the Counting Tape and the Percent Circle and guiding discussion by asking them to determine how many fourths and eighths there are in one half, or how many sixths there are in two thirds. Questions about how many tenths there are in one fifth and three fifths will also help students discover equivalent fractions.

▶ Frequently direct student attention to the decimal, fraction, and the equivalent percent. This is particularly important on days when the decimal can be written as tenths or hundredths, such as the 10th, 20th, 30th, 40th, 50th, and 60th days of school. Help students understand that 0.6 is the same as 0.60 and 60%.

▶ Pose questions that ask students to compare decimals, fractions, and percents. Is 60% closer to $\frac{1}{2}$ or 1 whole? Is $\frac{3}{5}$ more than or less than $\frac{1}{2}$? Which is larger, 60% or $\frac{3}{8}$?

EVERY DAY ELEMENT

DAILY CIRCLE

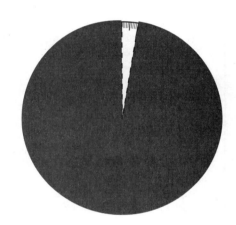

FOCUS

▶ Recognizing angles as measures of turn
▶ Recognizing angles of 10°
▶ Recognizing that circles have 360°
▶ Recognizing that 90° is a $\frac{1}{4}$ turn and that 180° is a $\frac{1}{2}$ turn

MATERIALS

November Circles (gray and white) cardstock, or November Circles (TR8 and TR9), scissors, thumbtack

FREQUENCY

Update daily. Discuss three or four times a week.

UPDATE PPROCEDURE

The Daily Circle will be used in November to help students visualize angles as measures of turn, to measure the number of degrees in a circle, and to recognize some common angles. Each day, the area of the white circle is increased by 10°, providing a visual model to help students develop a sense for degrees.

Cut out both of the November Circles and cut along the radius marked on each of them. Slip the radius of the gray circle (TR8), gray side up, into the radius of the white circle (TR9), printed side up. Each day, turn the gray circle 10° in a clockwise direction to expose more of the white circle, using the printed degree marks to determine the rotation. The degree marks have been printed to help make the angles as accurate as possible. It is not important that students see these marks. The goal is to enable the students to develop visual images for a variety of angle sizes. They need only to see the resulting display to achieve this. The November Circles can be displayed on the bulletin board using a thumbtack at the center point. After thirty days, the white circle will show 300°. Be sure to draw students' attention to the 60°, 90°, 120°, 180°, and 270° angles.

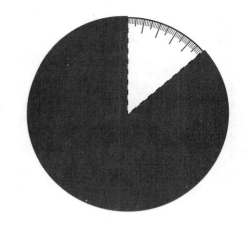

DISCUSSION FOR THE BEGINNING OF THE MONTH

Ask students to identify the name of the move a basketball player makes when turning completely around on the way to the hoop, or the name of the move a skateboarder or skier makes when turning completely around. Elicit the name " a 360." Ask if the students know why it is called "a 360." If the discussion does not result in an answer, explain that students will learn why it is called "a 360" during this month.

Ask the students to tell what they already know about angles. You may demonstrate angles with the opening and closing of a door. When the door is closed, the angle is 0°. As it is opened, it forms an angle between the door jamb and the door. Be sure that students recognize that an angle is a measure of turn and not a distance.

Show students the November Circles. Turn the gray circle 10° in a clockwise direction and explain that each day the circle will be turned 10° more. Ask, How many days will it take for $\frac{1}{4}$ of the white circle to show? What about $\frac{1}{2}$ of the white circle?

Draw a 10° angle on the chalkboard. You may want to demonstrate the use of a protractor. Otherwise, use the November Circles to measure the 10°. Point out and label the vertex and the two rays.

DISCUSSION FOR THE MIDDLE AND END OF THE MONTH

Continue turning the gray circle 10° in a clockwise direction each day. On the 9th day of the month, ask students to identify this special angle. In addition to measuring 90°, it is called a right angle. This might offer the opportunity to reinforce student understanding that an angle is a measure of turn. The angle tells you how far you turn from the origin or starting ray, but not in which direction you turn. To demonstrate this, ask the students to stand, face the front of the classroom, and then ask them to turn 90 degrees. Some students should end up facing left and others right, even though all of them turned 90 degrees.

Ask students to identify other right angles they can find in the room. Draw a large right angle on the chalkboard. Ask a student to estimate 45°. By increasing the angle 10° each day, students should begin to develop some familiar benchmarks for angle size, especially 10°, 30°, 60°, 90°, 120°, and 150° by the fifteenth day.

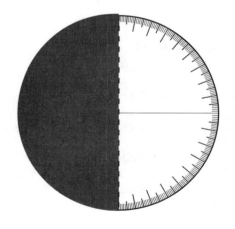

On the 18th day, ask students to identify this special angle. Some students may answer that there isn't an angle anymore. Help them see that while 180° does produce a straight line, it also is the result of turning 180°, or halfway around a circle.

The weekends provide an excellent moment for students to rotate the circle 30°, 10° for each day of the weekend and 10° for Monday. Encourage students to use their arms to estimate a 30° turn.

The days past the 18th are especially helpful for students to become familiar with larger angles which they may not have encountered previously. Students tend to think of angles enclosed in polygons. Moving past the 180° mark demonstrates these larger turns.

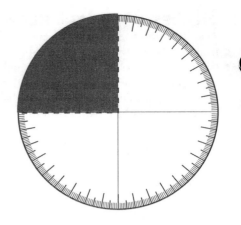

Teacher: Let's turn 10 more degrees. How many degrees is the angle today?

Student: 270°.

Teacher: How many more degrees until we have gone completely around the circle?

Student: 360.

Teacher: Yes, we will have turned 360 degrees, but how many more degrees until we reach an angle of 360°?

Student: Oh, 90 more degrees.

Teacher: So we have turned 270° moving clockwise. If we had started turning counterclockwise, how many degrees would we have turned to reach this same place?

Student: 90°.

Teacher: Yesterday, our angle measured 260°. How many degrees would we have turned counterclockwise to reach the same place?

Student: 100°.

Teacher: Yes. Can anyone tell me a general rule for determining the number of counterclockwise degrees that equal clockwise degrees? Talk to the person next to you and see if you can come up with a general rule to explain this problem.

Student: Well, you just subtract the counterclockwise degrees from 360.

Student: You just figure out how many more degrees until you reach 360.

Student: The sum of the counterclockwise angle and the clockwise angle must equal 360°.

Teacher: Can anyone tell me then why it's called "a 360" when Michael Jordan turns completely around before dunking the basketball?

EVERY DAY ELEMENT

FOCUS

▶ Recognizing triangular numbers
▶ Discovering relationships between area and perimeter
▶ Describing and analyzing mathematical relationships

MATERIALS

Centimeter Squared Paper (TR10), scissors, tape, paper for a chart

FREQUENCY

Students can update the pattern daily, including weekend days on Monday. Discuss the pattern once or twice a week.

UPDATE PROCEDURE

Because the area of the figures increases rapidly this month, use Centimeter Squared Paper (TR10) to make the larger figures easier to manipulate and display. Use tape to construct the figures near the end of the month.

DAILY PATTERN

Area = 1 cm^2
Perimeter = 4 cm

Area = 3 cm^2
Perimeter = 8 cm

Area = 6 cm^2
Perimeter = 12 cm

Area = 10 cm^2
Perimeter = 16 cm

This month, the area of the figure will increase daily by consecutive numbers. That is, the first figure will be one square centimeter, the next day we will add two square centimeters to make an area of three, and the next day we will add three square centimeters to make an area of six. This pattern will continue for the entire month. For the first three or four days, simply post the new figure. Keep a table showing the figure number, the area, and the perimeter of each figure.

DISCUSSION FOR THE BEGINNING AND MIDDLE OF THE MONTH

▶ Today is the 4th of November. What is the area of each of the first four figures? (1, 3, 6, and 10 square centimeters.)

▶ How much did the area increase today? (By 4 square centimeters.)

▶ What are the perimeters of the first four figures? (4, 8, 12, and 16 centimeters.)

▶ How much does the perimeter increase each day? (By 4 centimeters.)

▶ What do you predict the perimeter of the fifth figure will be, and why? (20 centimeters, because it increases by 4 each day.)

▶ What will the area of the fifth figure be, and why? (15 square centimeters because on the fifth day you add 5 square centimeters.)

▶ How many square centimeters will we add on the 10th day? (10)

▶ What will the area be? (55 square centimeters.)

▶ How can you figure that out? (1 + 2 + 3, . . . , + 10, or the area of the 9th figure plus 10 square centimeters.)

▶ What are some fast ways to figure out that amount ? (Add 1 to 10, 2 to 9, 3 to 8, and so on, to make five eleven's. Or add 0 and 10, 1 and 9, 2 and 8, 3 and 7, 4 and 6, and then 5 more. Or find combinations to make 10's such as 2 + 3 + 5, 1 + 9, and so on.) Later this month we will look for even more efficient ways to add these numbers.

▶ Today is the 15th of November. What is the perimeter today? (60 centimeters.)

▶ What are some different ways to measure this without counting? (4 times the date, or the perimeter of the previous figure plus 4.)

▶ Who can show us where the four extra centimeters appear each day?

▶ What is the area today? Who can tell us without counting each square centimeter? (120 square centimeters.)

▶ How did you do that? (Yesterday the area was 105 square centimeters, and 15 added to that is 120. Or 1 + 2 + 3, . . . , + 15 = 120.)

▶ Does the area always equal twice the perimeter? (No, look at the table.)

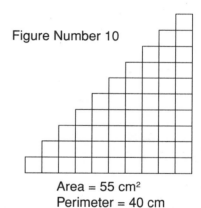

Figure Number 10

Area = 55 cm²
Perimeter = 40 cm

SAMPLE DISCUSSION FOR THE TWENTIETH DAY OF THE MONTH

Teacher: Today we are going to look at our table to see if we can discover some new insights into the increase in area each day. Who can summarize what we know about how the area and perimeter increase each day?

Student: The perimeter increases by four centimeters each day and the area increases by the date, or by the number of the figure.

Teacher: Yes. So the perimeter is easy to figure out. For example, if I asked for the perimeter of the 100th figure, what would you say?

Student: 400 centimeters.

Teacher: Why?

Student: Because each day you add 4. So for the 100th figure it would be 4 times 100.

Teacher: Yes. But if I asked you for the area of the 100th figure, could you do it?

Student: Yes. It will be the area of the 99th figure plus 100.

Teacher: But what is the area of the 99th figure?

Student: We won't know until we get there?

Student: Or you could add 1 + 2 + 3 all the way up to 100.

Teacher: True. These numbers are called consecutive numbers. We want to know the sum of the first one hundred consecutive counting numbers. Let's look at the first few figures. On the first day we had one square centimeter. Then we added two. Then we added three. Lets model that with some square tiles. (Demonstrate with tiles or graph paper.) Is there any way to figure out the area of this third figure without counting? What shape would make it easier to figure out?

Student: Well, if it was a rectangle we could do it easily.

Student: I know. What if we made this into a 3 × 3 rectangle and then found half of it?

Teacher: Try that.

Student: Oh, that would equal $4\frac{1}{2}$.

Teacher: Yes, but I think you are on the right track. We do want a rectangle that we can cut in half. What if we made another figure with the same number of tiles and then fit it into the existing figure to make a new rectangle? Try it.

Student: Well, you would take 6 tiles and fit it in like this.

Teacher: What size rectangle does it make?

Student: Let's see, it is a 3 × 4 rectangle.

Teacher: When we cut it in half, what is the area?

Student: 6 square centimeters.

Teacher: Yes, and that's the area we want to find for the 3rd figure. Let's try that same procedure with the 4th figure. We can use 10 tiles to make the 4th figure. Let's make the same figure with 10 more tiles and fit it into the 4th figure. What size rectangle does it make?

Student: A 4 × 5 rectangle.

Teacher: So to figure the area of the 4th figure, we make a rectangle that is 4 × 5, and then cut it in half. Pick out another figure and see if it works every time.

Student: It does. For the 10th figure, you would make a 10 × 11 rectangle, that's 110, and then cut it in half and it makes 55.

Teacher: So if this is the 20th day, how can we determine the area of the 20th figure? We know it is the sum of the first twenty consecutive counting numbers.

Figure Number	Area (cm²)	Perimeter (cm)
1	1	4
2	3	8
3	6	12
4	10	16
5	15	20
6	21	24
7	28	28
8	36	32
9	45	36
10	55	40
11	66	44
12	78	48
13	91	52
14	105	56
15	120	60
16	136	64
17	153	68
18	171	72
19	190	76
20	210	80
21	231	84
22	253	88
23	276	92
24	300	96
25	325	100
26	351	104
27	378	108
28	406	112
29	435	116
30	465	120

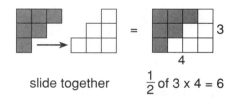

slide together $\frac{1}{2}$ of 3 x 4 = 6

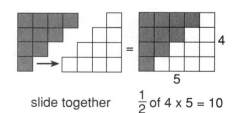

slide together $\frac{1}{2}$ of 4 x 5 = 10

Student: We'd make a 20 × 21 rectangle and then cut it in half.

Teacher: Who can do that quickly in their head?

Student: Well 20 divided by 2 is 10, and 10 times 21 is 210 square centimeters.

Teacher: Is 20 divided by 2 times 21 the same as multiplying 20 by 21 and then dividing by 2?

Student: Yes.

Teacher: Why?

Student: Because they have the same answer.

Teacher: Yes, and why is that?

Student: I'm not sure.

Teacher: I would like the you all to think about this tonight. For now, do you think we can come up with a general rule to explain how to determine the area of any figure, if it is made up of consecutive counting numbers? How can we describe the process we have used so far, in mathematical terms?

Student: You make a rectangle that is that number on one side and one more than that number on the other side. Find the area of the rectangle and divide that by two.

Teacher: Using mathematical symbols, we could say that it is the number, let's call it *n*, times one more than the number, let's call it *n* +1. This gives us the area of the rectangle. Now what?

Student: Divide by two.

Teacher: We write that in math symbols as $\frac{n \times (n+1)}{2}$ or even $\frac{n(n+1)}{2}$, because when two letters are placed next to each other, we multiply them even if there isn't a multiplication sign between them. Don't worry too much about these symbols. Just try to remember how we found the sum of these consecutive numbers by creating a rectangle, finding its area, and then dividing it in half.

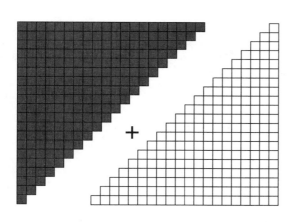

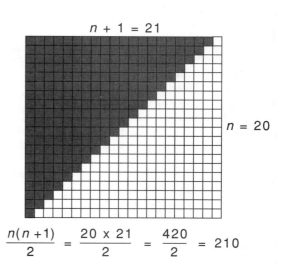

$n + 1 = 21$

$n = 20$

$$\frac{n(n+1)}{2} = \frac{20 \times 21}{2} = \frac{420}{2} = 210$$

EVERY DAY ELEMENT

FOCUS
▶ Understanding the concept of a variable
▶ Using mathematical symbols to record variables
▶ Evaluating mathematical expressions

MATERIALS
Paper for a chart

FREQUENCY
Update daily, including the weekend days on Monday. Discuss once each week.

UPDATE PROCEDURE
Students will continue to evaluate an expression tied to the date and the number of the month. In November, students will calculate the value for ten times the date plus 11, for the 11th month. Repeat the procedure used last month to evaluate the new expression. Keep a chart again this month and change the column headings over the course of the month. Begin with a verbal statement of this month's expression (*Ten times the date plus eleven equals Value*) and proceed to a mathematical equation (*10n + 11 = Value*) by the end of the month. Be sure to explain again that *n* in this case means the number of the day.

SAMPLE DISCUSSION FOR THE TWENTIETH DAY OF THE MONTH

Teacher: Today is the 20th of November. We want to find the value of $10n + 11$ where n is the number of the day. What is the value of the expression $10n + 11$ when n is 20?
Student: 211.
Teacher: How did you do that?
Student: Well, I multiplied 20 by 10 and then added 11.
Teacher: How did you multiply by 10?
Student: I just added a zero to 20.
Teacher: Why?
Student: Well because it works like that.
Teacher: Who can tell me why that works?
Student: I guess because what we are really doing is finding 20 tens, and that's 200.
Teacher: True. What will the value of the expression be tomorrow?
Student: 221.
Teacher: How do you know?
Student: It will be 10 times 21 plus 11.
Teacher: How much is 10×21?
Student: 210.
Teacher: Who can explain how to add 11 to this quickly?
Student: I think of it as $210 + 10 + 1$, so 221.
Student: I just think $200 + 10 + 11$.
Teacher: I hope you all can evaluate this month's expression mentally, without needing to write it down. Find a strategy of your own to help you do this.

DAILY VARIABLE

Ten times the date plus eleven equals Value		

10*d*	+ 11	= Value

10*n*	+ 11	= Value

10*n*	+ 11	= Value
10	11	21
20	11	31
30	11	41
40	11	51
50	11	61
60	11	71
70	11	81
80	11	91
90	11	101
100	11	111
110	11	121
120	11	131
130	11	141
140	11	151
150	11	161
160	11	171
170	11	181
180	11	191
190	11	201
200	11	211
210	11	221
220	11	231
230	11	241
240	11	251
250	11	261
260	11	271
270	11	281
280	11	291
290	11	301
300	11	311

$2325

FOCUS

▶ Developing an understanding of common percents
▶ Using and calculating percents

The MATERIALS and FREQUENCY continue from September. See page 14 for a detailed description.

UPDATE PROCEDURE

Each day, the date will be multiplied by $100. Students will then mentally calculate 5% of this amount and deposit it in the Daily Depositor. Ask students to mentally calculate the daily addition to arrive at the new total. The new total should then be written on the recording sheet each day. Students can update the weekend days on Monday. Ask the students if they can predict how much money will be deposited this month. Hopefully, they will use the data from the first two months. At the end of the month, be sure to add the total amount deposited in November to the chart showing the totals deposited in September and October.

SAMPLE DISCUSSION FOR THE END OF THE MONTH

Teacher: Today is the 30th of November. How much should we deposit today?

Student: 5% of $3000.

Teacher: Explain to me how to determine this amount. Pretend I don't know how to do this. Lead me through the steps.

Student: The easiest way, I think, is to find 10% and then divide it in half to find 5%. So to find 10% of $3000, you think of finding $\frac{1}{10}$ of $3000, or else divide $3000 by 10 to find 10%.

Teacher: How do I figure out $\frac{1}{10}$ of $3000?

Student: Just think, to divide $3000 into 10 equal parts, each part must have $300 in it. Or think, 10 times what number equals $3000? So if 10% of $3000 is $300, then 5% must be half of that, or $150.

Teacher: How much money have we deposited this month?

Student: $2325.

Teacher: How does that compare to what we had deposited on the same date in September?

Student: It's half as much.

Teacher: How does it compare to what we had deposited on the same date in October?

Student: It's a little less than $\frac{1}{4}$ as much.

Teacher: If we only have $100, $10, and $1 bills, what is the fewest number of bills we can use to make $2325?

Student: 30 bills.

Month	Operation	Total
September	(date x $100) x 10%	$4650
October	(date x $100) x 20%	$9920
November	(date x $100) x 5%	$2325
December		

DECEMBER

WINDING DOWN THE CALENDAR YEAR

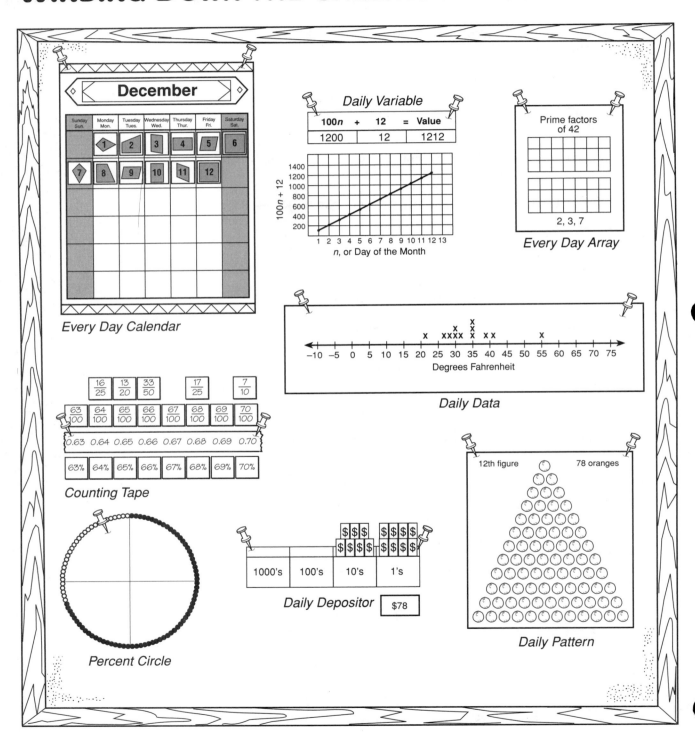

December

Sunday Sun.	Monday Mon.	Tuesday Tues.	Wednesday Wed.	Thursday Thur.	Friday Fri.	Saturday Sat.
	1	2	3	4	5	6
7	8	9	10	11	12	

Every Day Calendar

Daily Variable

100n	+	12	=	Value
1200		12		1212

$100n + 12$ vs. n, or Day of the Month

Prime factors of 42

2, 3, 7

Every Day Array

Daily Data — Degrees Fahrenheit

$\frac{16}{25}$ $\frac{13}{20}$ $\frac{33}{50}$ $\frac{17}{25}$ $\frac{7}{10}$

$\frac{63}{100}$ $\frac{64}{100}$ $\frac{65}{100}$ $\frac{66}{100}$ $\frac{67}{100}$ $\frac{68}{100}$ $\frac{69}{100}$ $\frac{70}{100}$

0.63 0.64 0.65 0.66 0.67 0.68 0.69 0.70

63% 64% 65% 66% 67% 68% 69% 70%

Counting Tape

Percent Circle

1000's	100's	10's	1's

Daily Depositor $78

12th figure   78 oranges

Daily Pattern

Because there are fewer teaching days this month, only one new element, Daily Data, will be added. The goal for this month will be to consolidate understanding of the major concepts introduced so far. All of the existing elements will be maintained and updated. In December, for the Daily Data element, students will collect and record temperature information and display it on a number line. Other types of graphs will be used in future months. Students will be asked to consider questions about the shape of the data they have collected and will be introduced to some useful terminology for interpreting the information they have gathered.

EVERY DAY ELEMENT

CALENDAR

FOCUS

▶ Analyzing and predicting patterns
▶ Recognizing and analyzing quadrilaterals
▶ Sorting and classifying shapes according to properties

MATERIALS

Every Day Calendar, December Month Strip, December Calendar Pieces, or Quadrilateral Cutouts (TR7) and marker; paper for a chart

SUGGESTED PATTERN FOR DECEMBER

In December, we will use a repeating six-day pattern of quadrilaterals in the following order: kite, trapezoid, parallelogram, rectangle, rhombus, and square. Each time the pattern repeats, rotate the quadrilateral 90° in a clockwise direction.

FREQUENCY

Update daily. Discuss at the end of each week.

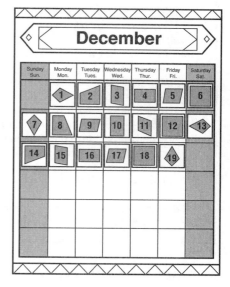

UPDATE PROCEDURE

Each day, post the Calendar Piece for the date. If you choose to use the Quadrilateral Cutouts (TR7), write the date on each piece before posting, remembering to rotate the pieces each time they repeat. Add the Calendar Pieces for the weekend dates on Monday. Ask the students to study each quadrilateral carefully, paying special attention to the sides and diagonals of each one. On the last school day of each week, discuss all the figures posted during the week, comparing their properties and looking for patterns.

Teacher: Let's review what we learned last month about quadrilaterals. What is a quadrilateral?

Student: A four-sided polygon.

Teacher: Let's look at the first four shapes we have put up this month. What is this first one called?

Student: A kite.

Teacher: What makes it a kite?

Student: Well, it looks like a kite.

Teacher: True. But what makes it a kite, and not a different kind of quadrilateral?

Student: Well, two sides are equal and then the other two sides are equal.

Teacher: I think I understand, but could you be even clearer so that even a person who didn't see the kite could visualize it from your description?

Student: The two top sides are equal and the two bottom sides are equal.

Teacher: What if I turned the kite sideways? Does it stop being a kite, since the top two sides are not equal?

Student: Well no.

Teacher: So what makes it a kite? How else could you describe the sides that are equal?

Student: They are next to each other.

Teacher: Yes, and they are called adjacent sides. So a kite is a quadrilateral with two sets of equal or congruent adjacent sides. It may seem picky, but mathematicians try to be as precise as possible. That makes it much easier to talk to one another about mathematical ideas. Are there any parallel sides in this kite?

Student: No. But it looks like there could be if you moved them a little.

Teacher: That's a good observation. Can a kite have parallel sides? Does it have to have parallel sides?

DISCUSSION FOR THE MIDDLE OF THE MONTH

Continue the discussion about the shapes you have posted during each week, focusing the student's attention on the presence or absence of parallel and congruent sides. These questions will facilitate discussion.

► How many parallel and congruent sides do all parallelograms contain? (Two sets of parallel sides and two sets of congruent opposite sides.)

► If a rectangle is a special parallelogram, what can we say about its sides? (Its opposite sides are parallel and congruent.)

► What makes a rectangle a special parallelogram? (It contains right angles.)

► Do all parallelograms have right angles? (No.) Why not? (Encourage students to say in their own words that since all rectangles are parallelograms, they have all the properties of parallelograms, but since not all parallelograms are rectangles, not all parallelograms have the properties of rectangles.)

► How many congruent sides are there in a rhombus? (4) How many parallel sides are there? (Two sets.) Which sides are parallel? (Opposite sides.)

Teacher: Let's make a table summarizing what we know about our quadrilaterals for this month. In the first column of this chart we will list the shapes. In the second column, we will write the number of parallel sides they each have. The third column will be used to record how many congruent sides each one has. In the fourth column, we will write the number of right angles they each have. The fifth column will be used to record something about the diagonals of each of these shapes. (Write *Diagonals* above the fifth column. Students should fill in the first four columns of the chart at this point.) I am going to use my straight edge to draw the diagonals of these quadrilaterals. Let's look at the diagonals of the kite. What can we say about these two lines?

Student: They cross each other.

Teacher: What is that called in mathematics?

Student: They intersect.

Teacher: What can you tell me about that intersection?

Student: It looks like right angles.

Teacher: Does anyone know what we call two lines that intersect at a right angle?

Student: Perpendicular?

Teacher: Yes. Can anyone spell that? It's a difficult word that confuses many people. (Write *Perpendicular* above *Diagonals* on the chart.) What else can you tell me about these diagonals? Are they congruent?

Student: Definitely not.

Teacher: Here's a tough question. Can the diagonals of a kite be congruent? Is there any kite where they are congruent? Draw some different kites and see if the diagonals are always perpendicular, and see if they are ever equal. Do you notice anything special? (Notice if any students realize that a rhombus is a special kind of a kite.)

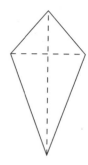

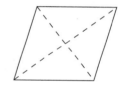

Perpendicular
diagonals

Shape	Number of Parallel Sides	Number of Congruent Sides	Right Angles	Perpendicular Diagonals
Kite	0	2 pair	0	Yes
Trapezoid	1 pair	0	0	No
Parallelogram	2 pair	2 pair	0	No
Rectangle	2 pair	2 pair	4	No
Rhombus	2 pair	2 pair (all equal)	0	Yes
Square	2 pair	2 pair (all equal)	4	Yes

HELPFUL HINTS

▶ Frequently, students are encouraged to memorize geometric terms routinely. For some students, this has led to a view of geometry as a vocabulary study rather than as a study of a field of mathematics. With the Every Day Calendar, we are trying to encourage students to spend more time on analyzing, conjecturing, and reasoning, with less emphasis on memorization. Posting vocabulary around the room and fostering speculation about different shapes may involve more students in this critically important topic. Sixth grade is often the first time that students begin to develop informal ideas of proof.

▶ Post the completed chart showing the properties of the sides and diagonals of the quadrilaterals in the room.

FOCUS
▶ Determining prime factors of a number
▶ Understanding that every number has a unique way of being factored into prime factors
▶ Using visual models to explain prime factors

The MATERIALS and FREQUENCY are the same as in November. See page 37 for a detailed description.

UPDATE PROCEDURE
In December, we will continue finding prime factors for numbers. In order to give students experience with larger numbers, add the 30 days of November to the date in December. Include the week-end days on Monday.

DISCUSSION THROUGHOUT THE MONTH
These questions provide points of departure for discussion on various days of the month.

▶ Today is the 10th of December, so we want to find the prime factors of 40. What rectangle should we begin with? (The 2×20, the 4×10, or the 5×8 rectangle.)

▶ Let's look at the 5×8 rectangle. We can see that one side is already a prime number. How will we divide the other side? (Into two 4×5 rectangles, or $2 \times 4 \times 5$.)

▶ Are these all prime numbers? (No, 4 is not a prime number.)

▶ How can we divide these rectangles further? (Divide each 4×5 rectangle into two 2×5 rectangles. Now we have $2 \times 2 \times 2 \times 5$.)

If you have already taught students exponential notation, this is a perfect time to reinforce it. Otherwise, you may wish to introduce it at this time.

▶ Another way to write $2 \times 2 \times 2$ is 2^3. This means $2 \times 2 \times 2$. Remember that it doesn't mean three 2's. It means two groups of two by two's.

▶ Today is the 12th of December, so what number do we want to find prime factors for today? ($12 + 30 = 42$.)

▶ What rectangle do you want to begin with? (The 2×21, the 6×7, or the 3×14 rectangle.)

▶ Does it matter which rectangle we begin with? Will we find the same prime factors no matter which rectangle we start with? (The prime factors will be the same. Only the order of $2 \times 3 \times 7$ might be different.)

▶ How many days are in a year? (365)

▶ It would be difficult to draw a rectangle for that number. If we did, what size rectangle would you begin with? (Perhaps a 5×73 rectangle.)

▶ How do you know that 5 is a factor? (The original number ends in a five.)

▶ What about the 73? Can it be divided or factored? (No.)

▶ When you see a large number like 73, how do you decide if it can be factored? (Try a variety of factors. There is no way to divide 73 into even groups.)

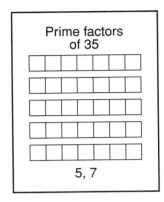

Prime factors of 35

5, 7

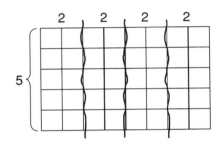

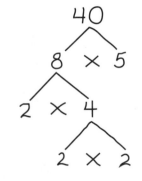

$2 \times 2 \times 2 \times 5$

FOCUS

▶ Counting with decimals, fractions, and percents
▶ Visualizing percents with both circular and area models
▶ Understanding percent as a fraction
▶ Comparing decimals, fractions, and percents; recognizing equivalencies
▶ Developing understanding with commonly used decimals, fractions, and percents

$\frac{17}{25}$		$\frac{7}{10}$		$\frac{18}{25}$		$\frac{37}{50}$	$\frac{3}{4}$

$\frac{68}{100}$	$\frac{69}{100}$	$\frac{70}{100}$	$\frac{71}{100}$	$\frac{72}{100}$	$\frac{73}{100}$	$\frac{74}{100}$	$\frac{75}{100}$

0.68	0.69	0.70	0.71	0.72	0.73	0.74	0.75

68%	69%	70%	71%	72%	73%	74%	75%

MATERIALS

Continue using the MATERIALS from the preceding months. In addition, the 10 by 10 Squared Paper (TR2) should be used to help students make connections between different models.

The FREQUENCY and UPDATE PROCEDURE continue from the preceding months. See page 7 for a detailed description.

DISCUSSION THROUGHOUT THE MONTH

By December, students will have been in school for fifty to eighty days. See the November Counting Tape and Percent Circle for a discussion of the 50th and 63rd days of school.

As we approach the end of the first one hundred days of school, it will prove helpful to students to have a good understanding of the connections between the three different models for decimals, fractions, and percents. Frequently draw their attention to the Counting Tape, the Percent Circle, and the 10 by 10 Squared Paper, and discuss how they relate to each other.

DISCUSSION FOR THE SEVENTY-FIFTH DAY OF SCHOOL

On the 75th school day, look at the 75 colored circles on the Percent Circle.

▶ How far around the large circle have the smaller circles been colored? (270°, or $\frac{3}{4}$, or 75% of the way.)
▶ How far along the Counting Tape have we come? (0.75, or $\frac{3}{4}$, or 75% of the way.)
▶ Since the Counting Tape is 200" long, how many inches are covered? (Encourage students to reason that 75 out of 100 is 75% and therefore 75 out of each 100 makes 150", 75% of 200.)
▶ What can we say about the position of the 75th day on the number line? How can we describe its location on the Counting Tape? (It is midway between the half and the whole, the same distance to the right of 50 as 25 is to the left of 50, and so on.)

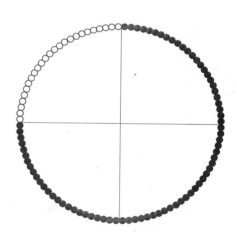

Introduce the 10 by 10 Squared Paper to the students.

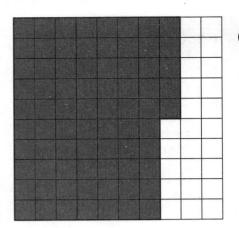

Teacher: How can we describe this figure as a whole?
Student: It's a square.
Teacher: What makes up the square?
Student: Lots of little squares.
Teacher: How many little squares? It may be hard for some of you to see so I'll tell you that it is a 10 × 10 grid.
Student: 100 small squares.
Teacher: How many squares would we color to show 50%?
Student: 50.
Teacher: Why?
Student: Well, 50 is half of 100, and 50% is $\frac{1}{2}$.
Teacher: Good. Is there any other way to solve this?
Student: 50% is the same as 0.50, or 50 out of 100.
Teacher: How many squares do we need to color to show 75%?
Student: 75 out of 100.
Teacher: Notice that when the Percent Circle is the whole, $\frac{3}{4}$ of the small circles are colored to show 75%. When the Counting Tape is the whole, $\frac{3}{4}$ of the line represents 75%. When the whole is a 10 × 10 grid, $\frac{3}{4}$ of the small squares are colored to show 75%.

FURTHER DISCUSSION DURING THE MONTH

▶ Before we talk about $\frac{2}{3}$, let's review what we know about $\frac{1}{3}$. If we divide 100 circles into 3 equal parts, how many whole circles will be in each part? (33) Three groups of 33 is 99. What do we have to do to the last circle to make it work? (Divide it into 3 equal parts.) What fraction is each part? ($\frac{1}{3}$) So each group now has $33\frac{1}{3}$ circles. How many circles must be colored to show $\frac{1}{3}$? ($33\frac{1}{3}$) How many circles must be colored to show $\frac{2}{3}$? ($66\frac{2}{3}$)

▶ What percent equals $\frac{2}{3}$ of the Counting Tape? ($66\frac{2}{3}$%)

▶ How would you color the 10 × 10 grid to show $\frac{2}{3}$? (Color $66\frac{2}{3}$ small squares.)

▶ What is the decimal equivalent of $\frac{2}{3}$? (0.6666...)

▶ How is this different from many of the other decimal equivalents we have been investigating? (It's a repeating decimal, a decimal that doesn't end, and so on.)

▶ If today is 67% of the first one hundred days, what percentage of days remain? (33%)

▶ What are some fast ways to compute the difference between 100 and another number? (Count up as if you are making change, or add the tens and then the necessary ones.)

▶ What are some ways we could we mark 75% of the space in our classroom?

▶ If $\frac{1}{4}$ is 25%, what percent is $\frac{1}{8}$? (To get $\frac{1}{8}$ we cut $\frac{1}{4}$ in half, so cut 25% in half to get 12.5%.)

▶ How can we find a percent equivalent to $\frac{5}{8}$? (Start with 50% for half and add 12.5% for $\frac{1}{8}$, which makes 62.5% to represent $\frac{5}{8}$, or midway between $\frac{1}{2}$ and $\frac{3}{4}$.)

▶ If today is 62.5% of the first one hundred days of school, what percent is left? (37.5%)

▶ What fraction does 37.5% equal? ($\frac{3}{8}$)

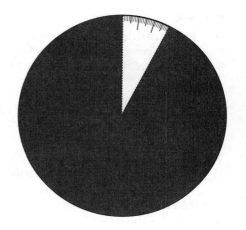

FOCUS

▶ Recognizing angles as measures of turn
▶ Recognizing angles of 10°
▶ Recognizing that circles have 360°

The MATERIALS and FREQUENCY are continued from November. See page 42 for a detailed description.

UPDATE PROCEDURE

Continue increasing the angle 10° each day. Since you have already moved 300° in November, it will take only six more days to go completely around the circle, or 360°. You may wish to stop at this point or you may continue adding 10° each day. Students will then see that turns of more than 360° begin the process of moving around the circle again. Turning 370° is the same as turning 10°, and so on.

Since it is the end of the year, this might be a good time to discuss with students why there are 360° in a circle. Why not 100°, or some other number? Invite students to investigate this question. The 360° comes from the base 60 system of the Babylonians. The Babylonians, thinking that the sun moved around the earth, thought that a year lasted 360 days. A circle therefore represented 360°. Luckily for us, the Babylonians didn't realize that a year has slightly more than 365 days. There are not nearly as many factors for 365 as there are for 360.

FOCUS

▶ Recognizing triangular numbers
▶ Using triangular numbers to solve problems
▶ Using a variety of strategies to discover terms in a series

MATERIALS

Triangular Oranges (TR11 and TR12), scissors, tape, construction paper (optional)

FREQUENCY

Update daily. Discuss once or twice a week.

UPDATE PROCEDURE

The pattern this month will focus again on triangular numbers. This is the same number sequence used last month, but presented in a new visual format. Allow the students to make the connection between this pattern and the one used last month. By reinforcing the lesson from last month, more students will develop a deeper understanding of this important number sequence. Since this is a short month for instruction, we will examine only the triangular shapes for the first twenty consecutive counting numbers.

You will need to make twenty copies of TR11 and ten copies of TR12. On the first day, cut the strip from TR11 showing one orange and post it. On each succeeding day, create the new arrangement by duplicating the previous display and adding the strip containing the next higher number of oranges. Post these each day. By the twentieth day of the month, all the configurations should be posted. You may choose to display the arrangements on construction paper and number them. It may also help the students if the total number of oranges is written with each figure after the class determines the new amount. Remember to include the weekend days each Monday.

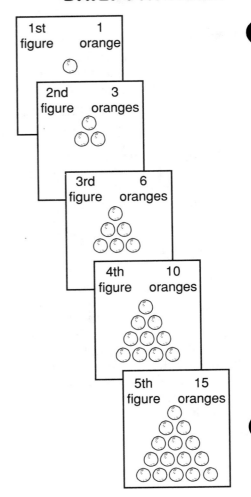

SAMPLE DISCUSSION FOR THE BEGINNING OF THE MONTH

Teacher: This month, we are going to look at a variety of problems that have similar patterns. The local grocer likes to stack her oranges in such a way that they form a triangle. On the 1st day, she stacks one orange. On the 2nd day, she puts two oranges under the first one. On the 3rd day, she adds three oranges under those. Can anyone tell me what the figure will look like on the 4th day, and how many oranges she will need to make it?

Student: It will be a triangle, and I think she will need ten oranges to make it.

Teacher: How do you know?

Student: Well you had 6 and then you add 4 more on the bottom.

Teacher: Good. Does anybody have any other ideas about the 4th figure?

Student: All the figures have a triangular shape except for the 1st one.

Teacher: You're right. But since we can draw a triangle around just one orange, or dot, we will call it the 1st figure. Does anyone have another way to determine the number of oranges in the 4th figure?

Student: This is like the pattern we did last month. The 4th figure is just 1 + 2 + 3 + 4 and we know some fast ways to add up the numbers because they are consecutive.

Teacher: Such as?

Student: I'm not sure that I can explain it.

Teacher: Last month, some of you suggested that we make a rectangle by adding a figure with the same number of oranges, or dots, and fitting it into the existing figure. This way, we get a rectangle that we can divide in half. To find the sum of the first four consecutive numbers then, what would you do?

Student: We would take half of a 4 × 5 rectangle, which is 10.

Teacher: How many oranges will there be in the arrangement on the 5th day?

Student: 15.

Teacher: How did you get that?

Student: Just add 5 to the 4th figure, or think 5 × 6 divided by 2.

Teacher: Who can explain these strategies in words?

Student: Well, if you want to know the 5th figure you just add 5 to the previous sum.

Student: Since we know the 5th figure is just the sum of 1 + 2 + 3 + 4 + 5, we can multiply 5 × 6 and divide that by 2 to find the sum.

Teacher: These are important strategies to remember. And why are these called triangular numbers?

Student: Because you can arrange them in a triangular shape.

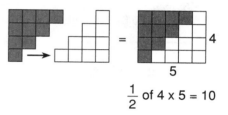

$\frac{1}{2}$ of 4 x 5 = 10

Teacher: Today is the 20th of December, so we will be examining the 20th triangular number. This is the last figure we will examine this month. How many oranges will there be on the bottom row?

Student: 20.

Teacher: Yes, it looks like 20. How many rows high will the stack be?

Student: 20.

Teacher: How many oranges will there be?

Student: We haven't done this in a while, so we have to go back to the 14th figure which was the last one we counted.

Teacher: So which strategy might be more useful in this circumstance, finding the previous sum and adding 20, or determining the sum of $1 + 2 + 3$ all the way to 20?

Student: Probably the second one.

Teacher: What is the general rule for adding consecutive numbers? (The diagram at right may help students recall this general rule.)

Student: The sum of all the consecutive numbers up to a certain number is the last number times one more than that number, all divided by two. If you want to add the numbers up to 20, you just multiply 20×21 and divide the product by 2.

Teacher: Yes. Mathematicians write this as $\frac{n(n+1)}{2}$. The 20th triangular number would be $\frac{20 \times 21}{2}$. How much is that? Are there some easy ways to solve this?

Student: 210. That's the same as 10×21, because you can divide the 20 by 2, which is 10, and then multiply by 21.

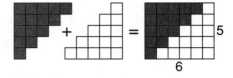

$\frac{1}{2}$ of $5 \times 6 = 15$

HELPFUL HINTS

To reinforce the concept of triangular numbers, it will be helpful to present a variety of problems that can be solved using the methods discussed during the month. Examples follow, some of which will need additional explanation to make the patterns clear to the students.

► If everyone in our classroom shook hands once with every other person in the room, how many handshakes are there in the class? (Explain that since people don't usually shake hands with themselves, the total number of handshakes will be the sum of the consecutive numbers from one to one less than the number of people in the classroom. So n = the number of people in the classroom, p, minus one, or $n = p - 1$.) Now that we have defined n, what is the total number of handshakes?)

► How many straight lines does it take to connect 1 point, 2 points, 3 points, and so on? (0, 1, 3, 6, 10, and so on. Like the preceding problem, n = the number of points, p, minus one, or $n = p - 1$, since one point can't be connected to itself by a line.)

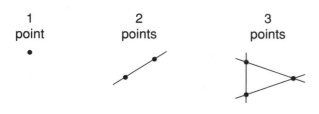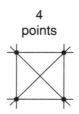

▶ How many diagonals are there in a polygon with three sides, four sides, five sides, and so on? (0, 2, 5, 9, 14, and so on. This problem is different from the first two. In this case, we are adding consecutive numbers but in each case we must omit the number 1. This is because we can't make a polygon with less than three sides, and the triangle has no diagonals. For a ten-sided polygon, we are really adding $0 + 2 + 3 + 4 + 5 + 6 + 7 + 8$, which works out to be 1 less than the sum of the first eight consecutive numbers. It might be interesting to some students to see this written out as an expression. If $n = 2$ less than the number of sides in the figure, the expression is: $[\frac{n(n+1)}{2}] - 1$.)

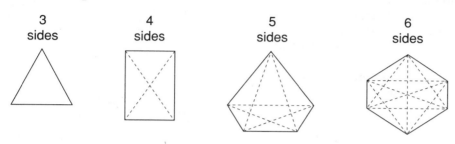

| 3 sides | 4 sides | 5 sides | 6 sides |

▶ A pizza is cut by a novice who can't seem to make each straight cut pass through a common point in the center. How many pieces of pizza are made with one cut, two cuts, three cuts, four cuts, and so on? (2, 4, 7, 11, 16, and so on. This problem is similar to the last one, but since even with zero cuts there is still one piece of pizza, we need to add 1 to the sum of the consecutive numbers equal to the number of cuts. For four cuts, we add one to the sum of the first four consecutive numbers. If $n =$ the number of cuts, the expression for this is: $[\frac{n(n+1)}{2}] + 1$.)

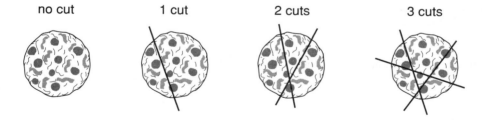

| no cut | 1 cut | 2 cuts | 3 cuts |

▶ With 10 baseball teams, how many games must be played if each team is to play every other team once? (The first team plays 9 other teams, the next team plays 8 other teams, and so on. This is the same problem as the first one, because no team plays a game with itself. So $n =$ the number of teams minus one.)

EVERY DAY ELEMENT

FOCUS
▶ Understanding the concept of a variable
▶ Using mathematical symbols to record variables
▶ Evaluating and graphing mathematical expressions

The MATERIALS and FREQUENCY continue from October. See page 30 for a detailed description.

UPDATE PROCEDURE
Students will continue to evaluate an expression tied to the date and the number of the month. In December, students will determine the value for one hundred times the date plus 12, for the 12th month. Repeat the procedure used last month to evaluate the new expression. Keep a chart again this month and change the column headings over the course of the month. Begin with a verbal statement of this month's expression (*One hundred times the date plus 12 equals Value*) and proceed to a mathematical equation ($100n + 12 = Value$) by the end of the month. Be sure to explain again that n in this case means the number of the day.

SAMPLE DISCUSSION FOR THE THIRTEENTH DAY OF THE MONTH

Teacher: Today is the 13th of December. We want to find the value of $100n + 12$ where n is the number of the day and 12 is the number of the month. What is the value of the expression $100n + 12$ when n is 13?

Student: 1312.

Teacher: How did you do that?

Student: Well, I multiplied 13 by 100 and then added twelve.

Teacher: How much did we increase from yesterday?

Student: Yesterday was 1212, which is 100 less.

Teacher: Let's look at the expression $100n + 12$. Each time we increase n by 1, how much does the value of the expression increase?

Student: What do you mean?

Teacher: How much does the expression $100n + 12$ increase each day?

Student: 100.

Teacher: Why?

Student: Because n increases by 1 each day, so that's one hundred more each day.

Teacher: How much does the value for this expression increase over the weekend?

Student: Do you mean from Friday to Monday?

Teacher: Yes, when n increases by three, for Saturday, Sunday, and Monday.

Student: Then the value increases by 300.

Teacher: Yes. How much does the value of the expression $100n + 12$ increase in one week?

Student: One week is 7 days, so that means it increases by 700.

DAILY VARIABLE

One hundred times the date plus 12 equals Value		
$100n$ +	12 =	Value
100	12	112
200	12	212
300	12	312
400	12	412
500	12	512
600	12	612
700	12	712
800	12	812
900	12	912
1000	12	1012
1100	12	1112
1200	12	1212
1300	12	1312
1400	12	1412
1500	12	1512
1600	12	1612
1700	12	1712
1800	12	1812
1900	12	1912
2000	12	2012
2100	12	2112
2200	12	2212
2300	12	2312
2400	12	2412
2500	12	2512
2600	12	2612
2700	12	2712
2800	12	2812
2900	12	2912
3000	12	3012
3100	12	3112

GRAPHING THE EXPRESSION

Make a graph this month for the Daily Variable.

● On a large piece of graph paper, label the x-axis *n, or Day of the Month* and label the y-axis *100n + 12*. Show students how to find the coordinates of the first few days. Ask students where the fifth point will be. By the thirteenth day, students should be able to see that these points can be connected with a straight line.

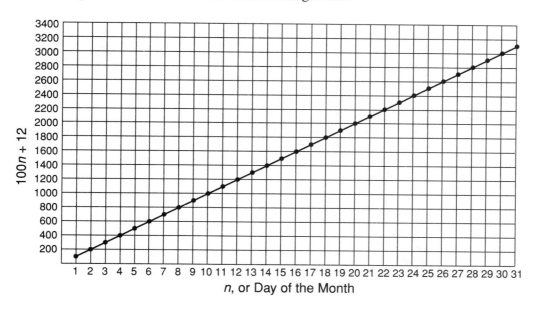

HELPFUL HINTS

▶ The ability to translate from table to graph to symbols is essential. The Daily Variable allows students to develop this ability by providing practice over an extended time.

▶ If you wish to allot additional time to this topic, it would be helpful to compare this month's graph to the one created for the Daily Variable in October. Students might also graph the expression for the November Daily Variable and compare that graph to the other two.

▶ A good homework assignment might be to graph the expressions $n + 12$ and $100n + 12$ on the same graph, and then compare the two lines. The x-axis should be labeled *n, or Day of the Month*. The y-axis should have numbers to 4000 at intervals of 100. See what the students notice about these two lines, especially with regard to their steepness when compared with each other. Suggest that the students graph the expression $100n + 12$ first. Then ask, Why is it easier to graph the second expression first? Check that students recognize that by graphing that expression first and setting up the graph for the larger numbers it requires means that they can graph the other expression at the same scale.

	$ $	$	
1000's	100's	10's	1's

$210

FOCUS

▶ Developing an understanding of common percents
▶ Using and calculating percents

The MATERIALS and FREQUENCY continue from September. See page 14 for a detailed description.

UPDATE PROCEDURE

Each day the date will be multiplied by $100. Students will mentally calculate 1% of this amount and deposit it in the Daily Depositor. By this time, students should be fairly comfortable with mental computation. They will quickly realize that the amount to be deposited equals the date in dollars. We are multiplying by $100 and then dividing by 100. The key concept for students is that 0.01, or $\frac{1}{100}$, of a number is easily calculated. If students can determine 0.01 of a number, then they can determine any percent.

Ask students to compute how much money will be deposited in December if the procedure is carried out for each day of the entire month. (The sum of 1, 2, 3, . . . , to 31.)

DISCUSSION THROUGHOUT THE MONTH

These questions can be used for discussion during December.
▶ Let's look at these examples:
  1% of $100 = $1   1% of $1000 = $10
  1% of $200 = $2   1% of $1600 = $16
  1% of $300 = $3   1% of $2000 = $20
  Who can describe some simple ways to find 1% of a number? (Divide by 100. Move the decimal point two places to the left.
▶ What is 1% of $10,000? ($100)
▶ What is 1% of $1,000,000? ($10,000)
▶ What is 1% of $10? ($0.10) Why?
▶ What is a simple way to compute 2%? (Find 1% and double it.)
▶ What is a simple way to compute 11% (Find 10% and add 1% to it.)
▶ What is 11% of $200? (20 + 2 = $22)
▶ What is 11% of $1000 (100 + 10 = $110)
▶ Display the chart showing the total amounts deposited for each of the first four months of school. Ask how many times greater the amount deposited in September is than the amount in November. (It is twice as much.) Ask, Can you think of a reason why the amount deposited in October is not twice the amount in September? (October has one more day than September.)

Month	Operation	Total
September	(date x $100) x 10%	$4650
October	(date x $100) x 20%	$9920
November	(date x $100) x 5%	$2325
December	(date x $100) x 1%	$496

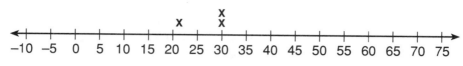

Degrees Fahrenheit

FOCUS

▶ Using a number line to collect and display data
▶ Analyzing data and interpreting graphs
▶ Using statistical terms to describe collected data

MATERIALS

Number line, outside thermometer

OVERVIEW

Analyzing data may be the most necessary and frequently used mathematics in an adult's life. From medicine to the stock market, from newspapers to consumer reports, from elections to sports, we are constantly exposed to data and graphs. By providing frequent opportunities for students to collect, organize, and interpret data, we will enable students to be successful in more advanced mathematics as well as in their daily adult lives.

With this Daily Data element, students will find and record data and display it using different kinds of graphs. They will learn what is meant by the middle, the average, and the typical and learn to compare different sets of data.

This month, students will use a simple number line to display the shape of the daily December temperature. Students will be asked to describe the data, while technical terms such as mean, mode and outlier are introduced as they are useful.

FREQUENCY

Discuss daily for the first three or four days and at least once a week thereafter.

UPDATE PROCEDURE

Make a number line showing the temperature range typical for your area in December. Use °F for the temperatures. Show the number line to the students. Each day, a student will note and record the temperature at a specific time. Assign one student to record the high temperatures for Saturday and Sunday as published in newspaper weather reports. Record the information on the number line. If an outside thermometer is not available, use newspaper reports to find the high temperature from the previous day and record that. You will need to wait until the second day to begin if you are using the newspaper. Show the students how to carefully mark an x above the appropriate number on the number line. It is important that each x be the same size, so you may want to specify that each x be 1 inch or 2 centimeters square.

Discussion for the First Three Days of the Month

Ask students what they think the typical temperature in December might be in your location. Allow students to provide ranges and single answers. Ask for suggestions as to how we could determine what the typical temperature is. Ask the students when they think it would be a good time to take a temperature reading, since it varies in the course of the day. Do we want the highest temperature of the day? The lowest? Or perhaps just the temperature in the morning or at lunch? Decide at which time the temperature will be read.

Explain that the class will be keeping track of the temperature all month long and recording the temperature on the number line. Ask a student to read the outside thermometer and to record the temperature. Show the students how to mark an *x* for the temperature. For example, if the temperature for the first three days is 32°F, 40°F, and 40°F, show it this way:

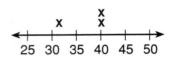

Degrees Fahrenheit

Discussion for the Middle of the Month

After recording 15 to 20 temperatures, the number line should have enough data to begin to make some generalizations. These questions will help with discussions.

► Where do most of the temperatures fall?
► How many are in this range?
► Are there any temperatures which seem particularly unusual, either higher or lower than the others?
► If someone asked you what the typical temperature was so far this month, what would you answer?
► Did any temperature occur more than once?
► Which temperature occurred most often? (Explain that this is called the mode.)
► What is the range of temperatures, from the lowest to the highest?
► Which temperature is right in the middle? (Explain that this is called the median.) How can it be found?
► What is the shape of the data? Are there any clumps of numbers? Are they spread all over?

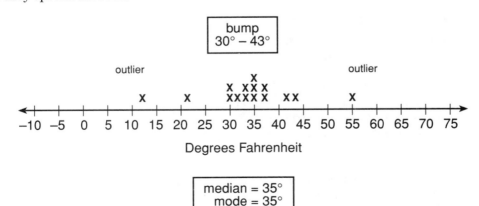

Degrees Fahrenheit

median = 35°
mode = 35°

HELPFUL HINT

Since the actual information that will be recorded is unknown, the graphs included here are only some examples of the possible results in your location. The recorded temperatures may not even lend themselves to providing answers for the discussion questions provided. In any case, explanations of some statistical terms used in interpreting data are given here, so that it is available for discussion with the students should the collected information allow.

► Mean—the average number. The mean is the sum of the numbers in a set divided by the number of numbers in the set. It is really a "balance point" for a set of numbers such that the numbers to the right of this point balance the numbers to the left in terms of distance.

► Median—the middle number when the numbers are arranged in order. If there is an even number of numbers in a set, the median is the average of the middle two numbers.

► Mode—the number that occurs most often in a set of numbers.

► Bump—a cluster of information on a graph.

► Outlier—a number that is very different from the others in a set of numbers.

► Range—the difference between the least number and the greatest number.

JANUARY

STARTING AGAIN

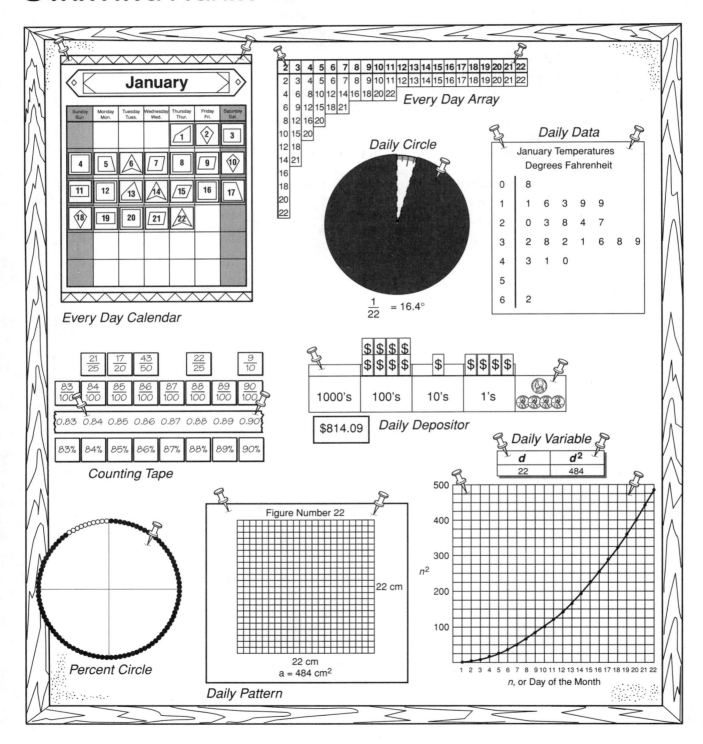

January

Every Day Calendar

Every Day Array

Daily Circle

$\frac{1}{22}$ = 16.4°

Daily Data

January Temperatures
Degrees Fahrenheit

0	8
1	1 6 3 9 9
2	0 3 8 4 7
3	2 8 2 1 6 8 9
4	3 1 0
5	
6	2

Counting Tape

Daily Depositor

$814.09

Percent Circle

Figure Number 22

22 cm

22 cm
a = 484 cm²

Daily Pattern

Daily Variable

d	d²
22	484

n, or Day of the Month

All of the Calendar Math elements introduced so far will be used again in January. This month, students will investigate the line symmetry of various quadrilaterals in the Calendar pattern. The focus will be on helping students to make conjectures and then to test their hypotheses. Students will use the Every Day Array to discover rules of divisibility. The Daily Circle will help students develop new understandings of the angles in a circle while reinforcing fractional concepts. The Daily Pattern will introduce the students to quadrangular numbers. The Daily Variable will expose students to exponential growth by squaring the number of the day. This month, the Daily Depositor will use the concept of interest to increase student understanding of percent. Finally, the Daily Data will introduce the use of a stem-and-leaf plot. It is a full month for students recovering from the fun of winter vacation.

EVERY DAY ELEMENT

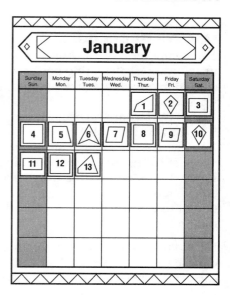

CALENDAR

FOCUS
▶ Analyzing and predicting patterns
▶ Using concepts of line symmetry to analyze quadrilaterals
▶ Recognizing properties of quadrilaterals
▶ Sorting and classifying shapes according to properties of symmetry

MATERIALS
Every Day Calendar, January Month Strip, January Calendar Pieces, or Quadrilateral Cutouts (TR7) and marker

SUGGESTED PATTERN FOR JANUARY
This month features a four-day repeating pattern based on the number of lines of symmetry of eight quadrilaterals. The four-day pattern begins with a figure with no lines of symmetry on day 1, one line of symmetry on day 2, two lines of symmetry on day 3, and four lines of symmetry on day 4. This means that day 1 will be a quadrilateral, a trapezoid, or a parallelogram, day 2 a kite or an arrowhead, day 3 a rectangle or a rhombus, and day 4 a square. It might take the students some time to recognize the rhombus as it appears in this month's Calendar Pieces. It is not the familiar diamond shape because it sits on a side rather than a vertex.

The January pattern is summarized below.

Quadrilateral on 1, 13, and 25
Kite on 2, 10, 18, and 26
Rectangle on 3, 11, 19, and 27
Square on 4, 8, 12, 16, 20, 24, and 28
Trapezoid on 5, 17, and 29
Arrowhead on 6, 14, 22, and 30
Rhombus on 7, 15, 23, and 31
Parallelogram on 9 and 21

FREQUENCY
Update daily. Discuss six to eight times during the month.

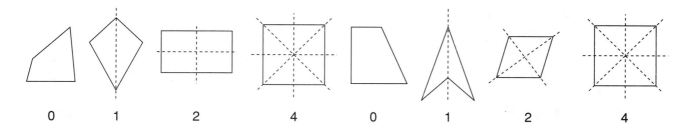

UPDATE PROCEDURE
The computer has transformed the world of work. In addition to its enormous calculating power, the computer also enables the user to manipulate visual and graphic images in extraordinary ways. Students need to be able to visualize the transformation of shapes as they are turned, flipped, and moved in other ways. Recognizing lines of symmetry is essential to this visualization. In January, students will analyze quadrilaterals for lines of symmetry. Some students may already be familiar with the concept of line symmetry. Incorporating mirrors and sketches into the lessons will enable more students to be successful. Just as students can be taught to develop number sense, they can be helped to improve their geometric sense.

Each day, post the January Calendar Piece for the date. If you choose to use the Quadrilateral Cutouts (TR7), write the date on each figure before posting. Add the Calendar Pieces for the weekend dates on Monday.

DISCUSSION FOR THE BEGINNING OF THE MONTH
While many sorting activities and informal conjectures can be undertaken, we will focus on questions of symmetry with the familiar quadrilaterals of the calendar. Ask students to explain or illustrate what they know about symmetry. Encourage students to be as precise as possible in their language. Folding a shape in half is often an easy way for students to demonstrate line symmetry. Explain that this month the students will examine the line symmetry of various shapes to discover a pattern in the order of the shapes.

SAMPLE DISCUSSION FOR THE MIDDLE OF THE MONTH

Teacher: You have had some time to examine these quadrilaterals for their properties of symmetry. Has anyone noticed a pattern to them?

Student: Well, every fourth one is a quadrilateral that doesn't seem to have any lines of symmetry.

Teacher: Do you mean that on every day that is a multiple of 4 there is a quadrilateral without a line of symmetry?

Student: No. But starting with the first day, and then every fourth day after that, there's a quadrilateral without a line of symmetry.

Teacher: Oh, I see what you mean. What else do you notice about the lines of symmetry of these figures?

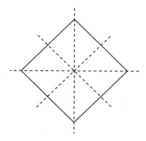

Student: The squares have the most lines of symmetry.

Teacher: How many?

Student: Four?

Teacher: Can everyone find all four? Describe them using the best mathematical language you can.

Student: One line is a vertical line in the middle of the square.

Teacher: If I tilted the square, would it still be vertical?

Student: Well, no.

Teacher: So how do I know where to put it?

Student: It's in the middle of the side, from one side to the other.

Teacher: Just in the middle of one side?

Student: No. Draw it from the middle of one side to the middle of the other side.

Teacher: Good. The middle is called the midpoint of the side. So I draw it from the midpoint of one side to the midpoint of the adjacent side?

Student: No, from the midpoint of one side to the midpoint of the opposite side of the square.

Teacher: Now I can draw it no matter how I tilt the square. And of course you have actually described two lines of symmetry. Does anybody notice anything special about these lines of symmetry?

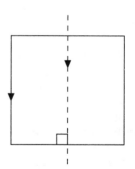

Student: They are parallel to the sides.

Teacher: I would like you to think about that for a while, and tell us why they must be parallel to the sides.

Student: Well we drew a line that is an equal distance from the original line on both ends, so everywhere we measure, it will be the same distance from the original line. It must be parallel.

Teacher: What kind of angle does it create when it intersects with the side?

Student: A right angle. It's perpendicular.

Teacher: Think some more about that, because I'm going to want to know why you think it must be perpendicular. But let's return to our square. Where are the other two lines of symmetry?

Student: A line drawn from one corner to the opposite corner.

Teacher: What is another name for corner?

Student: Vertex.

Teacher: How do you know this is a line of symmetry?

Student: If you folded the square along the line, the two parts match perfectly, they are congruent.

Teacher: Yes, they are mirror images of each other. If I put a mirror on this line, I can see the completed square in the mirror.

ADDITIONAL DISCUSSION FOR THE MIDDLE OF THE MONTH

These questions provide material for further discussion about line symmetry in quadrilaterals.

▶ How many lines of symmetry are there in the kite? (1) How many in the arrowhead? (1) How many in the rhombus? (2) How about in the parallelogram? (0) In the rectangle? (2)

▶ Why aren't the lines connecting the vertices in the rectangle and the parallelogram lines of symmetry? (Because the resulting sides are not mirror images of each other. They require rotation to match perfectly.)

▶ How can we describe the lines of symmetry of the rhombus? (They connect the opposite vertices.) How can we compare that to the lines of symmetry of the square? (The lines connecting the vertices are the same, but the lines connecting the opposite sides are not.)

▶ How do the lines of symmetry of the rectangle compare to those of the rhombus? (Both have two lines of symmetry, but in the rectangle they connect the midpoints of opposite sides and in the rhombus they connect the vertices.)

▶ Why does a square have four lines of symmetry? (It is both a rhombus and a rectangle, and has the same lines of symmetry as both.)

▶ Is there any trapezoid that has a line of symmetry? (Only an isosceles trapezoid.)

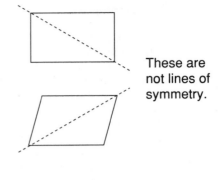

These are not lines of symmetry.

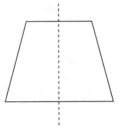

Isosceles trapezoid

DISCUSSION FOR THE END OF THE MONTH

▶ Can you describe the pattern of the January Calendar? (It is a four-day repeating pattern showing quadrilaterals with no lines of symmetry on the first day, one line on the second day, two lines on the third day, and four lines on the fourth day.)

▶ Which shapes can we use for the days showing figures with one line of symmetry? (The kite and the arrowhead.)

▶ Which shapes can we use for the days showing figures with two lines of symmetry? (The rectangle and the rhombus.)

▶ Are there any quadrilaterals other than the square that have four lines of symmetry? (No.)

▶ Where do the lines of symmetry meet in a square? (In the center.)

▶ If we use this same pattern in any month, how many squares will appear? (7) How do you know? (There will be one every four days.) Is there any month where 8 squares will appear? (No.)

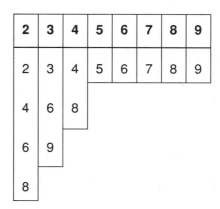

FOCUS
▶ Discovering rules of divisibility of numbers
▶ Recognizing factors
▶ Extending properties of divisibility to larger numbers

MATERIALS
30 strips of paper cut from adding machine tape, markers

FREQUENCY
Update daily. Discuss once each week for the first two weeks of the month, and two or three times each week thereafter.

UPDATE PROCEDURE
Students are often presented with rules of divisibility, asked to memorize them, and then to apply them to large numbers. Our approach will be different because students will be given opportunities to discover these rules for themselves.

Each day, students will write the date on the strips of paper labeled with numbers that are its factors. The Arrays from August/September and the 1 × 31 Array from the last day of October should be available to remind students about the divisibility of the numbers 1 through 31. The students can refer to the Arrays from August/September to discover the factors. For example, if the date is the 12th, that number will be added to the *2, 3, 4, 6,* and *12* columns. We will omit the number 1 and list prime numbers only under themselves. Include the weekend days on Monday.

Make strips of paper from the adding machine tape that will hang vertically near the Calendar on the bulletin board. In black marker, write the numbers 2 through 31 at the top of the strips. The length of each strip is determined by how many times the written number is a factor of the first 31 counting numbers. Allowing 2" for each number that will be written on the strips, their lengths are outlined below.

2 strip - 32"
3 strip - 22"
4 strip - 16"
5 strip - 14"
6 strip - 12"
7 strip - 10"
8 and *9* strips - 8"
10 through *15* strips - 6"
16 through *31* strips - 4"

As the lists grow longer, students will be asked to notice patterns they find for these numbers. If invited, students usually notice that multiples of 3 have digits whose sum is a multiple of 3, that multiples of 5 end in 5 or 0, and that all even numbers are divisible by 2. Sometimes students discover that numbers divisible by 6 must meet the requirements for divisibility by both 2 and 3. It is more difficult for students to discover rules of divisibility for 4, 7, and 8. They may need to examine additional numbers to discover these rules.

For the first two weeks, simply post the number of the date in the appropriate columns. In subsequent weeks, ask the students to decide under which columns the date should be listed.

SAMPLE DISCUSSION FOR THE BEGINNING OF THE MONTH

Teacher: This year is 1998. (Use the current year, whatever number it is.) You know how math teachers are. I was sitting around wondering whether 1998 could be divided by 3 without leaving a remainder. What do you think? Without computing this on paper, what would you suppose?

Student: Well it does have a lot of 9's, so probably yes.

Student: But it ends in a 8, and that can't be evenly divided by 3.

Student: I figured it out in my head, and there is no remainder.

Teacher: This month, we are going to examine the date each day to see if we can discover any rules for determining what numbers might be factors of larger numbers. We will list each date in all the columns of numbers that are its factors. Today is January 6th. Can 6 be evenly divided by 2?

Student: Of course.

Teacher: So we'll list 6 in the *2* column. Can 6 be evenly divided by 3?

Student: Yes.

Teacher: So we will list 6 in the *3* column as well. Can it be evenly dived by 4?

Student: No.

Teacher: So we can't list it in the *4* column. Of course 6 is not divisible by 5. Every number is divisible by itself, so we will list 6 in the *6* column. We will keep track this way during January to see if we can find any patterns of divisibility that we can use for larger numbers.

2	3	4	5	6
2	3	4	5	6
4	6			
6				

DISCUSSION FOR THE MIDDLE OF THE MONTH

Use these questions for discussion later in the month.

► Looking at the arrays we made in September, which numbers between 10 and 20 will be divisible by the most numbers? (12, 18, and 20.)

► What do you notice about numbers that are divisible by 5? (They end in 5 or 0.) Do you think that pattern may continue as the numbers get larger?

► What have you noticed about the numbers that are divisible by 2? (They are all even numbers.)

► In the *3* column, we have listed 3, 6, 9, 12, 15, and 18 so far. Does anyone see a pattern to these numbers? (See if students notice that the sum of the digits of these numbers equals a number divisible by 3. If no one notices this, ask questions that will lead them to discover this rule for themselves, such as "What is the sum of the digits of these numbers, and what do you notice about them?" Try not to point out the fact to the students.)

► Let's see if this rule works for the number of the new year. What is the sum of the digits? Is that number divisible by 3?

► What do we know about any number that is divisible by both 2 and 5? (It must end in a 0.) Why? (The number must be even to be divisible by 2, and end in 5 or 0 to be divisible by 5. Only numbers that end in 0 are divisible by both.)

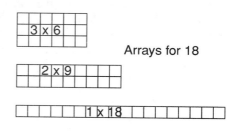

Arrays for 18

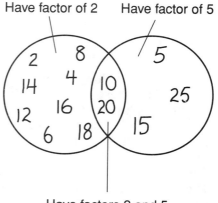

DISCUSSION FOR THE END OF THE MONTH

These questions can be used to initiate more discussion about patterns of divisibility.

▶ Let's look at the numbers divisible by 6. What do you notice about the digits of these numbers? (The sum of the digits equals a number divisible by 3.)

▶ When you compare the list of numbers divisible by 3 with those divisible by 6, what do you notice about the numbers in the 6 column that is not true of the numbers in the 3 column? (They are all even numbers.) Why is this true? (6 is 2 x 3, so the number must be divisible by both 2 and 3. Any number that is divisible by 2 is an even number.)

▶ Will 1999 be divisible by 6? (No, because it is not divisible by 3.)

▶ Do you think the number 35,274 is divisible by 6? (Yes, because it is an even number and the sum of the digits is 21, so it is divisible by 3.)

▶ There aren't many numbers on our chart that are divisible by 9. In fact, 9, 18, and 27 are the only ones we have listed. Since you know other multiples of 9, can anyone find a pattern for the digits of numbers divisible by 9? (The sum of the digits is a multiple of 9. Students may say that the sum of digits equals 9, since they are probably focusing on the first 10 multiples of 9. Encourage them to see if the pattern remains true by asking about 11 x 9, or 99, the sum of the digits equaling 18.)

▶ What is the latest year in the 20th century that is divisible by 9? (1998, because the sum of the digits equals 27.)

▶ Is every number that is divisible by 9 also divisible by 3? (Yes, because the sum of the digits is divisible by 9, and since 9 is divisible by 3, it will be divisible by 3 as well.)

EVERY DAY ELEMENT

COUNTING TAPE AND PERCENT CIRCLE

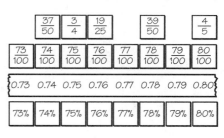

FOCUS

▶ Counting with decimals, fractions, and percents
▶ Visualizing percent with a circular model
▶ Understanding percent as a fraction
▶ Comparing decimals, fractions, and percents; recognizing equivalencies
▶ Developing understanding with commonly used decimals, fractions, and percents

The MATERIALS and FREQUENCY are the same as in preceding months. See page 7 for a detailed description.

UPDATE PROCEDURE

In January, students will have been in school for close to 100 days. See December if the 67th and 75th days of school fall in this month. In many schools, the 100th day of school will fall in January or February. As this day approaches, students have the opportunity to work with quantities close to 1 whole. As at the beginning of the year, this is a good opportunity to compare large fractions with small ones. Students should have a good grasp of the length of the whole. Since students have been in charge of this element for many months, you may choose to discuss it only once a week, while maintaining it daily.

Teacher: Today is the 80th day of school. I want you to write down all the ways you know to write this as a fraction of the first one hundred days. When you are done, look up. Let's list them.

Student: 0.80

Teacher: How do we read this?

Student: 80 hundredths.

Teacher: How about zero point 80?

Student: Not in our class. It just looks like that, but it means 80 hundredths.

Teacher: Good. How else can we write this fraction?

Student: $\frac{8}{10}$.

Student: $\frac{4}{5}$.

Student: 80% of the whole.

Teacher: (Drawing a line on the board.) If this represents 80% of a line, who can show us what the whole line looks like?

Student: (Dividing the line into 4 or 8 equal parts, and then adding either 1 or 2 more equal parts to make one whole.) You have to add this much.

Teacher: Why? Explain what you did.

Student: I knew that the line you drew was 80% of the whole line, which is the same as $\frac{8}{10}$ or $\frac{4}{5}$. So I knew that if I divided it into four equal parts, that would represent four of the five fifths, and all I needed to add was one more fifth to make the whole.

Teacher: What percent of the line did you draw?

Student: 20% or $\frac{1}{5}$.

Teacher: Which is larger, 0.80 or 0.20?

Student: 0.80, of course.

Teacher: I have a difficult question for you. How much bigger is it? What I mean is, how many times bigger?

Student: 0.60?

Teacher: Yes, it is $\frac{60}{100}$ more, but it is not $\frac{60}{100}$ times bigger. How many 0.20 will fit into 0.80?

Student: Oh, I get it, four of them, because 20 goes into 80 four times.

Teacher: One last question. Let's say that the line I drew was 180 centimeters long. Now that you have added the last 20%, how long is the line?

Student: 200 centimeters?

Teacher: How did you arrive at that solution?

Student: I don't know, I just guessed.

Teacher: So how can you tell whether you are correct?

Student: Is it?

Teacher: Is it?

Student: Let's see. If 180 is $\frac{4}{5}$, then finding four equal parts of 180 means that each part is 45 centimeters long, because four 40's is 160 and four 5's is 20. So each fifth is 45 centimeters. If we add another fifth it must be 45 centimeters also, so 180 and 45 is 225 centimeters.

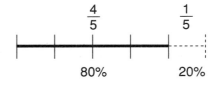

Teacher: What decimal does today represent?
Student: 0.87.
Teacher: How much less than 1 is 0.87?
Student: 0.13.
Teacher: How did you do that so fast?
Student: I counted up 0.03 to 0.9, or 0.90, and 0.10 more to 1.
Teacher: Counting up is a useful strategy for doing calculations in your head. Many people use it when computing how much change they will receive back at a store. It's a lot quicker than writing the subtraction problem on paper. For example, how much more is 2 than 0.87?
Student: 1.13.
Teacher: Why do you think that is the answer?
Student: Well we just decided that 0.87 is 0.13 less than 1, so I just added 1 more to it.
Teacher: That's clever. Could we use the same strategy for counting up, even if we had not done it already?
Student: Yes, just think 0.03 to 0.90, another 0.10 to 1 and 1 more to 2.
Teacher: How much more is 1.25 than 0.87?
Student: 0.38, because it's 0.13 to 1 and 0.25 more, so that is 0.38.

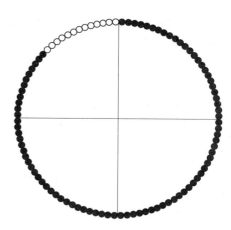

$$0.87 + 0.03 + 0.10 = 1.00$$

EVERY DAY ELEMENT

DAILY CIRCLE

FOCUS

▶ Relating fractions to degrees of a circle
▶ Practicing multiplication of fractions
▶ Recognizing common fractions on a circle

The MATERIALS for the Daily Circle continue from November. See page 42 for a detailed description.

FREQUENCY

Update daily. Include the weekend days on Monday. Discuss once each week.

UPDATE PROCEDURE

Each day, make a fraction using the date as the denominator and 1 as the numerator. Calculate the number of degrees of a circle that this fraction represents. For example, on the 3rd of January, we will consider $\frac{1}{3}$ of 360°, or 120°. On the 4th, we will consider $\frac{1}{4}$ of 360°, or 90°. Move the November Circles to the appropriate number of degrees to display the angle for the day. Make a chart showing the day, the fraction, and the number of degrees the fraction represents. You may also want to add a rough drawing of the appropriate circle.

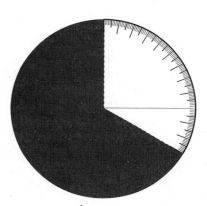

$$\frac{1}{3} = 120°$$

$$\frac{1}{4} = 90°$$

DISCUSSION FOR THE BEGINNING OF THE MONTH

These questions can be used to facilitate discussion.

▶ On the first day of the month, our fraction is $\frac{1}{1}$, or 1. The whole circle is 360°. The second day is $\frac{1}{2}$ of the circle, or how many degrees? (180°)

▶ Today is the 3rd day of January, so we want to show $\frac{1}{3}$ of the circle. How can we show $\frac{1}{3}$ of the circle? (One good way to think of $\frac{1}{3}$ of a circle is to picture a clock showing 4 o'clock or 8 o'clock. The angle made by the hands on the clock at those times shows $\frac{1}{3}$ of the circle.) How many degrees are there in $\frac{1}{3}$ of the circle? (120°) How do you know? (Accept answers such as 360 divided into 3 equal parts, 300 divided by 3 plus 60 divided by 3.)

▶ Look at the fraction and the degrees for January 7th. How is the number of degrees different from the other days? (It is not an even number of degrees.) Why is it different? (Because 7 is not a factor of 360.)

▶ When will this kind of result occur again? (On the 11th, the next number which is not a factor of 360.)

DISCUSSION FOR THE MIDDLE AND END OF THE MONTH

These questions can be used to guide discussion for the remainder of the month.

▶ What strategy is used to determine the number of degrees represented by the fraction? (Divide 360° by the denominator of the fraction and round to the nearest tenth.)

▶ If we know that $\frac{1}{8}$ of the circle is 45°, what is a fast strategy for determining the value for $\frac{1}{16}$? (Since $\frac{1}{16}$ is half of $\frac{1}{8}$, find half of 45°, which is 22.5°.)

▶ What are some strategies for finding $\frac{1}{12}$ of the circle? (360° divided by 12, or think of $\frac{1}{12}$ as half of $\frac{1}{6}$, or compare $\frac{1}{12}$ of the circle to the distance between each hour figure on a clock, and so on.)

▶ Since $\frac{1}{9}$ of the circle is 40°, what is $\frac{1}{18}$ of the circle? (Half of 40°, or 20°.)

▶ If $\frac{1}{18}$ of a circle is 20°, what is $\frac{4}{18}$ of the circle? (80°) What other fraction is equivalent to 80°? ($\frac{2}{9}$)

▶ How many degrees of the circle is $\frac{23}{24}$? ($\frac{1}{24}$ is 15°, so $\frac{23}{24}$ is 360° minus 15°, or 23 × 15°, which is 345°.)

▶ If $\frac{1}{30}$ of a circle is 12°, how many degrees are there in $\frac{1}{15}$ of a circle? (24°) How did you get that answer? (Since the fraction is twice as large, double the number of degrees as well.)

▶ Using the fact that $\frac{1}{30}$ of a circle is 12°, how can you figure out how many degrees are in $\frac{1}{6}$ of a circle? ($\frac{1}{6}$ is the same as $\frac{5}{30}$, so the number of degrees is 5 times larger than 12°, or 60°.)

▶ Since $\frac{1}{30}$ of a circle is 12°, how many degrees is $\frac{29}{30}$? (360° minus 12°, or 348°.)

▶ What fraction of the circle is 1 minute on a clock? ($\frac{1}{60}$) How many degrees is that? (6°)

▶ What fraction of the circle is 20 minutes past the hour? ($\frac{1}{3}$, or 120°.)

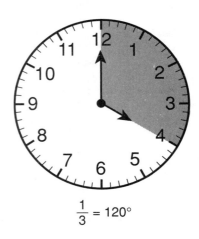

$\frac{1}{3}$ = 120°

Fraction	Degrees
$\frac{1}{1}$	360
$\frac{1}{2}$	180
$\frac{1}{3}$	120
$\frac{1}{4}$	90
$\frac{1}{5}$	72
$\frac{1}{6}$	60
$\frac{1}{7}$	51.4
$\frac{1}{8}$	45
$\frac{1}{9}$	40
$\frac{1}{10}$	36
$\frac{1}{11}$	32.7
$\frac{1}{12}$	30
$\frac{1}{13}$	27.7
$\frac{1}{14}$	25.7
$\frac{1}{15}$	24
$\frac{1}{16}$	22.5
$\frac{1}{17}$	21.2
$\frac{1}{18}$	20
$\frac{1}{19}$	18.9
$\frac{1}{20}$	18
$\frac{1}{21}$	17.1
$\frac{1}{22}$	16.4
$\frac{1}{23}$	15.7
$\frac{1}{24}$	15
$\frac{1}{25}$	14.4
$\frac{1}{26}$	13.8
$\frac{1}{27}$	13.3
$\frac{1}{28}$	12.9
$\frac{1}{29}$	12.4
$\frac{1}{30}$	12
$\frac{1}{31}$	11.6

HELPFUL HINTS

▶ Encourage students to use mental computation for these calculations, rather than pencil and paper.

▶ Encourage students to look for multiple strategies, such as using equivalent fractions and relationships between fractions, to determine the number of degrees represented by the fraction.

▶ Encourage students to use benchmarks such as $\frac{1}{2}$, $\frac{1}{3}$, and $\frac{1}{4}$ to determine other smaller fractions.

▶ Occasionally, use the November Circles as a visual model to encourage students to estimate both the fraction and the number of degrees. By the end of the month, students should have good visual benchmarks for estimating fractional pieces of circles.

EVERY DAY ELEMENT

FOCUS

▶ Analyzing and predicting patterns
▶ Recognizing quadrangular numbers
▶ Using a variety of strategies to discover the terms of a series

MATERIALS

Centimeter Squared Paper (TR10), scissors, tape

FREQUENCY

Update daily. Include the weekend days on Monday. Discuss once or twice each week.

UPDATE PROCEDURE

In January, the students will use this element to study quadrangular numbers. Each day, the date will be squared. Using Centimeter Squared Paper (TR10), create a square each day made up of square centimeters with the number of the date as the length of a side. Use additional copies of Centimeter Squared Paper (TR10) and tape to create the squares later in the month. This month, it's a good idea to display each figure on a piece of construction paper because we will use these figures again for the Daily Pattern in March. Each square should show a figure number, the length of two sides, and the area.

DISCUSSION FOR THE BEGINNING OF THE MONTH

▶ How many centimeter squares are in the second figure? (4) The third? (9) The fourth? (16) What shape do each of these figures make? (A square.)

▶ Last month, we studied numbers that we called triangular numbers. What do you think we will call the numbers this month? (Quadrangular numbers, from quad meaning four, as in a quadrangle on a college campus or as in quadrilateral. We can also call them square numbers.)

DAILY PATTERN

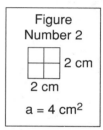

Figure Number 1

1 cm
1 cm
a = 1 cm²

Figure Number 2

2 cm
2 cm
a = 4 cm²

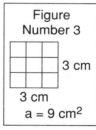

Figure Number 3

3 cm
3 cm
a = 9 cm²

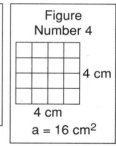

Figure Number 4

4 cm
4 cm
a = 16 cm²

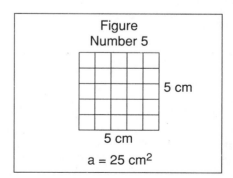

Figure Number 5

5 cm
5 cm
a = 25 cm²

▶ How many centimeter squares are on each side of the third figure? (3) The fourth? (4)

▶ What can you say about the date and the number of centimeter squares on a side? (They are the same number.)

▶ What do you think the figure will look like on the fifth day? (It will be a square with 5 centimeter squares on each side, or 25 centimeter squares all together.) How did you determine that it would be 25 centimeter squares? (There are five rows of five, or 5^2.)

▶ If we make a list of how many centimeter squares are in each figure, what is the difference between each number in the list? (3, 5, 7, 9) What do you notice about these numbers? (They are consecutive odd numbers.)

▶ How many centimeter squares will be added to this figure to make the 6th figure? (11, the next consecutive odd number.)

▶ How can I add centimeter squares to the fifth figure to make the sixth figure? (Add 5 centimeter squares on one side, five on the bottom, and one in the corner.)

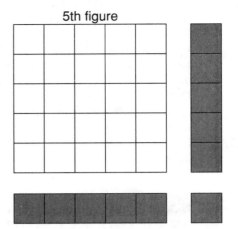

5th figure

SAMPLE DISCUSSION FOR THE MIDDLE OF THE MONTH

Teacher: Today is the 20th of January. What will the 20th figure look like, and how many centimeter squares will it have?

Student: It will be a square with 20 centimeter squares on each side.

Teacher: Yes, but how many centimeter squares will it have?

Student: 400, even though it is hard to count them.

Teacher: How do you know there are 400?

Student: Well you just multiply 20 times 20.

Teacher: Are there other strategies for finding this number?

Student: Yesterday the figure had 361 centimeter squares. Add 19 on one side, 19 on the bottom, and one in the corner. That's 39 more squares. Then 361 and 39 is 400, because 361 and 40 is 401.

Teacher: Wow, pretty impressive. Let's look a little more closely at these numbers. Looking back to the beginning of the month, what were the first five quadrangular numbers?

Student: 1, 4, 9, 16, and 25.

Teacher: What is another name for these numbers, if we don't want to call them quadrangular numbers? Think back to our calendar patterns from the beginning of the school year.

Student: Square numbers?

Teacher: Yes. Why are they called square numbers?

Student: They make squares when you arrange them in an array.

Student: The are a number times itself.

Student: They make a rectangle with the same number on each side.

Teacher: So the first figure has an area of 1 square centimeter. The second has an area of 4 square centimeters. The third figure has an area of 9 square centimeters. How should I add the square centimeters to make the next figure?

Student: Add three to one side and three to the bottom and one in the corner.

Teacher: How many squares is that?

Student: Three and three and one makes seven.

Teacher: Since it is the fourth figure, why can't we just add four squares to the side and bottom?

Student: Because that's one too many, you only need one in the corner to make the square.

Student: If you add four squares to the side and the bottom, you'll have an extra one.

Teacher: So, for the fourth square number you add one less than two fours?

Student: Yes.

Teacher: Then for the twentieth square number, how many centimeter squares should we add?

Student: We already did that.

Teacher: True, but I was wondering if you could use what you learned from these figures to discover another strategy.

Student: For the 20th square number, you add one less than two 20's, or 39.

Teacher: So how many centimeter squares would we add to the 99th figure to make the 100th square number?

Student: 199, or one less than two 100's.

Teacher: And how many centimeter squares will we use for the 100th square number?

Student: 100 times 100 or, let's see, 10,000.

Teacher: That would be a pretty large square, wouldn't it? Who can tell us a general rule for finding quadrangular or square numbers? For example, on the 30th day, how many centimeter squares will we need?

Student: 30×30, or 900 centimeter squares.

Teacher: So on the *n*th day, what would that number be?

Student: $n \times n$?

Teacher: Does everyone agree?

Students: Yes.

Teacher: What is another way to write that, using exponents?

Student: n^2.

Teacher: How much larger is the 30th quadrangular number than the 29th? How many more centimeter squares will it have?

Student: One less than two 30's, or 59.

Teacher: For the *n*th quadrangular number, how much larger is it than the previous number? You can use the same rule. Say it in your own words, and I'll write it with mathematical symbols.

Student: One less than two *n*'s.

Teacher: Good. We write that as $2n - 1$, which means one less than two *n*'s.

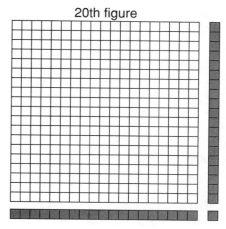

20th figure

Add 39 centimeter squares, or $(2 \times 20) - 1$.

DISCUSSION FOR THE END OF THE MONTH

▶ What is a fast way to figure out the number of centimeter squares in each figure? (Multiply the date by itself.)

▶ What is the formula for determining the value of the quadrangular number of the day? (Value = n^2.)

▶ How many consecutive odd numbers are added each day? (The number of the date.)

▶ If the number of centimeter squares in the figure on the 3rd day is the sum of the first three consecutive odd numbers, how many must be added on the 10th day? (The sum of the first ten consecutive odd numbers.)

▶ This quadrangular number is 100. On which day will it appear? (The 10th day.) How did you figure that out? (100 is the same as 10×10.)

▶ On which day will the quadrangular number 225 appear? (On the 15th day, because $15 \times 15 = 225$.)

▶ What is the sum of the first 20 consecutive odd numbers? (400, or 20×20.)

EVERY DAY ELEMENT

FOCUS

▶ Understanding the concept of a variable
▶ Using mathematical symbols to record variables
▶ Using exponential notation
▶ Evaluating and graphing exponential growth

MATERIALS

Paper for a chart, graph paper

FREQUENCY

Update both the chart and the graph daily. Include the weekend days on Monday. Discuss once each week.

UPDATE PROCEDURE

Since so many elements are used this month, you may want to skip this element in January. The variable this month reinforces the pattern in the Daily Pattern element by introducing exponential growth, rather than using linear relationships as in previous months. This month we will simply find the value of the date times itself. Students will quickly realize they are repeating the pattern of the quadrangular numbers. However, in the Daily Variable for January we will provide an opportunity for students to graph this function.

Evaluate the expression for the date times itself. As in previous months, create a chart with two columns and change the column headings each week. In the first week, write the expression *The date times the date equals value*. In the second week, write d and $d \times d$. In the third week, write d and d^2 and explain that d in this case means the date. In the fourth week, write n and n^2, explaining that n stands for the date or number.

Use a large piece of graph paper to create a graph of the expression. Label the x-axis n, *or day of the month* and the y-axis n^2. Each day, plot the values for the date. For example, in the first week, plot the points (1,1), (2,4), (3,9), (4, 16) and so on. Ask the students to speculate on the appearance of a line connecting these points.

Keep both the chart and the graph made this month handy. We will use them again in the Daily Variable element in April.

DISCUSSION THROUGHOUT THE MONTH

▶ How is the expression for the day determined? (The number of the date times itself.)
▶ What does the exponent 2 mean in the expression d^2, or n^2? (It means the number times itself, or n groups of n, not two sets of d or n.)
▶ As the date increases, what happens to the expression n^2? (Allow a variety of responses that express the fact that it increases much faster than just multiplying by 2.)
▶ On the graph paper, what do the numbers along the bottom represent? (The date.) What do the numbers along the side represent? (The value for the date squared.) Where should we place the information for the value on the first day? (1,1)

Date x date = Value	
d	$d \times d$
d	d^2
n	n^2
1	1
2	4
3	9
4	16
5	25
6	36
7	49
8	64
9	81
10	100
11	121
12	144
13	169
14	196
15	225
16	256
17	289
18	324
19	361
20	400
21	441
22	484
23	529
24	576
25	625
26	676
27	729
28	784
29	841
30	900
31	961

- ▶ We call the horizontal line on the bottom of the graph the x-axis and the vertical line the y-axis. What does the x-axis represent? (The date.) What about the y-axis? (The date squared, or n^2.)
- ▶ What numbers are along the x-axis? (1 to 31.) Can we use the same numbers on the y-axis? (No, they're too small.)
- ▶ Let's connect these points. Compare this line to the line in previous months. (The other graphs had straight lines, and this one is curved. This one bends up, the others didn't. The shape of this one is very different, more like half a "U.")
- ▶ What does this graph have to do with the growing squares we used when we discussed quadrangular numbers? (The graph is a picture of how the area grows with each centimeter square that is added to a side.)
- ▶ Today is the 15th of January. What are some mental strategies for determining the value of 15 squared? (Accept as many strategies as are offered. For example, 10×15 is 150, and half of that is 75. $150 + 75$ is 225. Or 20×10 is 200, and 5×5 is 25. $200 + 25$ is 225. Or 5×15 is 75, and 10×15 is 150. $75 + 150$ is 225.)

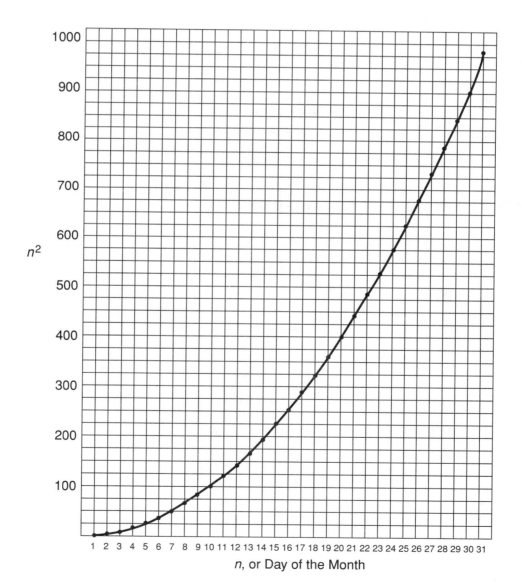

n^2

n, or Day of the Month

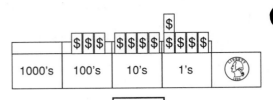

$345.25

FOCUS

▶ Developing the concept of interest
▶ Applying knowledge of percents to determine interest
▶ Recognizing the effect of compounding interest

MATERIALS

The MATERIALS for the Daily Depositor continue from September. See page 14 for a detailed description. In addition, you will need to use copies of Play Money-Coins (TR13), and an additional 3 × 6 clear pocket for the coins. Calculators will also be used this month.

The FREQUENCY continues from September. See page 14 for a detailed description. Remember to include the weekend days on Monday.

UPDATE PROCEDURE

We find examples of interest everywhere, from car dealers to banks offering deals for consumers. It is probably never too early for students to learn the advantages of saving money with interest. Encourage students to find advertisements in the newspaper which refer to interest rates.

This month, students will consider what happens to $100 when it is invested at a rate of 10% a year. To make this possible, we will treat each day of this month as one year. During the first "year" (January 1st), the $100 will grow to $110. On the 2nd day, this $110 will increase by $11, so it will be worth $121. It will be important for the students to notice that the daily increase is more than simply $10.

SAMPLE DISCUSSION FOR THE BEGINNING OF THE MONTH

Teacher: Why do you think people save money in a bank, instead of in a box in a closet? Obviously, a bank is safer, but what other reasons can you think of?
Student: They make money?
Teacher: How?
Student: The bank gives them money?
Teacher: Yes. Does anyone know what that money is called?
Student: Is it called interest?
Teacher: That's right. This month we will deposit money in the Daily Depositor as if it were a bank offering 10% interest a year. We are going to consider each day of January as one year. We started our account on January 1st by depositing $100. Each day the bank will increase the dollar amount by 10%. How much money do you think we will have by the end of the month?
Student: $400?
Teacher: How did you pick that number?
Student: I thought that 10% is $\frac{1}{10}$ of $100, so we add $10 each day.
Teacher: Any other good ideas?
Student: Maybe $1000.
Teacher: Why?
Student: Well 10 × $100 is $1000.

Teacher: Any other ideas? Let's write your guesses next to the Depositor and see what happens. We weren't in school for the first few "years" of January, so let's catch up by figuring out how much money is in our account as of today. Remember that we are treating each day as a year, so at 10% interest a year, how much interest do we earn by the end of the first "year?"

Student: $10.

Teacher: How do you know?

Student: 10% means $\frac{1}{10}$, and $\frac{1}{10}$ of $100 is $10.

Student: You can use your calculator to figure it out.

Student: You can multiply by 0.1.

Teacher: So in one year we earned $10 and we have $110 in our account. How much interest will we earn on January 2nd?

Student: Another $10.

Teacher: How do you know?

Student: Same as before, 10% of $100 is $10.

Teacher: But do we still have only $100 in the account?

Student: Oh I see, we want 10% of $110.

Teacher: Yes. What is 10% of $110?

Student: $11, because $11 × 10 = $110.

Teacher: Let's add this $11 to the $110 in the account. How much do we have now?

Student: $121.

Teacher: Do you think we will add $11 for the next day?

Student: No it will be more, because 10% of $121 is more than $11.

Teacher: Yes. On January 3rd we need to determine the interest on $121, which may be slightly more difficult. How can we do that? Which strategy will work best?

Student: A calculator will work.

Teacher: Yes, but I think you can do this in your head.

Student: Multiply by 0.1?

Teacher: Why is that a good strategy?

Student: 121 times 0.1 is 12.1. You just have to move the decimal to the left by one place.

Teacher: Yes, because multiplying by 0.1 means to divide by 10. What does 12.1 mean in terms of money?

Student: We would add 12 dollars and 10 cents.

Teacher: So how much money is in our bank account after three "years?"

Student: $133.10.

Day	Interest	Total
1	$10.00	$110.00
2	$11.00	$121.00
3	$12.10	$133.10
4	$13.31	$146.41
5	$14.64	$161.05
6	$16.11	$177.16
7	$17.72	$194.88
8	$19.49	$214.37
9	$21.44	$235.81
10	$23.58	$259.39
11	$25.94	$285.33
12	$28.53	$313.86
13	$31.39	$345.25
14	$34.53	$379.78
15	$37.98	$417.76
16	$41.78	$459.54
17	$45.95	$505.49
18	$50.55	$556.04
19	$55.60	$611.64
20	$61.16	$672.80
21	$67.28	$740.08
22	$74.01	$814.09
23	$81.41	$895.50
24	$89.55	$985.05
25	$98.51	$1083.56
26	$108.36	$1191.92
27	$119.19	$1311.11
28	$131.11	$1442.22
29	$144.22	$1586.44
30	$158.64	$1745.08
31	$174.51	$1919.59

DISCUSSION THROUGHOUT THE MONTH

These questions can be used to continue the discussion.

► How many "years" will it take to double our initial deposit of $100? (8 years.)

► As we continue to find 10% each day, the dollar amounts can sometimes extend three places to the right of the decimal point. That means thinking in terms of thousandths of dollars. In other words, it means adding amounts that are $\frac{1}{10}$ of a penny. Do you think it would make sense to round these figures to two places? What do you think the bank does with amounts like these?

 ► This is an excellent opportunity to explore the effective use of the calculator. Students will probably begin by using a two-step operation and multiply the total amount by 0.1 and then add the interest. It is worth spending some time in the middle of the month discussing how this operation can be performed in one step on the calculator. To do this, students must understand that multiplying by 0.1 and then adding this number to the original amount is the same process as multiplying the original amount by 1.1. Encourage students to try it both ways and ask them to explain why the answers are equal. The understanding of 100% and the addition of increments greater than 100% is very difficult at first. Once grasped, however, it is a useful piece of information throughout the student's life. Using money amounts to demonstrate this concept and repeating it each day helps students comprehend the concept more quickly.

► Once students are comfortable with this operation, they can begin to use the "constant" feature of the calculator to determine the new value for each "year." Students will enjoy entering 1.1 into the calculator, multiplying by $100, and then pressing the "=" key for each day of the month. Some will press ahead and find the total $1919.43 for the whole month by carefully counting and pressing "=" 31 times. Other students will keep their finger on the "=" key until the calculator screen fills with numbers and can hold no more. Others may enter the $100 before the 1.1. They will get very different results since the calculator uses the first number for the constant. Make sure that students understand that the order in which the numbers are entered into the calculator is important for finding the desired answer.

8 years = $214.37

100 x 1.1

110 x 1.1

121 x 1.1

| 1 | . | 1 | x |

| 1 | 0 | 0 | = |

| = | = | = |

Daily Depositor calculation
on the 4th day

Focus
▶ Analyzing data and interpreting graphs
▶ Using a stem-and-leaf plot to analyze and compare data
▶ Developing intuitions about "middle" and "typical"
▶ Recognizing medians

Materials
Paper for a stem-and-leaf plot

Frequency
Update daily. Discuss once each week.

Update Procedure
Students have probably had sufficient experience using bar and line graphs. In December, we introduced the number line. This month, we will introduce a special type of graph called a stem-and-leaf plot. The stem-and-leaf plot is particularly useful when working with a wide range of numbers, since it is difficult to fit information involving a wide range on a number line.

The stem-and-leaf plot is useful when the range extends over many tens or hundreds. The ten's or hundred's are listed vertically in the "stem," from lowest number at the top down to the highest number at the bottom. The "leaves" are the one's, and are listed next to the stem. Before using the information on the graph, the "leaves" are arranged into numerical order.

This format is especially helpful because it makes it easy to see the shape of the data, to see where the numbers clump together, and to see where the outliers are. For example, in the graph above, it is clear that a large number of days had temperatures between 23°F and 32°F and one warm day at 62°F that was unique.

Another useful feature of the stem-and-leaf plot is that data can be easily compared by inserting additional information on the opposite side of the "stem." Later this month, we will add the temperature data we collected in December to the left side of the "stem" and compare the range and shape of the data for both months.

Each day, at an agreed upon time, a student will read the class thermometer, or use the previous day's high temperature as reported in the newspaper, and record it on the stem-and-leaf plot. Assign one student to record the high temperatures for Saturday and Sunday as published in the newspaper. Record the information on the stem-and-leaf plot.

January Temperatures Degrees Fahrenheit	
0	8
1	1 6 3 9
2	0 3 8 4 7
3	2 8 2
4	3
5	
6	2

Teacher: How many temperatures have we recorded on our stem-and-leaf plot so far?

Student: 15.

Teacher: What are the coldest and the warmest temperatures so far?

Student: 8°F was the coldest and 62°F was the hottest.

Teacher: How many days had temperatures above 30°F?

Student: Five.

Teacher: Has any temperature occurred more than once?

Student: Yes, 32°F.

Teacher: Where do most of the temperatures seem to cluster?

Student: In the 20's.

Teacher: Any other ideas?

Student: Between 11°F and 43°F is where almost all the temperatures are.

Student: Most seem to be around 30°F.

Student: Which answer is right?

Teacher: Which one do you think?

Student: They could all be right.

Teacher: Why?

Student: All of them are true.

Student: So it depends on what you are looking for, the middle, or the typical temperature, or whatever.

Teacher: Yes. What is the range of temperatures so far?

Student: From 8°F to 62°F.

Teacher: Which of these temperatures seems really different from the others? In other words, which is an outlier?

Student: 62°F is much higher than any of the others.

Student: What about 8°F?

Student: It isn't very far from the others really.

Teacher: Which temperature is right in the middle?

Student: Do you mean which temperature happened in the middle?

Teacher: No. I want to know, which temperature is the middle temperature in the range? What is the median?

Student: 28°F.

Teacher: How did you get that?

Student: I know we've recorded the temperature for 15 days, so I counted 7 from each end.

Teacher: That's very good thinking, but be careful. If you have not arranged the "leaves" in numerical order, you can arrive at a wrong answer. It's important to remember to put the "leaves" into numerical order before trying to use the information on a stem-and-leaf plot. Since we have not rearranged the "leaves," we'll have to start by determining the lowest temperature and go from lowest to highest through the eighth temperature. It would also work to start with the highest temperature and proceed to the lowest. What is the lowest temperature?

Student: 8°F.

Teacher: And the next lowest?

Student: 11°F.

January Temperatures
Degrees Fahrenheit

0	8
1	1 3 6 9
2	0 3 4 7 8
3	2 2 8
4	3
5	
6	2

"leaves" rearranged

Teacher: If you keep proceeding this way, which number is the eighth lowest or eighth highest?

Student: 24F°.

Teacher: So 24°F is the median, or middle, temperature. We know that there are 15 temperatures on our chart. How many temperatures would $\frac{2}{3}$ of these be?

Student: 5 and 5, or 10, is $\frac{2}{3}$ of 15.

Teacher: What is the range of $\frac{2}{3}$ of the temperatures around the median?

Student: From 13° to 22°.

Teacher: Many people use the idea of the range of $\frac{2}{3}$ of the data to describe what is typical.

HELPFUL HINTS

▶ This dialogue contains many questions which really should occur over several weeks.

▶ It would be helpful for students to see the usefulness of arranging the temperatures in numerical order on the graph. Making a second chart to use on the 15th day of the month with the "leaves" in numerical order will allow students to see how quickly the median temperature can be found.

▶ Put the temperatures from the December number line on the left side of the stem-and-leaf plot. Be sure that both the December and January "leaves" are in numerical order. The December "leaves" will then display the lowest number near the "stem" and be read from right to left. Point out that many people get confused when the numbers are read this way, because it is not how we normally write or read numbers. For example, the first December temperature shown below is 13°F.

▶ By asking some of the same questions we used in the Sample Discussion, encourage students to discover how easy it is to compare the ranges and shapes of the data for both months when using the stem-and-leaf plot.

December Temperatures		January Temperatures
	Degrees Fahrenheit	

December "leaves"	stem	January "leaves"
	0	8
7 3	1	1 3 6 9 9
8 8 7 2 1 1	2	0 3 4 7 8
9 8 7 7 5 5 5 4 4 2 1 0 0	3	1 2 2 6 8 8 9
1	4	0 1 3 9
5	5	
	6	2

"leaves" rearranged

FEBRUARY

A MONTH FULL OF HEART

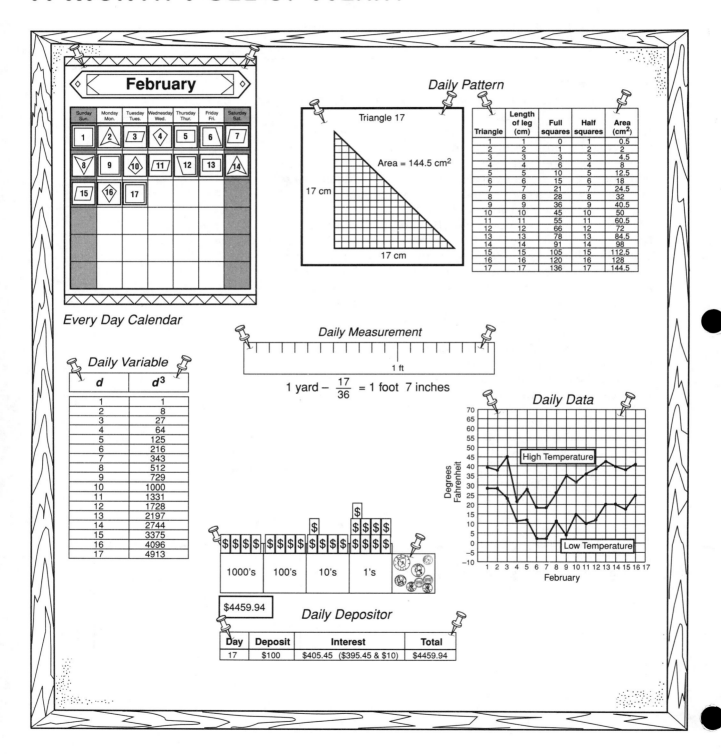

February

Sunday Sun.	Monday Mon.	Tuesday Tues.	Wednesday Wed.	Thursday Thur.	Friday Fri.	Saturday Sat.
1	2	3	4	5	6	7
8	9	10	11	12	13	14
15	16	17				

Every Day Calendar

Daily Pattern

Triangle 17

Area = 144.5 cm²

17 cm

17 cm

Triangle	Length of leg (cm)	Full squares	Half squares	Area (cm²)
1	1	0	1	0.5
2	2	1	2	2
3	3	3	3	4.5
4	4	6	4	8
5	5	10	5	12.5
6	6	15	6	18
7	7	21	7	24.5
8	8	28	8	32
9	9	36	9	40.5
10	10	45	10	50
11	11	55	11	60.5
12	12	66	12	72
13	13	78	13	84.5
14	14	91	14	98
15	15	105	15	112.5
16	16	120	16	128
17	17	136	17	144.5

Daily Variable

d	d^3
1	1
2	8
3	27
4	64
5	125
6	216
7	343
8	512
9	729
10	1000
11	1331
12	1728
13	2197
14	2744
15	3375
16	4096
17	4913

Daily Measurement

1 ft

$1 \text{ yard} - \dfrac{17}{36} = 1 \text{ foot } 7 \text{ inches}$

Daily Data

High Temperature

Low Temperature

Degrees Fahrenheit

February

Daily Depositor

1000's	100's	10's	1's

$4459.94

Day	Deposit	Interest	Total
17	$100	$405.45 ($395.45 & $10)	$4459.94

This month, the last new element of Calendar Math, the Daily Measurement, will be introduced. For the remaining months of the school year, only the specific content of each element will change. In February, we will examine the 180° turn symmetry of quadrilaterals with the Every Day Calendar. The Counting Tape and Percent Circle will be completed this month as we reach the one hundredth day of school. The Daily Pattern will focus on the area of an isosceles right triangle. The Daily Variable will introduce the dramatic effect of "cubing" a number, while compounding interest will again be explored in the Daily Depositor. The Daily Data element will introduce line graphs and their ability to display trends in data. The Daily Measurement will connect student understandings about customary linear measures to computations with fractions.

EVERY DAY ELEMENT

CALENDAR

FOCUS
▶ Analyzing and predicting patterns
▶ Using 180° turn symmetry to analyze quadrilaterals
▶ Recognizing properties of quadrilaterals
▶ Sorting and classifying shapes according to properties of symmetry

MATERIALS
Every Day Calendar, February Month Strip, February Calendar Pieces, or Quadrilateral Cutouts (TR7) and marker

SUGGESTED PATTERN FOR FEBRUARY
This month, the Calendar uses a pattern to study the 180° turn symmetry of seven different quadrilaterals. The odd-numbered days will feature the sequence square, parallelogram, rectangle, and rhombus. The even-numbered days will use the sequence arrowhead, kite, and trapezoid. These sequences will repeat throughout the month so that odd-numbered days will show figures that have 180° turn symmetry and even-numbered days will show figures that do not. The pattern for the month is shown below.

Square - 1, 9, 17, and 25
Parallelogram - 3, 11, 19, and 27
Rectangle - 5, 13, 21, (and 29 in leap year)
Rhombus - 7, 15, and 23
Arrowhead - 2, 8, 14, 20, and 26
Kite - 4, 10, 16, 22, and 28
Trapezoid - 6, 12, 18, and 24

FREQUENCY
Update daily. Discuss once or twice each week. Add the Calendar Pieces for the weekend dates on Monday.

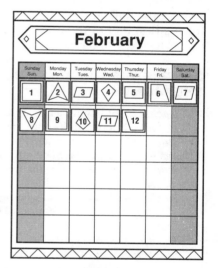

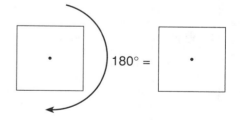

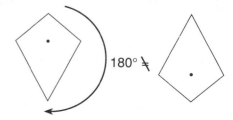

UPDATE PROCEDURE

Workers in many occupations, from doctors to carpenters, from engineers to costume designers, need good visualization skills and spatial sense. An essential part of this ability to visualize is to recognize the effect of turning or rotating a shape. Last month, students analyzed quadrilaterals for line symmetry, which required an understanding of reflection and congruence. This month, students will examine quadrilaterals for their ability to be rotated 180°, and to notice if the resulting figure looks the same or if it looks as though it has been turned upside down. This is called turn symmetry. A square can be turned 90°, 180°, and 270° around its center and all four shapes will match each other. However, a kite rotated in the same way will never match the original shape until it is turned a full circle.

This month, students will be asked to imagine rotating a figure 180° and to visualize the resulting figure before they actually see the rotation. Given enough practice, most students will develop stronger visualization abilities.

Each day, post the February Calendar Piece for the date. If you choose to use the Quadrilateral Cutouts (TR7), remember to rotate each shape 180° from its last appearance on the Calendar before writing the date and posting. The teacher should post the figure for the first half of the month. After that, students should be able to do the daily update.

SAMPLE DISCUSSION FOR THE BEGINNING OF THE MONTH

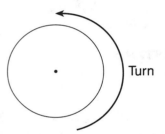

Turn

Still remains
the same

Teacher: (Holding up a circle) As I turn this circle around its center, does it look different in any position?

Student: Is this a trick question?

Teacher: Why do you ask that?

Student: We know how you are always trying to get us to think and see things differently.

Teacher: All I'm asking is whether the appearance of this circle changes as I turn it around its center.

Student: It doesn't seem to.

Teacher: Are you sure?

Student: No, but I don't think it does.

Teacher: No, I don't think so either. In January, we discussed quadrilaterals in terms of whether or not they had line symmetry. This month, we are going to examine a different kind of symmetry. We'll look at quadrilaterals to see if they have symmetry when they are rotated 180°. Let's call this looking for 180° turn symmetry. We could look at figures to see if they have turn symmetry when they are rotated at other degrees, like 90° or 270°. Notice that this circle has turn symmetry no matter how many degrees I rotate it. But in February, we'll look only for 180° turn symmetry. We'll notice what happens to the appearance of various quadrilaterals as we turn them upside down. We are going to rotate each figure a half turn, meaning halfway around a circle. How many degrees are in a half circle turn?

Student: 180°.

Teacher: (Holding up a square) So if I turn this square upside down, or 180°, does the new figure look exactly like the original square?

Student: Yes.

Teacher: (Holding up an arrowhead) How about this figure? If I turn it upside down, does it appear the same as the original quadrilateral?

Student: No, it looks upside down.

Teacher: Good. We can say that, when rotated a half turn, it doesn't match the original figure. So it doesn't have 180° turn symmetry. This month, we will use 180° turn symmetry to determine the pattern on the calendar. I'm going to put a square on the first day of February, an arrowhead on the 2nd, a parallelogram on the 3rd, and a kite on the 4th. Today is the 5th day of February. What shape should I choose? Do you see any order or pattern in the figures I have chosen?

Student: Does it have to do with lines of symmetry?

Teacher: It could, but not this month. This month we are looking for what happens to a shape when it is turned upside down, or 180°.

Student: Well, the square looks the same when you turn it 180°. So does the parallelogram. But the arrowhead doesn't.

Teacher: How about the kite?

Student: I'm not sure. It looks the almost the same.

Student: It does look like the original. But when you turn it upside down, the long sides are on top, not on the bottom where they were in the original figure. So it doesn't work.

Teacher: Is there a pattern to how the shapes have been selected ?

Student: Looks the same upside down, doesn't look the same, looks the same, doesn't look the same.

Teacher: What should the next figure do?

Student: It should have 180° turn symmetry.

Teacher: I need a new quadrilateral shape. What should we use?

Student: A square?

Teacher: Can anyone suggest a shape we haven't used yet?

Student: A rectangle?

Teacher: Does a rectangle have 180° turn symmetry?

Student: Yes, because when you turn it 180° it still looks the same as the original shape.

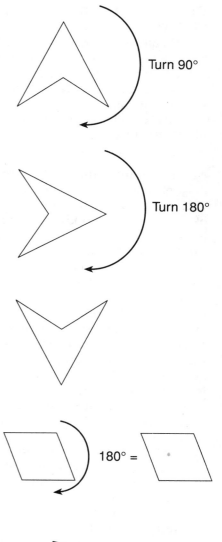

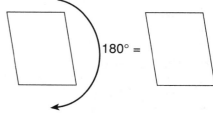

DISCUSSION FOR THE MIDDLE AND END OF THE MONTH

▶ Do all parallelograms have 180° turn symmetry? (Yes.)
▶ Since that is true, what does that tell us about all rectangles? (They must also have 180° turn symmetry, because a rectangle is a special kind of parallelogram.)
▶ Which quadrilaterals don't have 180° turn symmetry? (Kites, arrowheads, and trapezoids.)
▶ Does any trapezoid have 180° turn symmetry? How about an isosceles trapezoid? (No.)

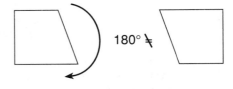

As time permits, students will benefit from a discussion about the diagonals of the seven quadrilaterals that make up the February Calendar pattern. For some of the quadrilaterals, the intersection of the diagonals defines the center point around which the figure is rotated. The discussion below focuses on the rectangle, but these questions can be used with all the quadrilaterals that make up the pattern this month. A good visual model would be to create a large copy of each figure, draw in the diagonals, and demonstrate the rotation of the figure around its center point by posting the figure with a pin at that point and actually rotating it. The arrowhead is an interesting figure, since its diagonals do not meet. Showing this to the students will clarify the concept of turn symmetry and provide new points of comparison of the different quadrilaterals.

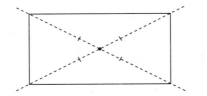

▶ Examine the rectangle. What do we mean by the center point of the rectangle? (The distance from this point to each set of opposite sides is the same.) The center point of a rectangle is also the point at which the diagonals intersect. What can we say about the intersection of the diagonals? (The diagonals bisect each other, or meet at the midpoint of each diagonal. If the students are not familiar with these terms, or do not volunteer them in the discussion, be sure to introduce them and offer explanations about their meaning.) As I rotate this rectangle on the bulletin board with a pin at its center point, you can see that the rectangle has turn symmetry only when it has been rotated 180°.

HELPFUL HINTS

▶ Have the students close their eyes and imagine turning each quadrilateral and stopping after a half turn. Ask them to draw each quadrilateral in the air when it is turned 180°.
▶ Invite students to find shapes in nature or in architecture that have 180° turn symmetry.
▶ Experiment with other shapes, such as different kinds of triangles, and examine them for 180° turn symmetry.

EVERY DAY ELEMENT

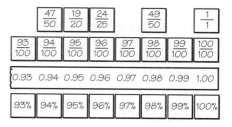

FOCUS

▶ Counting with decimals, fractions, and percents
▶ Visualizing percent with a circular model
▶ Using common decimals, fractions, and percents close to one whole
▶ Recognizing equivalencies between fractions, decimals, and percents

The MATERIALS and FREQUENCY continue from September. See page 7 for a detailed description.

UPDATE PROCEDURE

As the Counting Tape approaches 1.00, students can focus on decimals, fractions, and percents close to the whole. When discussing this element, remember to include discussion about the circles that have been colored on the Percent Circle.

This is the last month the Counting Tape and Percent Circle will be included as an element, since the one hundredth day of school usually occurs in this month. After the one hundredth day, you may choose to continue using this element to expose students to decimals, fractions, and percents greater than 1, or 100%.

DISCUSSION THROUGHOUT THE MONTH

▶ What fraction of the first one hundred days has passed? What fraction is left? How did you figure that out? How many circles have been colored? How many are left?
▶ Which is larger, 0.9, or 0.87?
▶ What are some equivalent fractions for 0.96? ($\frac{48}{50}$, $\frac{24}{25}$) What strategies did you use to figure that out?
▶ Which is larger, $\frac{24}{25}$, or $\frac{99}{100}$? Can you explain why?
▶ What is 100% of 100? Of 1000? Of 0.1?
▶ What is a fast way to find 99% of a number? (Find 1% and subtract that amount from the number. For example, 99% of 160 is 160 − 1.6, or 158.4.)
▶ How do we write 101% as a decimal? (1.01) As a mixed number? ($1\frac{1}{100}$) As an improper fraction? ($\frac{101}{100}$)
▶ If we added another Percent Circle with one hundred circles around it, how many circles would be colored to show 101%? (101)

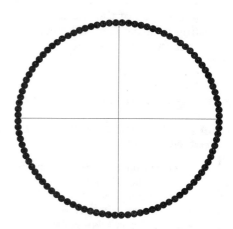

100 small circles = 1.0

EVERY DAY ELEMENT

FOCUS
▶ Recognizing the area of a right triangle as half of a square
▶ Using visual clues and numerical tables to predict patterns
▶ Generating formulas to predict the next term in a series

MATERIALS
Centimeter Squared Paper (TR10), scissors, tape, paper for a chart

FREQUENCY
Update daily. Include weekend days on Monday. Discuss once or twice a week.

UPDATE PROCEDURE
By giving students enough time to discover a rule for finding the area of a right triangle, teachers support learning that is more likely to be remembered and understood. This month, students will share a variety of strategies for finding the area of a right triangle and for predicting the area of the next triangle in a series.

Each day, a right isosceles triangle will be constructed from the Centimeter Squared Paper. You may choose to display each triangle on a piece of construction paper. The length of the legs of the triangle will equal the date. Students will use this model to determine the area of the triangle and will share their strategies for finding its area. General rules for predicting the pattern will be investigated at the end of the month.

Make a chart showing the number of the triangle, the length of each leg, the number of full squares, the number of half squares, and the area. Update the chart each day.

SAMPLE DISCUSSION FOR THE BEGINNING OF THE MONTH

Teacher: I have put up a figure for each of the first four days of February. What do you notice about these triangles?
Student: They are all right triangles.
Student: Two sides are the same length.
Student: Every triangle has full squares and half squares.
Teacher: What is the area of the first triangle?
Student: Half a square centimeter.
Teacher: What is the area of the next three?
Student: 2 square centimeters.
Student: 4.5 square centimeters.
Student: 8 square centimeters.
Teacher: How did you figure that out?
Student: The second triangle has 1 full square and 2 half squares, or 2 square centimeters in all.
Student: The third one has 3 full squares and 3 half squares, so it's 4.5 square centimeters.
Student: The fourth triangle has 6 full squares and 4 half squares, which is 8 square centimeters in all.
Teacher: What do you predict the area of the next triangle will be? What will the triangle look like?

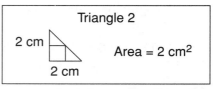

Triangle 1
1 cm — 1 cm   Area = 0.5 cm²

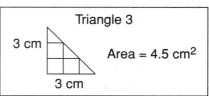

Triangle 2
2 cm — 2 cm   Area = 2 cm²

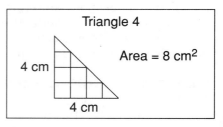

Triangle 3
3 cm — 3 cm   Area = 4.5 cm²

Triangle 4
4 cm — 4 cm   Area = 8 cm²

Triangle	Length of leg (cm)	Full squares	Half squares	Area (cm²)
1	1	0	1	0.5
2	2	1	2	2
3	3	3	3	4.5
4	4	6	4	8
5	5	10	5	12.5
6	6	15	6	18
7	7	21	7	24.5
8	8	28	8	32
9	9	36	9	40.5
10	10	45	10	50
11	11	55	11	60.5
12	12	66	12	72
13	13	78	13	84.5
14	14	91	14	98
15	15	105	15	112.5
16	16	120	16	128
17	17	136	17	144.5
18	18	153	18	162
19	19	171	19	180.5
20	20	190	20	200
21	21	210	21	220.5
22	22	231	22	242
23	23	253	23	264.5
24	24	276	24	288
25	25	300	25	312.5
26	26	325	26	338
27	27	351	27	364.5
28	28	378	28	392
29	29	406	29	420.5

DISCUSSION FOR THE MIDDLE AND END OF THE MONTH

These questions can be used for further discussion.

► How many full squares are in the fifth figure? (10) How many half squares? (5)

► How many full squares are on one side of the fifth figure? (4)

► How many full squares are on one side of the fourth figure? (3) The third triangle? (2)

► Do you see a pattern? Can you describe it? (The number of full squares on each side of the triangle is one less than the number of the figure.)

► Is there a pattern for the number of half squares in each figure? What is the pattern? (Each triangle has the same number of half squares as the number of the figure.)

► How much did the area increase between the first two triangles? (By 1.5 square centimeters.) Between the second and third triangles? (By 2.5 square centimeters.)

► Can you describe the pattern for the amount the area grows between one day and the next? Use the area of the fifteenth figure to explain your answer. (The area increases by the number of the figure minus one half square. To find the total area, just add that number to the area of the preceding figure. For the fifteenth figure, the area increases by 15 squares minus one half square, or 14.5 square centimeters. Add that amount to the area of the fourteenth figure, which is 98 square centimeters, and you get 112.5 square centimeters.)

► What will the twentieth triangle look like? (Two sides of 20 centimeters each, 19 full squares on each side, and 20 half squares on the hypotenuse. Check that all students understand that the hypotenuse is the side of a right triangle opposite the right angle.)

► How many full squares are in the twentieth triangle? (190) How did you figure it out? (Use the formula for triangular numbers, $\frac{n(n+1)}{2}$, and let n be the number of full squares on each side of the triangle. So it can be 1, 2, 3, . . . ,19, or ($\frac{19 \times 20}{2}$.)

► What is the area of the 20th triangle? (190 full squares and 20 half squares, or 200 square centimeters.)

► How is the area of the triangle related to the length of the leg? Can you describe this relationship in a formula? (The area is the length of a leg times itself, and divided by two, or $\frac{L^2}{2}$.)

► Why does this work? (The area of these triangles is the same as half the area of a square with sides the same length as the sides of the triangle.)

► What is a triangle with two equal legs and a right angle called? (An isosceles right triangle.)

► Can the area of any right triangle be found in this way? (Yes, even if the two legs are not the same length. The area of any right triangle is half of the rectangle or square formed by the length of its two legs.)

► How many times larger is the area of the twentieth triangle than the area of the tenth one? (4 times larger, or an area of 200 square centimeters compared to 50 square centimeters, because each leg is twice as long.)

► If February had thirty days, what would the area of the thirtieth triangle be? (One half of 30 × 30, or 450 square centimeters.)

► How many times larger is the area of the thirtieth figure than the area of the tenth figure? (9 times larger, because each leg is three times as long.)

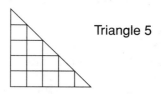

Area = 12.5 cm²

Triangle 5

4 + 3 + 2 + 1 = whole squares
5 half squares

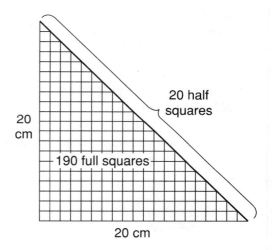

20 cm

20 half squares

190 full squares

20 cm

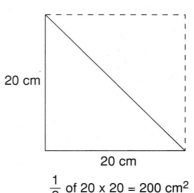

20 cm

20 cm

$\frac{1}{2}$ of 20 x 20 = 200 cm²

EVERY DAY ELEMENT

FOCUS
▶ Using exponents
▶ Using mental math strategies to multiply two-digit numbers
▶ Understanding volume
▶ Recognizing the relationship of length to volume of a cube
▶ Using mathematical symbols to express exponential growth

MATERIALS
Paper for a chart, calculators

FREQUENCY
Update daily, including the weekend days on Monday. Discuss once a week.

UPDATE PROCEDURE
Each day, students will calculate the "cube" of the date, using the volume of a cube as a model. In the first week, students will compute mentally to determine the quantity for the date raised to the third power. As the number of the date increases, students can choose to practice paper and pencil multiplication or to use calculators. Keep a chart as in previous months, changing the labels over the course of the month as shown in the diagram.

SAMPLE DISCUSSION FOR THE BEGINNING OF THE MONTH

Teacher: (Drawing a cube on the chalkboard) Let's say that the length of one edge of this cube is 1 centimeter. What is its volume?
Student: What does volume mean?
Teacher: Does anyone know?
Student: The space inside something?
Teacher: Inside what?
Student: Inside a box?
Teacher: Only inside a box?
Student: Inside a shape.
Teacher: Inside a square?
Student: No, inside a three-dimensional shape.
Teacher: Yes. Volume is the space inside a three-dimensional shape. One way we measure this space is to consider how many standard cubes will fit in it. For example, if our standard is a one-centimeter cube, how many standard cubes will fit in this one-centimeter cube?
Student: One, of course.
Teacher: Let's build a cube with a length of 2 centimeters. What is the volume of that cube? How many one-centimeter cubes will fit inside?
Student: 8.
Teacher: How do you know?
Student: There are four cubes on the bottom and four on top of those.
Teacher: Yes, the base is 2 centimeters by 2 centimeters, and there are 2 of those, so 8 cubes will fit inside. This is $2 \times 2 \times 2$, or 2 to what power?
Student: 2 to the third power.
Teacher: Yes, and sometimes we call this 2 cubed. This month, we will use the date as the length of one edge of a cube and then determine its volume. In other words, we will be calculating the date raised to the third power, or n^3.

DAILY VARIABLE

Date x Date x Date = Value	
d	$d \times d \times d$
d	d^3
n	n^3
1	1
2	8
3	27
4	64
5	125
6	216
7	343
8	512
9	729
10	1000
11	1331
12	1728
13	2197
14	2744
15	3375
16	4096
17	4913
18	5832
19	6859
20	8000
21	9261
22	10,648
23	12,167
24	13,824
25	15,625
26	17,576
27	19,683
28	21,952
29	24,389

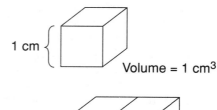
1 cm Volume = 1 cm³

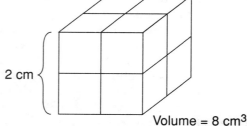
2 cm Volume = 8 cm³

DISCUSSION FOR THE MIDDLE AND END OF THE MONTH

▶ What is 6 cubed? (216) How can you do this in your head? (6 × 6 is 36, and 6 × 36 is 6 × 30, or 180, plus 6 × 6, or 36, so it is 216.)

▶ What is the volume of a cube when the length of an edge is 9 centimeters? (729 cubic centimeters.) How can you do that in your head? (9 × 9 × 9 is the same as 81 × 9. So 9 × 80 is 720 and 9 x 1 is 9, so it is 729. Or, 10 × 81 is 810. 810 minus 80 is 730, and minus 1 more is 729. Encourage students to develop their own strategies for calculating these mentally.)

▶ What if each edge of the cube has a length of 10 centimeters? (10 × 10 × 10 is 1000 cubic centimeters.)

▶ What do you notice about 10^3 and the answer 1000? (10^3 is 1 followed by 3 zeros.) What do you think 10^4 will be? (10,000, or 1 followed by 4 zeros.)

▶ What is 11 × 11 × 11? (11 × 121 is 1210 plus 121 more, or 1331.)

▶ If 11 × 11 is 121, and 11 × 11 × 11 is 1331, what do you think 11^4 will be? (Students will guess that it will be 14,441, and will be surprised to discover that it isn't. They will be even more surprised when they examine 11^5. Encourage students to check their predictions when searching for patterns, for it is easy to assume that a pattern exists when none does.)

▶ What is the volume of a cube with an edge of 17 centimeters? Let's each work this out using paper and pencil. (4913 cubic centimeters.)

▶ What is 20 to the third power? (20 × 20 is 400, and 10 × 400 is 4000. Double that to get 8000.)

▶ What do you notice about 2^3 and 20^3? (20^3 is 1000 times, or 10 × 10 × 10, larger than 2^3.)

▶ How is the volume of a cube related to the length of one edge? (It is the cube of the edge.)

▶ If we know that 3^3 is 27, what is 30^3? (1000 times larger, or 27,000. 30^3 is the same as $(3 × 10)^3$, or $3^3 × 10^3$.)

$$11^2 = 121$$
$$11^3 = 1331$$
$$11^4 = 14,641$$
$$11^5 = 161,051$$

Fun with 11

▤ EVERY DAY ELEMENT

DAILY DEPOSITOR

FOCUS
▶ Developing the concept of interest
▶ Calculating interest
▶ Recognizing the effect of compounding interest

The MATERIALS and FREQUENCY continue from January. See page 84 for a detailed description. You will need another 3 × 6 clear pocket for the 10,000's place.

UPDATE PROCEDURE
The interest calculations this month are more complex. We will continue to treat each day of the month as a year. Each "year," students will deposit $100 and receive a rate of 10% interest a year. On February 1, students will deposit $100 and receive $10 interest, making a total of $110. On February 2, students will deposit another "yearly" $100 and receive the interest on the $210 in the

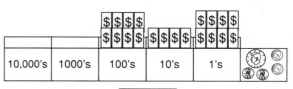

10,000's	1000's	100's	10's	1's	

$848.72

bank so far, or $21, for a cumulative total of $231. Another way to do this is to add the $100 each day and multiply by 110%, or 1.1, to determine the new total. For example, on February 2, take the $110 in the account, add the new $100 and multiply the total by 1.1 ($210 × 1.1 = $231) to determine the cumulative total. Students should be encouraged to realize that this is much easier and quicker than calculating and adding the interest on the previous day's total, adding $100, and then adding the 10% interest on that amount to determine the new total. Round all money amounts to the nearest penny. Students will be surprised to see how much money accumulates after 28 or 29 days. It is important to update the Depositor every day because it is complicated to catch up when several days have been skipped. Remember to update the weekend days each Monday.

DISCUSSION FOR THE SIXTH DAY OF THE MONTH

These suggested questions can be used throughout the month to help students determine the new total for each day.

► How much money will be in the Depositor by the end of the month? What are some reasonable estimates? (Accept a wide range of responses.)

► What is the least amount possible? (Answers should be no less than 28 days times $110, or $3080.)

► Today is February 6th. How much money is in our Depositor today? ($671.56)

► When we add $100, how much do we have? ($771.56)

► What is 10% of that? ($77.16) How did you figure that? (By moving the decimal one place to the left, or dividing by 10, and rounding.)

► Why did we round the number 77.156? (Because when using money amounts we round to the nearest penny.)

► How much do we have in the Depositor now? ($848.72)

► Is this more or less than you expected for the sixth day?

► How can we use a calculator to determine the amount we will have in the Depositor tomorrow? (Add $100 to the Depositor amount and multiply by 1.1, or 110%.)

Day	Deposit	Interest		Total
1	$100	$10.00		$110.00
2	$100	$21.00	($11.00 & $10)	$231.00
3	$100	$33.10	($23.10 & $10)	$364.10
4	$100	$46.41	($36.41 & $10)	$510.51
5	$100	$61.05	($51.05 & $10)	$671.56
6	$100	$77.16	($67.16 & $10)	$848.72
7	$100	$94.87	($84.87 & $10)	$1043.59
8	$100	$114.36	($104.36 & $10)	$1257.95
9	$100	$135.80	($125.80 & $10)	$1493.75
10	$100	$159.38	($149.38 & $10)	$1753.13
11	$100	$185.31	($175.31 & $10)	$2038.44
12	$100	$213.84	($203.84 & $10)	$2352.28
13	$100	$245.23	($235.23 & $10)	$2697.51
14	$100	$279.75	($269.75 & $10)	$3077.26
15	$100	$317.73	($307.73 7 $10)	$3494.99
16	$100	$359.50	($349.50 & $10)	$3954.49
17	$100	$405.45	($395.45 & $10)	$4459.94
18	$100	$455.99	($445.99 & $10)	$5015.93
19	$100	$511.59	($501.59 & $10)	$5627.52
20	$100	$572.75	($562.75 & $10)	$6300.27
21	$100	$640.03	($630.03 & $10)	$7040.30
22	$100	$714.03	($704.03 & $10)	$7854.33
23	$100	$795.43	($785.43 & $10)	$8749.76
24	$100	$884.98	($874.98 & $10)	$9734.74
25	$100	$983.47	($973.47 & $10)	$10,818.21
26	$100	$1091.82	($1081.82 & $10)	$12,010.03
27	$100	$1211.00	($1201.00 & $10)	$13,321.03
28	$100	$1342.10	($1332.10 & $10)	$14,763.13
29	$100	$1486.31	($1476.31 & $10)	$16,349.44

HELPFUL HINTS

▶ Keeping track of the amounts and calculations can prove difficult. Students may need help with the calculations. It may be helpful to give the task of updating the Daily Depositor to two students each day. Their work may then be checked by two other students.

▶ Be sure to record the amount in the Depositor each day so you don't lose track. In addition to posting the new total for each day, it will probably be helpful to keep a chart showing the amount deposited and the interest earned for each "year."

▶ You may want to invite someone from a bank to discuss savings and interest. You may also ask students to see if local banks round the money amounts or truncate them.

▶ You may choose to use the Daily Depositor element through March. Students will be surprised at how large the numbers become. By the end of March, the Depositor will contain $304,122.25. In leap years, the amount will be $334,644.48.

EVERY DAY ELEMENT   DAILY DATA

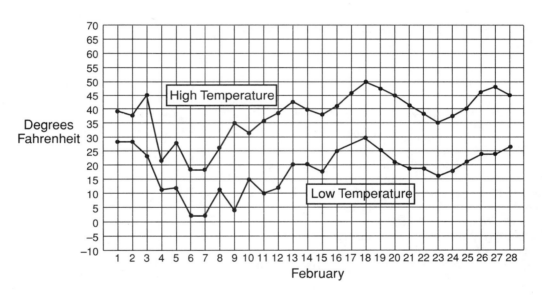

FOCUS

▶ Recognizing trends with a line graph
▶ Recognizing the advantages of line graphs in displaying trends over time
▶ Using a double-line graph to display and analyze data

MATERIALS
Paper for a graph, markers of two different colors

FREQUENCY
Update daily, including weekends. Discuss once or twice a week.

UPDATE PROCEDURE
This month, students will record both the high and low temperature of the preceding day on the graph. A line connecting the highs and another connecting the lows will be drawn and extended daily so that students can observe temperature trends over time. Discussion should focus on these trends, rather than on middles. We want to draw the student's attention to rises and drops. By using a double-line graph, students can compare trends in high temperatures to trends in low temperatures.

The days of the month will be listed on the x-axis and temperatures on the y-axis. Beginning on the second day, a student will be responsible for recording the high and low temperatures for the preceding day, as published in the newspaper. The student will then connect these points with lines to the previous day's high and low temperatures. It is best to use two different colors for these lines.

SAMPLE DISCUSSION FOR THE ELEVENTH DAY OF THE MONTH

Teacher: We have used the graph to display the high and low temperatures for the last ten days. Which day had the highest temperature?

Student: February 3.

Teacher: How do you know?

Student: It is the highest number on the line.

Teacher: Which line?

Student: On the up and down line that is the temperatures.

Teacher: The name of that line is the y-axis, or the vertical axis. As we go up this line the temperatures are higher. What numbers are on the x-axis, or the horizontal axis?

Student: Those are the days of February.

Teacher: What day(s) had the lowest temperature so far?

Student: February 6 and 7.

Teacher: Which day had the greatest drop in high temperatures from the previous day?

Student: February 4.

Teacher: How do you know?

Student: The numbers drop the most.

Teacher: True. How does the graph help you see that?

Student: You can see it drop down a lot. On other days it doesn't go down as steeply.

Teacher: Steepness is an excellent word to use with this kind of graph. What would a steep rise mean on this graph?

Student: The temperature rose a lot.

Teacher: What about a steep fall or decline?

Student: The temperature dropped a lot.

SAMPLE DISCUSSION CONTINUED

Teacher: Here's a more difficult question. Forget about the numbers for right now. Can you tell which day had the biggest difference between the high and the low temperatures? How does the graph help you see that?

Student: I don't understand.

Teacher: If there is hardly any difference between the high and low temperatures, what happens to the two lines?

Student: They are close together.

Teacher: And if there is a big difference between the high and low temperatures?

Student: The lines are far apart?

Teacher: Is that right?

Student: Yes, the bigger the difference between temperatures, the more space between the two lines.

Teacher: So which day so far has had the biggest difference between the high and low temperatures?

Student: February 9, because the two lines are farthest apart on that day.

DISCUSSION FOR THE REMAINDER OF THE MONTH

Use two or three of these questions each time you discuss the graph.

▶ On which days did the high temperature remain almost the same?

▶ On which days did both the high and the low temperatures increase?

▶ On which day did the high temperature increase while the low temperature decreased?

▶ On which two consecutive days did the low temperature decline? On which three consecutive days did it increase?

▶ What does the line look like when the high temperature remains the same for two days?

▶ Do the high and low temperatures rise and fall by the same amount each day?

▶ Can you describe the trend of the high temperatures this month? How does a line graph help you see these trends?

▶ Think about some other graphs we have studied this year. Do you think it is as easy to see what the average temperature for the month is on this kind of graph as it is on some other kinds of graphs?

At the end of the month, it is a good exercise to have students write a short description of the trends of the temperature over the month. This encourages interpretation of the data recorded on the graph as well as stressing communication skills.

EVERY DAY ELEMENT

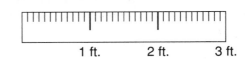

1 ft.   2 ft.   3 ft.

FOCUS
▶ Using, converting, and comparing standard linear measures
▶ Performing operations with fractions
▶ Developing visual images for fractions

MATERIALS
Eight yard-length strips of adding machine tape, with inches marked

OVERVIEW
This is the last new Calendar Math element we will add this year. Each month, a different measurement will be explored with an emphasis on understanding fractional parts of the measurement. This month, we will begin with a yard-length strip, and subtract $\frac{1}{36}$ of the yard each day. Students will write an equation such as $1 - \frac{1}{36} = \frac{35}{36}$, or 1 yard $- \frac{1}{36} = 2$ feet and 11 inches.

FREQUENCY
Update twice each week. Discuss once each week.

UPDATE PROCEDURE
The students can create the yard-length strips from the adding machine tape using the classroom yardstick, adding the inch marks to each one.

Post one of the one-yard strips. Twice each week ask the students to create a fraction using the date as the numerator and 36 for the denominator. Subtract this fraction from the one yard and determine the number of feet and inches that remain. Fold the subtracted portion behind the new length and post the strip, recording the fraction each time. Be sure to begin each session with a new one-yard strip.

DISCUSSION THROUGHOUT THE MONTH
▶ What is $\frac{5}{36}$ of one yard? (5 inches.)
▶ What is $1 - \frac{5}{36}$? ($\frac{31}{36}$)
▶ If we take $\frac{5}{36}$ from one yard, how much is left? (31 inches.)
▶ How many feet is that? (2 and $\frac{7}{12}$, or 2 feet and 7 inches.)
▶ What is $\frac{31}{36}$ of one yard? (31 inches.)
▶ If we simplify $\frac{6}{36}$, what do we get? ($\frac{1}{6}$)
▶ What is $\frac{1}{6}$ of a yard? (6 inches, or $\frac{1}{2}$ foot.)
▶ How much is $\frac{5}{6}$ of a yard? (30 inches.)
▶ What is $\frac{1}{2}$ of a yard? (18 inches.) How many feet is that? (1 foot and 6 inches, or $1\frac{1}{2}$ feet.)
▶ How much is left if we subtract $\frac{3}{4}$, or $\frac{27}{36}$, of one yard? (9 inches.)

1 ft.   2 ft.

1 yard $- \dfrac{5}{36}$ = 31 inches

or 2 feet, 7 inches

MARCH

MORE TO THINK ABOUT

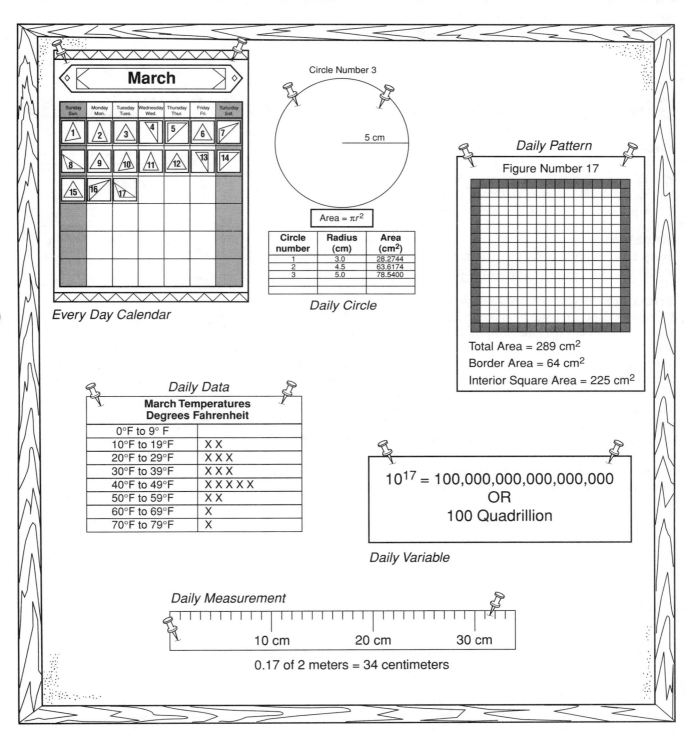

March

Sunday Sun.	Monday Mon.	Tuesday Tues.	Wednesday Wed.	Thursday Thur.	Friday Fri.	Saturday Sat.
1	2	3	4	5	6	7
8	9	10	11	12	13	14
15	16	17				

Every Day Calendar

Circle Number 3

5 cm

$$Area = \pi r^2$$

Circle number	Radius (cm)	Area (cm^2)
1	3.0	28.2744
2	4.5	63.6174
3	5.0	78.5400

Daily Circle

Daily Pattern

Figure Number 17

Total Area = 289 cm^2
Border Area = 64 cm^2
Interior Square Area = 225 cm^2

Daily Data

March Temperatures Degrees Fahrenheit	
0°F to 9° F	
10°F to 19°F	X X
20°F to 29°F	X X X
30°F to 39°F	X X X
40°F to 49°F	X X X X X
50°F to 59°F	X X
60°F to 69°F	X
70°F to 79°F	X

$$10^{17} = 100,000,000,000,000,000$$
OR
100 Quadrillion

Daily Variable

Daily Measurement

10 cm   20 cm   30 cm

0.17 of 2 meters = 34 centimeters

During March, the Calendar will feature a pattern using a variety of triangles. Students will analyze the angles, sides, and properties of these triangles to discover the pattern. The Daily Circle will be used in March to explore strategies for determining the area of a circle. The Daily Pattern, in which students calculate the area of a growing square, emphasizes multiple patterns and the use of symbols and variables. The Daily Variable introduces powers of 10. Students will construct a circle graph displaying the range of March temperatures in the Daily Data element. The Daily Measurement will focus on decimal multiplication using the meter stick.

EVERY DAY ELEMENT

FOCUS
► Analyzing and predicting patterns
► Recognizing and comparing triangles
► Analyzing sides and angles of triangles
► Understanding and using geometric terms relating to triangles

MATERIALS
Every Day Calendar, March Month Strip, March Calendar Pieces, or Triangle Cutouts (TR14) and marker

SUGGESTED PATTERN FOR MARCH
Triangles take center stage on the Calendar this month. Students will analyze the posted triangles and make observations about their angles and sides. Two patterns will run simultaneously. The first, a repeating three-day pattern, will focus on the sides of the triangles, beginning with a scalene triangle (three unequal sides), followed by an isosceles triangle (two sides equal), and ending with an equilateral triangle (three equal sides). The second, a nine-day repeating pattern, will focus on the angles of the triangles, with every third triangle being an acute triangle. The pattern is acute, acute, acute; right, right, acute; and obtuse, obtuse, acute. Using these patterns, the scalene and isosceles triangles will alternate between acute, right, and obtuse triangles. Every third triangle will be an equilateral triangle.

CALENDAR

scalene 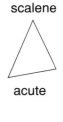 acute

isosceles acute

equilateral acute

scalene  right

isosceles 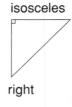 right

equilateral  acute

scalene 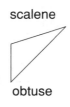 obtuse

isosceles 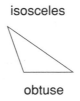 obtuse

equilateral 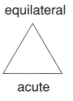 acute

Students will discover what makes a triangle an obtuse scalene triangle and what makes it different from an acute isosceles triangle. If time allows at the end of the month, students can examine other attributes of triangles, such as lines of symmetry and turn symmetry.

FREQUENCY

Update daily. Post the Calendar Pieces for the weekend dates on Monday. Discuss twice a week.

UPDATE PROCEDURE

Each day, post the March Calendar Piece for the date. If you choose to use the Triangle Cutouts (TR14), write the date on each piece before posting. Ask the students to study the posted figures, to be prepared to compare and contrast the triangles, and to discover what determines the order in which they are posted.

SAMPLE DISCUSSION FOR THE FIRST DAY OF THE MONTH

Teacher: The pattern this month features different kinds of triangles. Let's find out what you already know about triangles. What makes a triangle a triangle?

Student: It has three sides.

Teacher: (Drawing a three-sided open figure.) Like this?

Student: No. A triangle is a three-sided polygon, a closed figure with straight sides.

Teacher: How many angles are there in a triangle?

Student: Three.

Teacher: Hence the name triangle, which means three angles. We know there are many different kinds of triangles. Does anyone remember any other words connected to triangles?

Student: We learned about equilateral and right triangles last year.

Teacher: What is an equilateral triangle?

Student: Is that the one where all the sides are equal?

Teacher: Yes. What is a right triangle?

Student: A triangle with a right angle in it.

Teacher: Can an equilateral triangle have a right angle in it?

Student: I think it can.

Teacher: Why don't you try to draw it.

Student: I don't think you can because as soon as you draw a right angle the line connecting the two sides of the angle has to be longer.

Teacher: The term equilateral refers to the sides of the triangle. Other terms, such as right triangle, refer to the angles. I will use a variety of triangles this month to create a pattern. I would like you to examine the triangles, and decide what distinguishes them from each other. Pay attention to their sides and their angles.

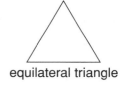

equilateral triangle

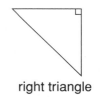

right triangle

Teacher: What do you notice about the triangles we have posted so far?

Student: The ones on the 3rd and the 6th look like equilateral triangles.

Teacher: What makes them equilateral?

Student: All the sides are the same.

Teacher: What other kinds of triangles do you see?

Student: The triangles on the 2nd, 5th, and the one we put up today all look like they have two equal sides.

Teacher: How could you check to see if you're right?

Student: You could measure them with a ruler.

Teacher: What if we didn't have a ruler?

Student: You could fold the triangle in half and see if the sides match.

Student: You could use something else like a piece of paper to measure them.

Teacher: Good. Does anybody remember what a triangle with two congruent sides is called? No? It's called an isosceles triangle. We haven't talked about the triangles we posted on the 1st, 4th, and 7th. How many sides are congruent or equal in length on those triangles?

Student: It looks like every side is different on those.

Teacher: Yes it does. But they all have a characteristic that is the same. Can anyone tell me what it is?

Student: Yes. In these triangles no sides are equal.

Teacher: We call a triangle with no equal sides a scalene triangle. Is every triangle either a scalene triangle, an isosceles triangle, or an equilateral triangle?

Student: Yes because every triangle has either no sides equal, two sides equal, or all three sides equal.

Teacher: Good. Now let's look at the angles of these triangles. What do you notice?

Student: The triangles on the 4th and 5th have right angles in them.

Student: On the 7th and 8th there's a big angle in the triangle.

Teacher: What do you mean by a big angle?

Student: The angle is greater than 90 degrees.

Teacher: An angle greater than 90 degrees is called an obtuse angle. A triangle with an obtuse angle is called an obtuse triangle. On the 7th, the scalene triangle is obtuse. Are all scalene triangles obtuse?

Student: No. On the 1st and 4th the scalene triangles don't have obtuse angles.

Teacher: Are any isosceles triangles obtuse?

Student: The one we put up today is an isosceles and obtuse triangle.

Teacher: What about the triangles with angles less than 90 degrees? Does anyone remember what they are called? They are cute little triangles, aren't they?

Student: Very funny! They're called acute triangles, aren't they?

Teacher: Yes. What is the pattern of angles in the triangles so far?

Student: Acute, acute, acute, right, right, acute, obtuse, and obtuse.

Teacher: Yes, so what do you think will come next?

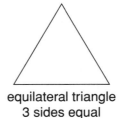

equilateral triangle
3 sides equal

isosceles triangle
2 sides equal

scalene triangle
no sides equal

DISCUSSION FOR THE REMAINDER OF THE MONTH

These questions can be used to continue the discussion throughout the month. Be sure to encourage the students to use the geometric terms that have been introduced.

▶ Looking at all the scalene triangles, what pattern do you see to their angles? (Acute, right, obtuse, acute, right, obtuse, and so on.)

▶ Can you describe the pattern of the triangles in terms of their sides? (Scalene, isosceles, equilateral, scalene, isosceles, equilateral, and so on.)

▶ What do you notice about the pattern of the angles? (There are three acute, two right, one acute, two obtuse, one acute. The scalene and isosceles triangles alternate between acute, right, and obtuse angles while the equilateral triangles are always acute.)

▶ What do you notice about the days that have equilateral triangles? (They are all multiples of three.)

▶ What do you notice about the angles of the equilateral triangles? (They are all equal.) Why do you think that is so? How can we find out if they are equal? (We can fold an equilateral triangle along a line of symmetry and line up the angles to prove they are equal.)

▶ How many degrees would you guess are in each of the angles in an equilateral triangle? (There are 60 degrees. Do not confirm this until most students are convinced that 60 degrees is close to the right size.)

▶ Can a triangle be both scalene and obtuse? (Yes.)

▶ Can a triangle be isosceles and obtuse? (Yes.)

▶ Which angle can be obtuse in an isosceles triangle? (Only the one between the two equal sides.)

▶ Can an equilateral triangle be obtuse? (No, because all the angles are 60 degrees.)

HELPFUL HINT

▶ If time allows, you may want to ask the students to consider whether these triangles have lines of symmetry or turn symmetry. Doing this will help the students in their spatial thinking and visualization abilities, reminding them that the properties of polygons remain the same no matter what their orientation. This emphasis on symmetry is not part of the pattern this month, but you can use a Calendar Piece to demonstrate the rotation. You may simply choose to draw the figures on the chalkboard. Be sure to point out that the equilateral triangle has three lines of symmetry and 120° turn symmetry, that scalene triangles have neither, and that isosceles triangles have one line of symmetry but no turn symmetry. Repeated exposure to these concepts is critical for a good understanding of symmetry.

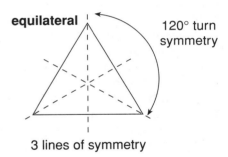

equilateral — 120° turn symmetry — 3 lines of symmetry

scalene — no line symmetry, no turn symmetry

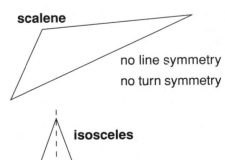

isosceles — 1 line of symmetry, no turn symmetry

EVERY DAY ELEMENT

FOCUS
▶ Investigating the relationship between the length of the radius and the area of a circle
▶ Using the formula for the area of a circle

MATERIALS
Four or five of the October Circles, calculator (optional)

FREQUENCY
Measure and discuss weekly.

UPDATE PROCEDURE
Students should have many experiences with approximating the area of a circle. These might include laying small grid paper over circles of different sizes, measuring the size of squares inscribed inside and outside a circle, or cutting up a circle to make it into an easily measured shape. Once students have had such experiences, they can compare these approximations to the value derived when the formula for the area of a circle is used. Hopefully this will lead students to a better understanding of how the formula works than they might have if they are just given the formula and told that it works.

This month, students will use the formula πr^2 to find the area of different circles. If the students are using calculators, use the value 3.1416 for π. If computing with pencil and paper, they should use 3.14. It might prove interesting to compare the difference between these two means of calculating.

Each week, measure the radius of one of the October Circles and have the students compute the area. It makes no difference which of the circles are used, but begin with a small circle and proceed to the larger ones. Make a chart with the formula at the top and columns for the circle number, radius length, and area. Update the chart each time a different circle is measured. Repeating this activity four or five times during the month should help students use and remember the formula for the area of a circle. It will also help them to recognize that as the radius increases, the area of the circle increases by the square of the radius.

DISCUSSION THROUGHOUT THE MONTH
These questions should be used to increase students' understanding of the formula for calculating the area of a circle.
▶ Does the word "area" mean the same thing for a circle as it does for polygons? (Yes, it means the space inside the figure.)
▶ Why is it more difficult to determine the area of a circle than it is to determine the area of a square? (The circle has a curved perimeter or circumference.)
▶ The area of a circle is equal to one half the circumference times the radius. This comes out to be πr^2. If the radius of a circle is one inch, what is the area of the circle? (3.14 or 3.1416 square inches, using 3.14 or 3.1416 for pi.)
▶ What is the area of a circle with a radius of 2 inches? (12.5664 square inches, using 3.1416 for pi.)

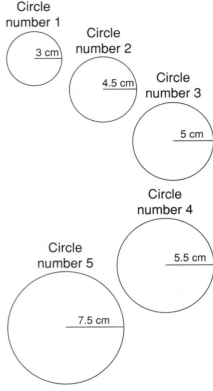

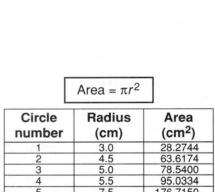

Circle number	Radius (cm)	Area (cm²)
1	3.0	28.2744
2	4.5	63.6174
3	5.0	78.5400
4	5.5	95.0334
5	7.5	176.7150

Area = πr^2

- ▶ What happens to the area when we double the length of the radius? (It increases by four times. This can be checked with a calculator.)
- ▶ Is this the exact area? (No, because we are approximating π.)
- ▶ What is the area of a circle with a radius of 3 inches? (28.2744 square inches.)
- ▶ How much larger is the area of a circle that has a radius of 3 inches than a circle with a radius of 1 inch? (Nine times larger. This should be checked using a calculator.)
- ▶ Which has the larger area, a square with a side of 1 inch or a circle with a radius of 1 inch? (The circle, because the 1 inch is multiplied by 3.14 instead of by 1.)
- ▶ Which has the larger area, a square with a side of 1 inch or a circle with a diameter of 1 inch? (The square. Check this with a calculator. This can also be simply demonstrated by drawing a circle inside a square whose side is the same as the diameter of the circle.)

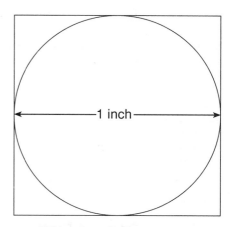

Which has the larger area, the circle or the square?

EVERY DAY ELEMENT

DAILY PATTERN

FOCUS

- ▶ Recognizing patterns involving increasing areas of a square
- ▶ Solving problems using multiple strategies
- ▶ Recording mathematical relationships with mathematical symbols
- ▶ Using variables to generalize patterns

MATERIALS

Squares created in January for the Daily Pattern, colored marker

FREQUENCY

Update daily. Post the weekend figures on Monday. Discuss once or twice a week.

UPDATE PROCEDURE

As in previous months, this month's pattern involves the growing area of a square. This month, we will place special emphasis on recording different mathematical expressions for describing a variety of solutions for the same problem. Students will analyze a square with each side having a length in centimeters equal to the date. Students will determine the number of square centimeters in the border of the large square, the number of square centimeters in the interior, and the total number of square centimeters in the figure. Some students will simply count. Others will use strategies such as determining the area of the entire figure and subtracting the interior area to determine the area of the border. As students repeat these procedures through the month, they can begin to generalize these procedures and connect their generalizations to mathematical language. For example, a student who calculates the border of a 5 centimeter × 5 centimeter figure by multiplying 5 × 5 and then subtracting the area of the interior 3 centimeter × 3 centimeter square will see that this procedure can be recorded as $5^2 - 3^2$. Eventually, students will generalize this to $n^2 - (n - 2)^2$.

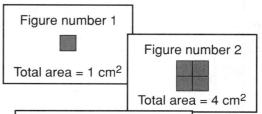

Figure number 1
Total area = 1 cm²

Figure number 2
Total area = 4 cm²

Figure number 3
Total area = 9 cm²
Border area = 8 cm²
Interior square area = 1 cm²

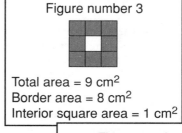

Figure number 4
Total area = 16 cm²
Border area = 12 cm²
Interior square area = 4 cm²

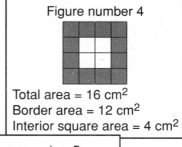

Figure number 5
Total area = 25 cm²
Border area = 16 cm²
Interior square area = 9 cm²

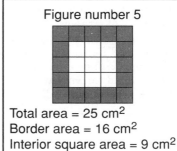

Since the daily figure is a square with side lengths equal to the date, you can use the same pattern squares created in January for the Daily Pattern in March. If you choose to do this, they should be displayed on construction paper. You may also choose to create a new set of squares this month. In either case, you will need to color the row of square centimeters around the perimeter of each figure to make the border. Color the total area of the squares for the first two days of this month.

For the first few days, simply post the figure. After several days, ask students to begin to think about the number of square centimeters around the border of the figure, and the number of square centimeters inside the border. Ask them to describe any patterns they might notice.

SAMPLE DISCUSSION FOR THE SIXTH DAY OF THE MONTH

Teacher: How many square centimeters are in this square, and how did you figure it out?

Student: It looks like 6 rows of 6, so 36 square centimeters.

Teacher: Why do you think each side has 6 square centimeters?

Student: It looks like each side always has the same number of square centimeters as the date.

Teacher: That's right. How many square centimeters are there in the border or frame of the figure? I would like you to think of as many different ways as you can to figure it out.

Student: I know there are 6 square centimeters on a side and 4 times 6 is 24.

Student: I counted 6 on two sides and 4 on the other two, so that is 20.

Teacher: Why did the two of you come up with different answers?

Student: I'm not sure.

Teacher: Does anyone have a suggestion?

Student: Even though each side has 6 square centimeters, the corners use the same ones. There really aren't four sides of 6, but two sides of 6 and two sides of 4.

Teacher: Does that make sense to everyone? Check with your neighbor to see if they agree with this explanation. If we write this as a mathematical expression, (writing on chalkboard) we'll get *area = (2 × 6) + (2 × 4)*. Since we are writing a mathematical expression, we could use the variable *a* to mean the area. Are there any other strategies we can use to determine the area of the border?

Student: If you count only one corner for each side, then there are four sides of 5 square centimeters in the border, so 4 × 5 = 20 square centimeters.

Teacher: Let's write that as an expression, too. We have (writing on chalkboard) *a, or area = 4 × 5.* What do the parentheses mean in the first expression?

Student: You do the multiplication first.

Teacher: Good. It also means "the quantity of." When you see parentheses in a mathematical expression, think that it means "the quantity of whatever is inside the parentheses." Does anyone have another strategy to determine the area of the border?

Student: Well there is 1 square centimeter in each corner and 4 more square centimeters on each side.

Teacher: How would we write that as a mathematical expression?

Student: (Writes on chalkboard) *a = (4 × 1) + (4 × 4).*

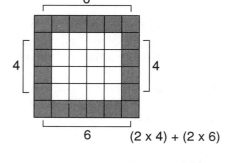

(2 x 4) + (2 x 6)

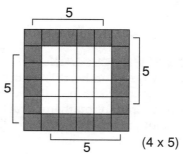

(4 x 5)

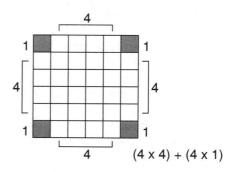

(4 x 4) + (4 x 1)

Teacher: What does the *a* stand for?

Student: It means the area.

Teacher: So how would we read that expression?

Student: The area is the quantity of 4 × 1 plus the quantity of 4 × 4.

Teacher: What do all these expressions equal?

Student: Twenty.

Teacher: We call these equivalent expressions because they all equal the same amount.

Student: I have another strategy, but it is pretty complicated. The area of the whole figure is 36 square centimeters, and the area of the inside square is 4 × 4 or 16 square centimeters, so if you subtract that you still get 20 square centimeters in the border.

Teacher: How will we write this expression?

Student: 36 − 16?

Teacher: Yes, but how did we get the 36 and 16?

Student: The whole square is 6 by 6, and the square inside the border is 4 × 4, so that is 36 − 16.

Teacher: Good. How should I record all of that on the chalkboard?

Student: a = (6 × 6) − (4 × 4). The area is the quantity of 6 × 6 minus the quantity of 4 × 4.

Student: I have another solution. Since we don't want to count the corner squares twice, we can say the area is (4 × 6) − 4. That way we count each corner only once.

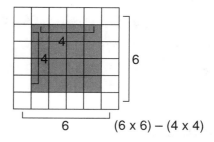

(6 x 6) − (4 x 4)

DISCUSSION FOR THE REMAINDER OF THE MONTH

These questions will help the students move from specific number situations to generalizing what they know into new mathematical expressions.

► What was the area of yesterday's figure? What is the area of today's figure? What will the area of tomorrow's figure be? What do you notice about these numbers? (They are all squares. The difference between them is consecutive odd numbers.)

► If you know the date, how can you determine the total area of the figure? (Since the date is the number of square centimeters on a side, the area will be the date squared.)

► What is a general rule for figuring out how many square centimeters there are in each figure? (Think that the date is squared, or $n \times n$.)

► If you know the date, how can you determine the area of the interior square? (Take 2 from the date and square that number.)

► Can you find a general rule for determining the area of the interior square? (It's 2 less than the date squared, or $(n - 2)^2$.)

► If you know the date, how can you figure out the area of the border? (Subtract 1 from the date and multiply by 4, or 4 times the date minus 4, or 2 times the date plus 2 times the date minus 2.)

► What are the general rules for each of those strategies for figuring out the area of the border? ($4(n - 1)$, or $4n - 4$, or $2n + 2(n - 2)$.)

► Tomorrow will be the 20th of March. What will the 20th figure look like? (It will be a square with 20 centimeters on each side, 76 square centimeters in the border, and 324 square centimeters in the interior.)

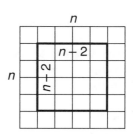

- What are some different ways to determine the area of the interior of the 25th figure? (The area of the total figure (25 × 25) minus the area of the border (4 × 24), or the area of the total figure (25 × 25) minus 4 times the number of centimeters on a side (4 × 25) minus the four corners (4), or the square of the number of the figure minus two $(25 - 2)^2$.)
- Encourage the students to explain their reasoning. For example, in the last strategy, try to elicit the phrase "two less than the number of the figure" rather than just the number 23.

EVERY DAY ELEMENT

DAILY VARIABLE

$$10^6 = 1,000,000$$
one million

$$10^9 = 1,000,000,000$$
one billion

$$10^{12} = 1,000,000,000,000$$
one trillion

$$10^{15} = 1,000,000,000,000,000$$
one quadrillion

$$10^{18} = 1,000,000,000,000,000,000$$
one quintillion

$$10^{21} = 1,000,000,000,000,000,000,000$$
one sextillion

$$10^{24} = 1,000,000,000,000,000,000,000,000$$
one septillion

$$10^{27} = 1,000,000,000,000,000,000,000,000,000$$
one octillion

$$10^{30} = 1,000,000,000,000,000,000,000,000,000,000$$
one nonillion

FOCUS
- Understanding powers of 10
- Using exponents
- Reading large numbers

MATERIALS
Paper for a chart

FREQUENCY
Update the chart daily. Discuss occasionally during the month.

UPDATE PROCEDURE
This month, students will evaluate the expression 10^n, using the date as the exponent. The base will remain 10 throughout the month. On the first day of the month, students will evaluate 10^1, on the second 10^2, on the third 10^3, and so on. Students will be encouraged to read the large numbers and to provide examples for the quantities named. For example, a large stadium such as the one the Rose Bowl is played in holds around 100,000 (10^5) people, or a million (10^6) seconds is a little more than eleven and a half days, or the sun is almost 100,000,000 (10^8) miles away from the earth, and so on. The teacher or a student should write the number and the word for the number, it if it is known.

This element does not need to be updated daily. You can catch up on days that you think are important, such as 10^6 or 10^9. Remember to include the numbers for the weekend dates and discuss them when appropriate.

DISCUSSION FOR THE BEGINNING OF THE MONTH
- This month we will evaluate the expression 10^n. We will use the number of the date for n. What does 10^n mean? (10 raised to the nth power, or 10×10, n times.)
- How do we read it? (10 to the nth power.)
- Today is the 3rd of March, so what will our expression be? (10^3.) What does 10^3 mean? ($10 \times 10 \times 10$.) So what is the value of today's expression? (1000)
- Who can give an example of a thousand of something? (There are a thousand milliliters in a liter, or the number of students in a small high school, or the approximate number of days in three years, and so on.)

► Today is the 5th, so what will today's expression be? (10^5.) What is the value of 10^5? (100,000) How do we write it as a number? (100,000) How do we write that in words? (One hundred thousand.)

► What is the value of 10^9? (1,000,000,000. It might be interesting to point out that in the United States 1000 million is called a billion, or 10^9, while in England a million million is called a billion, or 10^{12}.)

► What do you notice about the value of the expression 10^n? (The number of zeros equals n.) On which day then will we write the number 1 followed by 15 zeros? (On the fifteenth.)

► The word bi means two as in billion, and tri means three as in trillion, so what do you think 10^{15} will be called? (A quadrillion.)

► A million is a 1 followed by six zeros. A billion is a 1 followed by 9 zeros. A trillion is a 1 followed by 12 zeros. What is the pattern for the time a new name is used? (The new name is used at every 1000, or at each point where we put a comma, or every three zeros.)

► Does every large number have a name? (No. Allow students to speculate. Certainly every counting number that can be described could be named, but it is simply impractical and unnecessary.)

► The large number 1 followed by a 100 zeros is called a googol, a name suggested by the son of a famous American mathematician, Edward Kasner. The largest named number is a googolplex, or a 1 followed by a googol of zeros. It is expressed as $10^{10^{100}}$. There is nothing in the universe that is a googol because it has been estimated that there are only 10^{87} particles in the universe.

► Why do you think that scientists and engineers use notations such as 10^{20} to describe a large number? (It is much easier than writing a 1 followed by 20 zeros.)

HELPFUL HINTS

► Encourage students to investigate the names of very large numbers.

► Ask students to find large numbers that are used in the newspaper and books.

► Encourage students to think of examples for each 10^n you discuss.

FOCUS

▶ Using a circle graph to display and analyze data

▶ Recognizing when a circle graph is appropriate for displaying data

▶ Comparing circle graphs to other kinds of graphs

▶ Using percents and fractions with circle graphs to recognize relative sizes of parts

▶ Connecting percents to angles of a circle graph.

March Temperatures	
0°F to 9° F	
10°F to 19°F	X X
20°F to 29°F	X X X X X
30°F to 39°F	X X X X
40°F to 49°F	X X X X X X X X
50°F to 59°F	X X X
60°F to 69°F	X X
70°F to 79°F	X

MATERIALS

A 100-centimeter length of adding machine tape, paper for a graph, metric rulers, a thermometer or newspaper weather report

─── 100 cm ───

FREQUENCY

Record the temperature daily. Discuss three or four times during the month.

UPDATE PROCEDURE

Circle graphs are useful when discussing the relative size of parts of a whole when the whole is known. For example, in a survey of the students in the class, the whole is the number of students. The whole may be the number of days in the month, or any other known whole. Circle graphs are not useful for representing trends over time, or for depicting the middle of a set of data.

This month, students will collect daily temperature information for 25 days. If you are using the newspaper, use the high temperature reading of the previous day. The temperatures should be sorted into 10 degree ranges (20°F to 29°F, 30°F to 39F°, and so on) and recorded in table form until all 25 temperatures are collected. Students will then create a circle graph using the 100-centimeter strip. Students should first figure out how much space will be allotted for each of the 25 days on the strip (4 centimeters). The strip will be turned into a circle and the fractional parts labeled. Percentages and degrees can be added as well.

Have a student be responsible for reading and recording the temperature at the same time each day, or noting and recording the temperature from the newspaper. One student should be responsible for collecting and recording the high temperature readings from the newspaper for the weekend days. Tally each temperature in the appropriate range. After 25 days, the class creates a circle graph using the 100-centimeter strip.

─── 100 cm ───

8 cm	20 cm	16 cm	32 cm	12 cm	8 cm	4 cm
10° to 19°	20° to 29°	30° to 39°	40° to 49°	50° to 59°	60° to 69°	70° to 79°

March Temperatures
Degrees Fahrenheit

Teacher: The temperatures in March are hard to predict because they change so often. You have heard the expression "March roars in like a lion and leaves like a lamb." This month, let's see if we can determine what range of temperatures occurs most often in March. If we divide the temperatures into 10 degree ranges, like 20 to 29 degrees, 30 to 39 degrees, and so on, in which range do you think the highest number of days will fall?

Student: 40 degrees.

Teacher: Which range is that?

Student: 40 to 49 degrees.

Student: I think it might be a lot colder than that, like 20 to 29 degrees.

Student: Well I hope it will be a lot warmer than that. Let's hope for 50 to 59 degrees.

Teacher: We are going to keep track of the temperatures this month and then use a circle graph to show what fraction of the month falls into each range. We'll use only the temperatures of the first 25 days of March, including weekends, and we'll record them on a chart until we're ready to make the circle graph.

THE CIRCLE GRAPH

To create the circle graph, connect the ends of the 100-centimeter strip to each other and place the resulting circle on a piece of paper. The information recorded on the strip should face out, away from the center of the circle. Estimate the location of the center of the circle and mark it. Trace the outline of the strip to form the circumference of the circle graph. Make marks along the circumference to show the location of the temperature ranges as they appear on the strip. Remove the strip and draw lines connecting the center point to each mark indicating the temperature ranges. This procedure will probably work best if only two or three students are in charge of creating the outlines of the circle graph. All the students should be encouraged to participate as the sectional lines are drawn and the data is entered in each section.

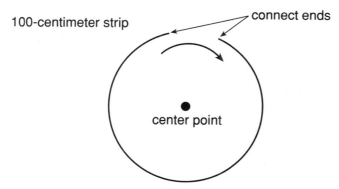

Trace outline on a piece of paper to create a circle graph with a circumference of 100 centimeters. Mark temperature ranges as points on the circumference.

SAMPLE DISCUSSION FOR THE END OF THE MONTH

Teacher: This strip is 100 centimeters long and it represents the whole 25 days. Five days this month had temperatures that were between 30 and 39 degrees Fahrenheit. How many centimeters of the tape should represent these five days?

Student: I don't understand.

Teacher: This strip stands for the whole 25 days for which we have recorded temperatures. Five of those 25 days had temperatures between 30 and 39 degrees Fahrenheit. How much of this 100-centimeter strip should represent these five days? How long a section?

Student: $\frac{5}{25}$ of the strip?

Teacher: How long will that be?

Student: $\frac{5}{25}$ is $\frac{1}{5}$, and $\frac{1}{5}$ of 100 centimeters is 20 centimeters.

Teacher: What length should represent each day?

Student: 1 out of 25.

Teacher: If the whole 25 days is 100 centimeters, what length represents one day?

Student: 4 centimeters?

Teacher: Why?

Student: Because there are 25 fours in 100.

Teacher: Good. Four days this month had temperatures between 20 and 29 degrees Fahrenheit. How long a section of the strip should represent these four days?

Student: 4 times 4 is 16, so 16 centimeters.

Teacher: Lets mark the sections for each of the temperature ranges. We could cut each of these sections and make a bar graph, but instead we are going to make this strip into a circle graph. Then we are going to make lines from the center of the circle to the marks we have made on our strip. What fraction of the area of the circle represents the temperature range from 30 to 39 degrees Fahrenheit?

Student: $\frac{1}{5}$.

Teacher: What percent of the circle will represent this range?

Student: 20%.

Teacher: Why?

Student: $\frac{1}{5}$ is 20%.

Teacher: Since the circumference of our circle graph is 100 centimeters, 20 centimeters along the circumference will represent the 30 to 39 degree temperature range. 20 out of 100 is 20%. What fraction of the circumference is represented by this temperature range?

Student: $\frac{1}{5}$.

Teacher: How many degrees of the circle is that? Remember that there are 360 degrees in a circle.

Student: $\frac{1}{5}$ of 360 degrees is 72 degrees.

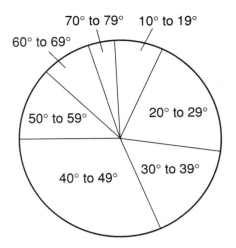

March Temperatures
Degrees Fahrenheit

FURTHER DISCUSSION FOR THE END OF THE MONTH

These general questions will guide the students in interpreting the data collected during the month. Because the actual recorded temperatures will vary, responses to the questions will be different, but the usefulness and limitations of the circle graph will be clear in any case.

► What fraction of the circle graph represents each temperature range?

► What percent of the area of the circle is that?

► Which temperature range is the largest fraction? Which is the smallest?

► Let's combine two of our temperature ranges and then figure out what fraction of the circle graph represents the combined ranges. For example, what fraction of the circle graph represents the combined ranges of 20 to 39 degrees Fahrenheit?

► Is there any range that is twice as large as another?

► What kind of information do you think circle graphs show really well? (Accept a variety of responses, but try to encourage the students to notice that circle graphs are good for showing the relative size of the parts in relation to the whole.)

► Using our graph, who can tell me what temperature range was most common this month? Which range was least common?

► What kind of information is hard to see from a circle graph? (Accept a variety of answers, including that the change in temperature over time is not visible like it is on a line graph, and that the general shape of the data is not clear like it is on a number line.)

HELPFUL HINTS

► You may want to include other circle graphs in future months. Student surveys provide excellent data for such graphs, with the whole being the number of students in the class.

► Ask students to find circle graphs in newspapers and magazines, and to explain what the graph shows. You might also ask them why they think the format of a circle graph was used to show the particular information.

EVERY DAY ELEMENT

DAILY MEASUREMENT

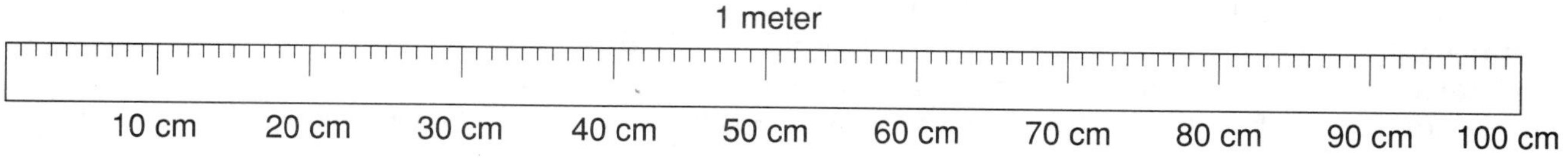

1 meter

| 10 cm | 20 cm | 30 cm | 40 cm | 50 cm | 60 cm | 70 cm | 80 cm | 90 cm | 100 cm |

FOCUS

► Using linear metric units
► Multiplying with decimals
► Developing linear models for decimals

MATERIALS

Eight strips of adding machine tape cut into one-meter lengths with centimeters marked

FREQUENCY

Update and discuss twice a week.

UPDATE PROCEDURE

While the effort to introduce metric measurement into the United States has been met with much skepticism and resistance, in fact it has slowly pervaded the everyday consumer world as well as serving as the standard in the scientific world. For example, most drinks other than milk, juice, and soda in cans are now sold in metric containers. Most cars sold in the United States use metric parts and require the use of metric tools for their maintenance. No one swims or runs the 440-yard race any more, but rather the 400-meter race. The United States seems to be evolving into a country using a dual measuring system, retaining some of the common English standards such as inches, pounds, and miles, while introducing centimeters, liters, and cubic centimeters into daily activities. The best approach for today's students may be to encourage them to become familiar with both systems, without the need to convert from one to the other, as most adults were taught. Students can learn to use benchmarks for commonly used metric units such as one meter, one centimeter, and ten centimeters.

In March, students will use the date to represent a number of hundredths, and then record this as a fraction of a metric linear measurement. For example, on the 3rd of March, students will consider 0.03 of a meter and record the number of centimeters this represents. This process will help students to develop benchmarks for centimeters and to understand how centimeters relate to meters.

The students can create the meter-length strips the same way they made the yard-length strips in February. Be sure to indicate groups of ten centimeters with a slightly longer mark. Post one of the meter strips to provide a visual model for discussion during the first fifteen days of the month. Each time you update this element, use the date to determine the number of hundredths of a meter. For example, on March 10th, determine 0.10 of the meter, or 10 centimeters. Since students will quickly realize that the date is also the number of centimeters, add a second meter strip about halfway through the month. Continue to use the date to create a fractional measurement of the total distance. For example, on the 16th, ask students to determine 0.16 of 2 meters, or 32 centimeters.

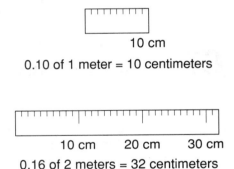

10 cm

0.10 of 1 meter = 10 centimeters

10 cm   20 cm   30 cm

0.16 of 2 meters = 32 centimeters

DISCUSSION THROUGHOUT THE MONTH

These questions can be used to guide the discussion during the month.

► This strip is 1 meter long. What are some things in our classroom that appear to be about 1 meter long?

► Today is the 5th of March, so we want to determine 0.05 of the meter strip. How many centimeters is that? (5) How did you determine that? (Since there are 100 centimeters in a meter, 0.05 of 100 is 5, or 0.05 × 100 is 5, or $\frac{1}{20}$ of 100 is 5.) How many of these 5 centimeter lengths will fit into the meter? (20)

► What do you see in the classroom that might be 5 centimeters long?

► What are we measuring when we use meters and centimeters? (Length, or distance, or how long an object is.)

► How do we write 0.05 of 100 centimeters as an expression? (0.05 × 100 cm.)

► What percent of 1 meter does 0.05 represent? (5%) What percent does 95 centimeters represent? (95%)

► What is 0.16 of 2 meters? (32 centimeters.) How do you know? (Take 16 centimeters of each meter, or 0.16 × 200, or 4 out of each 25 centimeters, so 8 × 4.) How can we write this as an equation? (0.16 × 200 cm = 32 cm.)

► What is 0.28 of 200 centimeters? (56 centimeters) Why? (0.14 of 200 centimeters is 28 centimeters and double that, or 0.28 of 100 centimeters is 28 centimeters and double that.)

► What percent of the 2 meters does 56 centimeters represent? (28%) Why? (56 out of 200 centimeters is the same as 28 out of 100 centimeters, which is 28%.)

► How many centimeters are in $2\frac{1}{2}$ meters? (250)

► What do you think your height might be in meters and centimeters? (Students should be encouraged to measure themselves to discover their height. Average height is probably about 155 centimeters.)

► About how many centimeters long is a baby? (Average is about 50 centimeters.)

► About how many meters tall is Shaquille O'Neal? (About 2 meters 20 centimeters, or 220 centimeters, would be a good estimate.)

APRIL

SPRING INTO THE MONTH

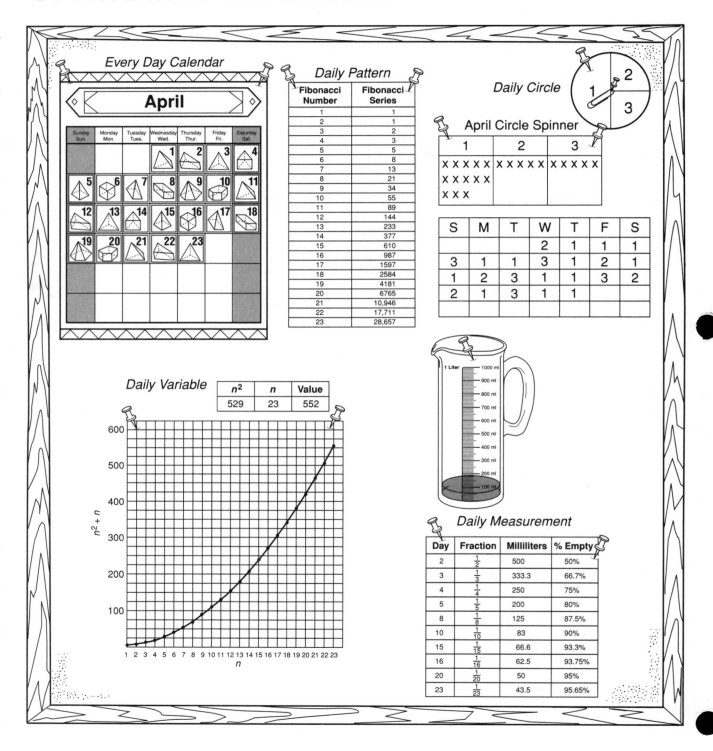

Every Day Calendar

April

Sunday Sun.	Monday Mon.	Tuesday Tues.	Wednesday Wed.	Thursday Thur.	Friday Fri.	Saturday Sat.
			1	2	3	4
5	6	7	8	9	10	11
12	13	14	15	16	17	18
19	20	21	22	23		

Daily Pattern

Fibonacci Number	Fibonacci Series
1	1
2	1
3	2
4	3
5	5
6	8
7	13
8	21
9	34
10	55
11	89
12	144
13	233
14	377
15	610
16	987
17	1597
18	2584
19	4181
20	6765
21	10,946
22	17,711
23	28,657

Daily Circle

April Circle Spinner

1	2	3
x x x x x x x x x x x x x	x x x x x	x x x x x

S	M	T	W	T	F	S
			2	1	1	1
3	1	1	3	1	2	1
1	2	3	1	1	3	2
2	1	3	1	1		

Daily Variable

n^2	n	Value
529	23	552

$n^2 + n$ vs n

Daily Measurement

Day	Fraction	Milliliters	% Empty
2	$\frac{1}{2}$	500	50%
3	$\frac{1}{3}$	333.3	66.7%
4	$\frac{1}{4}$	250	75%
5	$\frac{1}{5}$	200	80%
8	$\frac{1}{8}$	125	87.5%
10	$\frac{1}{10}$	83	90%
15	$\frac{1}{15}$	66.6	93.3%
16	$\frac{1}{16}$	62.5	93.75%
20	$\frac{1}{20}$	50	95%
23	$\frac{1}{23}$	43.5	95.65%

Like the weather this month, Calendar Math for April is a mixture of new and old. The elements introduced during the year will be continued, some new concepts will be introduced, and concepts from previous months will be developed. The Every Day Calendar will highlight three-dimensional shapes, with an emphasis on analyzing their faces, vertices and edges. The Daily Circle will focus on circle spinners and probability. The Daily Pattern introduces students to the famous Fibonacci sequence, encountered in numerous mathematical and natural environments. In the Daily Variable, students will calculate the value of the expression $n^2 + n$, where n is the date. The Daily Measurement will allow students to work with fractions and percents of a liter. It is a full month as students welcome spring.

EVERY DAY ELEMENT

FOCUS
▶ Recognizing three-dimensional shapes
▶ Recognizing properties of polyhedra
▶ Analyzing faces, edges, and vertices of polyhedra
▶ Distinguishing regular polyhedra
▶ Developing informal deductive reasoning

MATERIALS
Every Day Calendar, April Month Strip, April Calendar Pieces, or Polyhedra Cutouts (TR16) and marker; paper for a chart

SUGGESTED PATTERN FOR APRIL
So far, students have spent the year identifying and analyzing two-dimensional shapes. This month, they will turn their attention to three-dimensional shapes, specifically the polyhedron. Polyhedra are three-dimensional figures whose faces are all polygons. The Calendar will focus on pyramids and prisms, including a few regular polyhedra. A regular polyhedron uses only one regular polygon and the same number of polygons meet at each vertex. The most commonly known example is the cube.

The Calendar pattern for April will alternate between pyramids and prisms. Pyramids and prisms are defined by their bases, and it is these bases that determine the Calendar pattern this month. It is a ten-day repeating pattern with the bases in the order isosceles triangle, equilateral triangle, square, rectangle, and pentagon. Each of these five shapes will be used as the base of both a pyramid and a prism. The ten-day pattern is outlined below.

Day 1-Isosceles triangular pyramid
Day 3-Equilateral triangular pyramid
Day 5-Square pyramid
Day 7-Rectangular pyramid
Day 9-Pentagonal pyramid

Day 2-Isosceles triangular prism
Day 4-Equilateral triangular prism
Day 6-Cube (square prism)
Day 8-Rectangular prism
Day 10-Pentagonal prism

CALENDAR

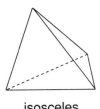
isosceles
triangular pyramid

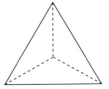
equilateral
triangular pyramid

square
pyramid

rectangular
pyramid

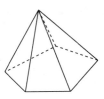
pentagonal
pyramid

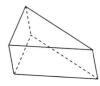
isosceles
triangular prism

equilateral
triangular prism

square prism
(cube)

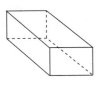
rectangular
prism

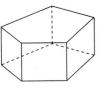
pentagonal
prism

This month, students will analyze a variety of pyramids and prisms. They will examine the faces, edges, and vertices of the shapes for purposes of comparing, contrasting, and classifying them. By studying a variety of polyhedra, students will develop mathematical language for defining them.

Many students may be unfamiliar with two-dimensional representations of these solid figures. It is critical that students have experiences with actual three-dimensional figures. If these are not available in the classroom, students will benefit greatly from time allotted to constructing solid figures from toothpicks, straws, clay balls, or gum drops. By comparing these models to the pictorial representations of the figures, students can develop a better understanding of the two-dimensional pictures.

As with previous concepts, it is not critical for students to memorize many geometric terms. The goal is to encourage students to carefully observe and reason as they study these three-dimensional figures.

FREQUENCY
Update daily. Discuss once or twice each week.

UPDATE PROCEDURE
Each day, post the April Calendar Piece for the date. If you choose to use the Polyhedra Cutouts (TR16), write the date on each piece before posting. Update the weekend dates on Mondays. Ask the students to study the posted figures, to be prepared to compare and contrast the polyhedra, and to discover what determines the order in which they are posted.

Teacher: What do all these shapes have in common?

Student: They are all three-dimensional.

Teacher: Yes. They are all pictures of three-dimensional solids, sometimes called space figures because they fill space. Are they really solid or space figures?

Student: No, just pictures of them.

Teacher: (Indicating the Calendar Piece for the first day of the month.) What is this first one called? Does anyone know?

Student: A pyramid?

Teacher: Yes. It's a special pyramid called a triangular pyramid because its base is a triangle. What shapes do you see in this first pyramid?

Student: Three triangles.

Student: And another triangle on the bottom.

Teacher: Are all the triangles the same?

Student: No.

Teacher: Does anyone remember what we call the flat surfaces in solid figures?

Student: Faces.

Teacher: How many faces does the first figure have?

Student: Four.

Teacher: Do all pyramids have four faces?

Student: No. I think the fifth figure is a pyramid, but it has more sides.

Teacher: What do you mean by sides?

Student: You know, flat shapes.

Teacher: So you mean faces. Why don't we call them sides?

Student: Because sides are the lines between the faces?

Teacher: Those are called edges. But you're on the right track. In order to avoid confusion, mathematicians use the word "sides" to refer to the line segments of polygons. But because this line is the segment where two faces meet, they call it an edge. In other words, edges are shared by two faces. No face has an edge all to itself, but shares an edge with another face. What do we call the points where the edges meet?

Student: Corners.

Teacher: Yes. The mathematical word is vertex. Looking at the first pyramid, how many edges does it have?

Student: Six.

Teacher: How did you count them?

Student: There are three on the triangle base and three more coming up.

Teacher: How many vertices are there?

Student: Four.

Teacher: What do we call the shapes represented by the 2nd and 4th figures?

Student: They look like prisms, like the ones that make rainbows.

Teacher: They are both called triangular prisms. But not all prisms have triangles. How many faces are on the 2nd and 4th figures?

Student: Five. Two triangles on the top and bottom and three rectangles connecting them.

Teacher: How many vertices do they have?

Student: Six, three on the bottom and three on the top.

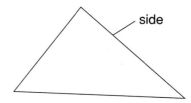

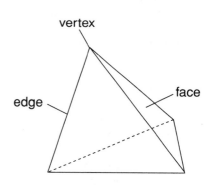

FURTHER DISCUSSION FOR THE BEGINNING OF THE MONTH

These questions can be used to continue discussion early in the month.

► What is the same about the 1st and 3rd figures? (Both are triangular pyramids.) How are they different? (In the 3rd figure, the triangles are all regular, having all faces and edges the same. It is a regular polyhedron, and is called a tetrahedron, meaning "four-faced.")

► What is the name of the 5th shape? (It is a square pyramid.)

► What is the name of the 6th shape? (A cube, or a square prism. It is also a regular polyhedron, and is called a hexahedron, meaning "six-faced.")

► What shapes do you see in the 5th and 6th figures? (Squares and triangles in the square pyramid, and only squares in the square prism or cube.)

► What is the same about the 3rd and 6th figures? (They are polyhedra made from one regular shape in which all faces and edges are congruent.)

DISCUSSION FOR THE MIDDLE OF THE MONTH

These questions can be used to continue the discussion about polyhedra.

► What do all prisms have in common? (Two parallel congruent bases. Students should be encouraged to say this in their own words.)

► How many faces are there on a rectangular prism? (6) How many vertices? (8) How many edges? (12)

► How is a rectangular prism the same as a cube, and how is it different? (It has the same number of faces, edges, and vertices as the cube. The cube is just a special kind of rectangular prism because all the faces are squares.)

► The triangular pyramid has 6 edges and the rectangular pyramid has 8 edges. What do you predict for the number of edges in the pentagonal pyramid? (10) Why? (There is one more vertex on the base, so there are two more edges.)

► What is a fast way to count the edges of the pyramid? (Count the edges of the base and the vertices of the base and add them. Another way is to double the number of vertices of the base.)

► What do you predict the number of edges will be on an octagonal, or eight-sided, pyramid? (16)

► How many vertices are there on the pentagonal pyramid? (6)

► The triangular pyramid has 4 vertices, the rectangular pyramid has 5, and the pentagonal pyramid has 6. What do you predict the number of vertices will be for an octagonal pyramid? (9) Why? (It seems that the number of vertices in a pyramid is the number of vertices in the base plus one.)

► How many vertices are there in a pentagonal prism? (10) What is a fast way to count them? (There are 5 on each base.)

► The triangular prism has 6 vertices, the rectangular prism has 8, and the pentagonal prism has 10. What seems to be the pattern? (The number of vertices is twice the number of sides of the polygon base, or twice the number of vertices of the base.)

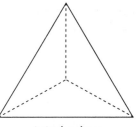
tetrahedron

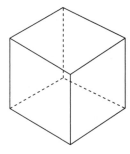
hexahedron

▶ How many faces are there on a triangular prism? (5) On a rectangular prism? (6) On a pentagonal prism? (7) What would you predict for the number of faces on a hexagonal prism? (8)

▶ What seems to be a fast way to count the number of faces on a prism? (It is the number of sides of the base polygon plus two for the faces of the bases.)

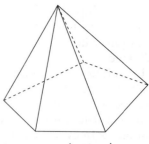

pentagonal
pyramid

DISCUSSION FOR THE END OF THE MONTH

Near the end of the month, make a chart showing the number of faces, vertices and edges for each shape used in the Calendar pattern. The chart can be used with the following questions to help students understand the similarities and differences between these shapes.

Polyhedron	Number of faces	Number of vertices	Number of edges
Isosceles Triangular Pyramid	4	4	6
Isosceles Triangular Prism	5	6	9
Equilateral Triangular Pyramid (Tetrahedron)	4	4	6
Equilateral Triangular Prism	5	6	9
Square Pyramid	5	5	8
Cube, or Square Prism (Hexahedron)	6	8	12
Rectangular Pyramid	5	5	8
Rectangular Prism	6	8	12
Pentagonal Pyramid	6	6	10
Pentagonal Prism	7	10	15

▶ What is the lowest number of faces that can meet at a vertex? (3)

▶ Can more than three faces meet at a vertex? (Yes. The vertex opposite the base of a square or pentagonal pyramid has more than three faces meeting.)

▶ What are some everyday examples of prisms or pyramids in the world ? (Allow a variety of responses which should include skyscrapers, pyramids, hatboxes, cereal boxes, and so on.)

▶ How many of the polyhedra used on our Calendar are regular, that is made up of one regular polygon? (Two, the equilateral pyramid, or tetrahedron, and the square prism, or hexahedron.)

▶ How many faces, vertices, and edges would a hexagonal pyramid include? (7 faces, 7 vertices, and 12 edges.) What about a hexagonal prism? (8 faces, 12 vertices, and 18 edges.)

▶ Why are the numbers on the chart the same for a cube and a rectangular prism? (A cube is a special kind of rectangular prism.)

▶ Is there any pattern or relationship between the number of faces, vertices, and edges of these figures? (The sum of the number of faces and vertices is two more than the number of edges for all polyhedra. If students don't discover this

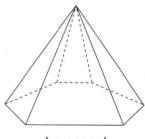

hexagonal
pyramid

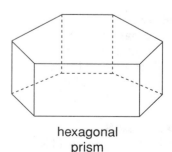

hexagonal
prism

relationship, don't provide the answer, but allow the students to continue to conjecture and explore. This formula is a famous relationship, called Euler's Formula, which states that F (faces) + V (vertices) = E (edges) + 2. Students will encounter this relationship again in their mathematical careers.)

▶ What other patterns can be discovered in this chart? Use the shapes to prove your answers. (The number of faces is the same as the number of vertices in all pyramids. The number of edges in every pyramid is twice the number of vertices in its base. The number of faces in a prism is two more than the number of sides in its polygon base, and so on.)

HELPFUL HINTS

▶ You may want to construct these three-dimensional figures using toothpicks, straws, or other materials. There are also a number of commercial materials available that will allow students to construct these figures. This will help the students visualize each figure and facilitate making comparisons between them.

▶ You may want to construct some other regular polyhedra as well. There are only five of these figures, also called Platonic solids. In addition to the tetrahedron and the hexahedron, they include the octahedron (8 triangle faces), the dodecahedron (12 pentagon faces), and the icosahedron (20 triangle faces). It is remarkable that while every polygon can be regular (have equal sides), only five polyhedra are regular.

▶ Encourage the students to make their own observations and conjectures about these solids. The intent should not be to memorize the technical terms, but to understand the relationships between the various parts of these three-dimensional figures.

▶ It might be interesting to see how many different everyday examples of these shapes can be collected and displayed in the classroom.

▶ Invite the students to cut out 6 adjacent squares from the Inch Squared Paper (TR4) that can be folded to form a cube. How many different nets can be found? (There are 11 such nets.)

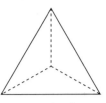
tetrahedron

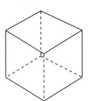
hexahedron

octahedron

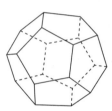
dodecahedron

icosahedron

EVERY DAY ELEMENT

FOCUS

▶ Recognizing probability based on the circumference of a circular spinner
▶ Recognizing the difference between theoretical and experimental probability
▶ Identifying the role of sample size in experimental probability

MATERIALS

April Circle Spinner (TR17) or cardstock, a paper clip or bobby pin for the spinner, a pencil or pin to hold the spinner in place, paper for two charts.

DAILY CIRCLE

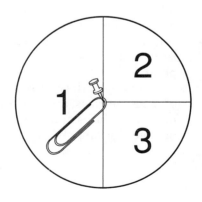

FREQUENCY
Update daily. Discuss once a week.

UPDATE PROCEDURE
The mathematics of probability plays an increasingly important role in every day life. Doctors design treatments based on the probability of success. Scientists use probability to describe the universe and the structure of the atom. Political polls and commercial surveys depend on sample sizes for accuracy. Newspapers and magazines are filled with statistics describing probabilities. But probability may be the least understood of all mathematical concepts.

Students need many experiences in which they deal with the slippery concept known as probability. They need to know the difference between certain and likely, between the odds of an occurrence and the actual occurrences in a trial, and the importance of the sample size or number of trials necessary to achieve the theoretical probability of an event.

This month, the Daily Circle will be a spinner. Each day, a student will spin and record the resulting number. Students will keep two charts this month, one listing the numbers as they appear on the spinner each day, and the other tallying the results. In order to increase the sample size, be sure to include the weekend days by spinning and recording three times on Monday.

At the beginning of the month, students will be invited to speculate on the likelihood of each number appearing, and to predict the number of occurrences for each number during the month. At the end of the month, students will discuss the relationship between their predictions and the actual results of the spins. The emphasis will be on how the number of trials, or sample size, effects the results of the probability experiment.

While it may appear obvious that spinning a 1 will occur more often than spinning either a 2 or a 3 since half the circumference is allowed for the 1, it is important to remember other supposedly obvious predictions about the likelihood of an event. People often bet on lucky numbers, or believe that after three heads it is more likely that tails will appear on the next toss of a coin. These are difficult ideas, and deserve time to enable understanding.

The April Circle Spinner cardstock or copies of (TR17) may be placed on a piece of cardboard and the spinner held in place with a pin. It may also be run off on acetate and used as an overhead transparency. In this case, use a pencil to hold the end of the spinner. In either case, be sure that it lies as flat as possible when spinning.

SAMPLE DISCUSSION FOR THE FIRST WEEK OF THE MONTH

> *Teacher:* This month, we are going to spin this circular spinner each day and record whether the spinner lands on the 1, the 2, or the 3. Which number do you think the spinner will land on most often?
>
> *Student:* On the 1, of course!

Teacher: Why?

Student: Because there is more space on the spinner for that number than either the 2 or the 3.

Teacher: So why will 1 be more likely than the other numbers?

Student: There are more ways for 1 to occur than either 2 or 3.

Teacher: Will spinning a 1 definitely occur?

Student: No. It's just more likely to occur.

Teacher: Is spinning a 1 more likely to occur than spinning a 2 or a 3?

Student: What do you mean?

Teacher: What if I said that spinning a 2 or a 3 is as likely to occur as spinning a 1. Would that be correct?

Student: Yes, because there is as much space for the 2 and 3 on the spinner as there is for the 1.

Teacher: If I spin ten times, how many times do you think the number 1 will result?

Student: 5, or half the time.

Teacher: Why half?

Student: The number 1 is half the circle, so half the time the number 1 should result, and half of 10 is 5.

Teacher: Yes. The number 1 occupies half the circumference of our spinner, so it should occur half the time. That seems to be a reasonable prediction for what will happen. We'll see if our prediction actually occurs. Each day this month, we will spin and record the results on the charts. How often do you predict the number 2 will occur?

Student: One quarter of the time, because it is one quarter of the circle.

Teacher: Which will occur more often, spinning a 2 or a 3?

Student: It should be the same.

Teacher: Exactly the same?

Student: Well, they're the same size.

Teacher: Does that mean they will occur exactly the same number of times?

Student: Does it depend on where we start the spinner?

Teacher: That's an interesting question. Just to be fair, let's make sure we start from many different positions and spin it hard, so we won't influence the result at all. Then will spinning a 2 and a 3 occur the same number of times?

Student: Probably.

Teacher: If spinning a 1 should occur half the time, does that mean with every two spins a 1 will result?

Student: The odds are that it will.

Teacher: What do you mean by the odds?

Student: Well, the chance that it will happen.

Teacher: What are the odds that spinning a 1 will occur?

Student: 1 out of 2?

Teacher: Even though there are three possibilities?

Student: Yes. We already said that half the circle is taken up by the 1, so half the time 1 should result.

Teacher: What percent of the time should we spin a 1?

Student: 50% of the time.

Teacher: So 50%, or 1 out of 2 spins, is the chance that we will spin a 1. Let's wait and see if 1 really occurs once every two spins. Let's see what happens this month and then talk later on about all these ideas that you have had. Each day, I want you to write the number that is spun on the chart and then record the number on the tally sheet.

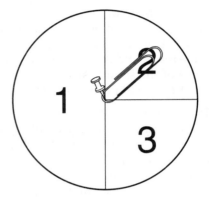

DISCUSSION THROUGHOUT THE MONTH

These questions can be used to discuss the numbers that actually occur and to compare them against the predictions that were made.

▶ Which number did we spin first?

▶ What fraction of the spins so far have resulted in 1? In 2? In 3?

▶ Why doesn't spinning a 1 happen once out of every two spins? (The chances are that 1 will result half of the time, but not that 1 will regularly appear every two spins. The more we spin, the number of times the spinner will land on the 1 approaches one half of the spins.)

▶ We have spun a 2 twice in a row. Is there a better chance now that we will spin a 1 next time? (No. The odds are always one out of two times we spin. The spinner doesn't remember what happened before. Every event is a separate event.)

▶ If we spin twenty times, how often do you predict that we will spin a 1? (10)

▶ Is it more likely that fifty out of one hundred spins will be a 1, or that 5 spins out of 10 will be a 1? (It is more likely that fifty out of one hundred spins will be a 1. The greater the number of experiments, the closer the experimental probability will be to the theoretical probability.)

▶ Have spinning a 2 and a 3 happened the same number of times? Why not? (Again, the more times we spin, the more likely it is that spinning a 2 and a 3 will occur equally.)

▶ Can we predict the order that the numbers will occur? (No, only the percentage of times that a particular number should occur if we spin it sufficient times.)

▶ How many times do we have to spin in order to get the percentages we predicted? (Responses will vary, but stress that the more times we spin, or the larger the sample size, the closer to the expected values we will be.)

▶ Is there any pattern to how the numbers appear? (There may be numbers that seem to make a pattern, but it is really a random sequence. Every time students try this experiment, they will produce a different order of numbers. Only the percentages for spinning each number will resemble each other as the sample size grows large enough.)

▶ Will thirty spins be enough to get the results we anticipated? What if we spin another thirty times? Is there any definite number of spins that will guarantee the results we predicted? (No.)

▶ How can you explain the difference between the theoretical probability, or what we thought was a reasonable prediction, and the actual experimental probability? (Theoretical probability tells us the chances of an event occurring, not the certainty that it will happen. The more experiments or trials we do, the closer the actual or experimental probability will be to the theoretical probability.)

April Circle Spinner

1	2	3
x x x x x	x x x x x	x x x x x
x x x x x	x x	x
x x x x x		
x x		

S	M	T	W	T	F	S
			2	1	1	1
3	1	1	3	1	2	1
1	2	3	1	1	3	2
2	1	3	1	1	2	1
3	2	1	1	1		

EVERY DAY ELEMENT

FOCUS
▶ Recognizing the Fibonacci number series
▶ Discovering number patterns in nature
▶ Connecting mathematical patterns to the real world

MATERIALS
An envelope, paper for a chart, calculators

FREQUENCY
Update daily. Discuss once or twice a week.

UPDATE PROCEDURE
The Fibonacci series (1, 1, 2, 3, 5, 8, 13, 21, 34, 55, 89, 144, 233, 377, . . .) begins with the numbers 1 and 1 again, and each subsequent number is obtained by adding the two preceding numbers. This series was first discussed in 1202 by Leonardo Pisano Bigolla of Pisa, the greatest European mathematician of the middle ages. Leonardo's major accomplishment was to introduce Hindu-Arabic numerals and calculations into Italy to replace Roman numerals. His nickname was Fibonacci, and that is the name attached to this number pattern. Leonardo introduced the pattern by formulating a mathematical problem. Suppose a pair of adult rabbits breeds a pair of rabbits each month. Each new rabbit pair produces another pair of rabbits from the second month on. How many pairs of rabbits will there be each month, or at the end of one year?

The reason the Fibonacci series continues to play such a prominent, almost magical, role in mathematical lore is that it has so many connections to the natural world. It also has other unexpected mathematical properties. The Fibonacci numbers appear in the strangest of places. For example, if you look closely at a pineapple, you will find three sets of spirals, 8 going to the right, 13 to the left, and 21 vertically. Sunflower seeds grow in two sets of spirals. One spirals clockwise and has 55 seeds, and the other spirals counterclockwise and, in larger plants, has 89 seeds. In smaller sunflower plants, the number of seeds is always two consecutive Fibonacci numbers. A giant sunflower has spirals of 89 and 144 seeds. A daisy plant almost always has 13, 21, or 34 petals on its flowers. On a piano, there are 5 black keys, 8 white keys, and 13 keys altogether in an octave. Note cards come in 3 × 5 inch and 5 × 8 inch sizes. The proportions in many famous buildings and paintings contain ratios of Fibonacci numbers. We will look at these ratios more closely next month. Examples of Fibonacci numbers abound in both the natural and the artistic world. Students may enjoy the many books that have been written about this number sequence. The World Wide Web is another good source for anecdotes and information about the Fibonacci numbers.

DAILY PATTERN

Fibonacci Number	Fibonacci Series
1	1
2	1
3	2
4	3
5	5
6	8
7	13
8	21
9	34
10	55
11	89
12	144
13	233
14	377
15	610
16	987
17	1597

Create a chart with two columns, one labeled *Fibonacci Number* and the other *Fibonacci Series*. Each day, record the new number in the Fibonacci series and record which Fibonacci number it is. Include the weekend days so that the first thirty Fibonacci numbers can be discussed. Students will consider this sequence and discover the pattern that generates it. It may take 10 to 15 days before students discover the pattern. As students think they have solutions, encourage them to write their solutions and keep them in a "Fibonacci Envelope" near the chart. When most of the students have submitted solutions, review the conjectures, test them, and consider which seem accurate. After two weeks, discuss the pattern. Place a different student in charge each day for finding the next Fibonacci number. Students may generate the number with a calculator, by computing the number mentally, or with paper and pencil. Students should read the number aloud to practice reading large numbers.

The completed chart shows the first thirty Fibonacci numbers. Each number is the sum of the two previous numbers. Save the completed chart for use in the May Daily Pattern element.

DISCUSSION FOR THE BEGINNING OF THE MONTH

These questions will encourage the students to speculate on the numbers in the Fibonacci series.

▶ How do you think these numbers are generated?

▶ What number do you think will come next? Why?

▶ How big do you think these numbers will be by the end of the month?

▶ Can you write an explanation for the rule for this pattern?

DISCUSSION FOR THE MIDDLE OF THE MONTH

▶ This pattern is a famous number sequence called the Fibonacci series. What will the Fibonacci number be for today? How can you figure it out? (By adding the numbers from the previous two days.) What will it be tomorrow? (The sum of yesterday's and today's numbers.)

▶ Today is the sixteenth day of April. To find the next number in the series, we will need to add 377 and 610. What do you think is the fastest way to add those numbers? Should we use a calculator or pencil and paper? Can you think of a fast strategy for doing this mentally? (377 + 600 + 10, or 300 + 600 + 77 + 10, and so on.)

▶ What is a fast strategy for calculating the next number mentally? (610 and 987 can be thought of as 600 + 997, or as 600 + 1000 – 3.)

HELPFUL HINTS

▶ Explain Leonardo's original mathematical problem about pairs of breeding rabbits for discovering the numbers in the series. You can create a chart on the chalkboard showing the number of baby pairs born each month and the total number of pairs of rabbits. The Fibonacci series appears in the column showing the number of baby pairs.

Fibonacci Number	Fibonacci Series
1	1
2	1
3	2
4	3
5	5
6	8
7	13
8	21
9	34
10	55
11	89
12	144
13	233
14	377
15	610
16	987
17	1597
18	2584
19	4181
20	6765
21	10,946
22	17,711
23	28,657
24	46,368
25	75,025
26	121,393
27	196,418
28	317,811
29	514,229
30	832,040

Using this chart, various questions can be asked during the course of the month that will make the process of determining the next number in the series easier for the students. For example, using the pattern on this chart, if in the 12th month there are 144 baby pairs produced, how many total pairs are there? (377, or two more Fibonacci numbers.)

▶ Invite students to research Fibonacci numbers in the library and on the computer on-line. Make a list of examples of Fibonacci numbers in nature and art that the students discover through their research. No one knows why so many kinds of plant and marine life display Fibonacci numbers, but it is an interesting discussion to pursue.

▶ The patterns that can be found in the sequence of Fibonacci numbers seem almost endless. If students are interested, encourage them to continue to look for patterns. For instance, the sums of consecutive Fibonacci numbers reveals a curious relationship. Copy the chart at right on the chalkboard. You can continue the pattern as far as you want. Referring to the chart, notice that the sum of the first five Fibonacci numbers is the seventh Fibonacci number minus 1. What would the sum of the first ten Fibonacci numbers be? (The twelfth Fibonacci number, 144, minus 1.)

Month	Baby Pairs	Total Rabbit Pairs
1	1	2
2	1	3
3	2	5
4	3	8
5	5	13
6	8	21
7	13	34
8	21	55
9	34	89
10	55	144
11	89	233
12	144	377

1	$= 1 = 2 - 1$
$1 + 1$	$= 2 = 3 - 1$
$1 + 1 + 2$	$= 4 = 5 - 1$
$1 + 1 + 2 + 3$	$= 7 = 8 - 1$
$1 + 1 + 2 + 3 + 5$	$= 12 = 13 - 1$

EVERY DAY ELEMENT

DAILY VARIABLE

FOCUS
▶ Evaluating and graphing complex expressions
▶ Comparing simple and complex exponential expressions
▶ Recognizing the effects of squaring a number

MATERIALS
Paper for a chart, large piece of graph paper

FREQUENCY
Update the chart and the graph daily, including the weekend days. Discuss once each week.

UPDATE PROCEDURE
This month, students will use their understanding of exponential and linear variables to evaluate the expression of the date squared plus the date, or $n^2 + n$. Since the students have been working with variables in mathematical expressions all year, this will not prove to be difficult. As students determine the value for the expression, they will notice that the exponential part of the expression influences the value much more than the addition of the date as n increases.

Make a three-column chart for the Daily Variable this month. Label the columns n^2, n, and *Value*. The x-axis of the graph should be labeled n, or *Day of the Month*. The y-axis should be labeled $n^2 + n$.

n^2	n	Value
1	1	2
4	2	6
9	3	12
16	4	20
25	5	30
36	6	42
49	7	56
64	8	72
81	9	90
100	10	110
121	11	132
144	12	156
169	13	182
196	14	210
225	15	240
256	16	272
289	17	306
324	18	342
361	19	380
400	20	420
441	21	462
484	22	506
529	23	552
576	24	600
625	25	650
676	26	702
729	27	756
784	28	812
841	29	870
900	30	930

DISCUSSION THROUGHOUT THE MONTH

These questions can be used to provide opportunities to discuss the expression and its value.

▶ The expression we are evaluating this month is the date squared plus the date. Today is the 2nd of April. What is the value of 2 squared plus 2? (6)

▶ If n is the number of the date, how do we write the expression for the date squared plus the date? ($n^2 + n$)

▶ Looking at our chart, notice the values of the expression for the first five days of April. (2, 6, 12, 20, and 30.) How much does the value increase each day as n increases by 1? (It increases by consecutive even numbers (4, 6, 8, 10, . . .) or by an amount equal to the date times 2.)

▶ Today is the ninth day of the month, so the value of $n^2 + n$ is 90. What will the value of the expression be tomorrow? Can you figure this out without using a calculator or pencil and paper? (Tomorrow's date will be the 10th, so the value will increase by 20, to 110.)

▶ Can you describe how we will determine the value of the expression on the last day of the month? (It will be 60 more than the previous day.)

▶ Today is the 25th day of the month. What is a fast way to multiply 25×25? (Multiply 25 times 100 and then divide by 4. Encourage students to discover other ways to do this.)

▶ Display the chart created for the January Daily Variable (see page 82). How do the values for this month's expression compare to the values of the expression we used in January, when we found the value of only the square of the date? (The value for each day is larger by the amount of the date, or n.)

▶ As n increases, what happens to the difference between n^2 and $(n^2 + n)$? (While the difference increases, the relative difference between the two values decreases. For example, 2 is twice as large as 1, but 420 is only 5% larger than 400.)

▶ When we graph the expression this month, does it make a straight line? (No, it curves upward. See chart, page 136.)

▶ How does that compare to the graph of the expression n^2? (It's almost the same, but it begins a little higher on the y-axis.)

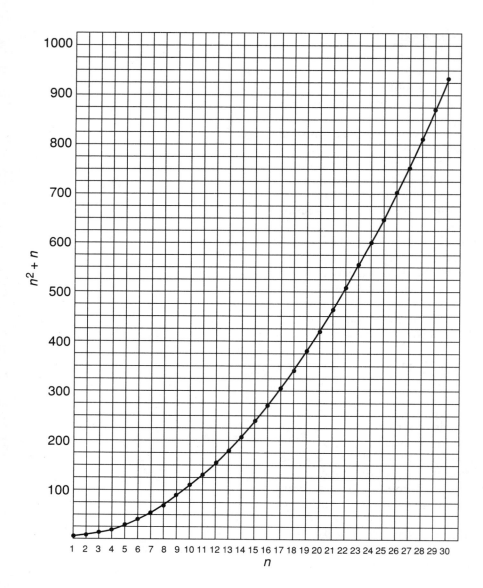

FOCUS

▶ Measuring capacity with metric units
▶ Converting between milliliters and liters
▶ Multiplying with fractions
▶ Connecting fractional parts to percents
▶ Using mental subtraction strategies

MATERIALS

Liter measuring container and water; or Liter (TR15) and colored marker; paper for a chart

DAILY MEASUREMENT

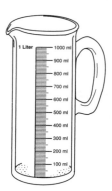

FREQUENCY

Update and discuss two or three times a week.

UPDATE PROCEDURE

While most people in the United States don't easily recognize a liter bottle or know how many milliliters there are in a can of soda (355), our grocery stores are full of such containers. Most soft drinks are now sold in one- and two-liter bottles. As with linear measures, metric measures for capacity have become part of our every day world. Given this situation, our goal as instructors should not be to eliminate the study of customary measures such as cups and quarts. After all, it is still rare to find an American cookbook recipe that requires 240 milliliters of milk. Rather, the goal should be to enable students to comfortably recognize and use both metric and English customary measures.

For this element to be most effective, it is preferable that an actual liter measuring container and water be used. This gives the students real experience with capacity and provides knowledge of how large a liter is, and how milliliters relate to that size. The alternative is to use the Liter (TR15), either under acetate or copied each day, and a colored marker. The drawback with this is that the students will actually be working only with linear measurements, due to the two-dimensional nature of the chart. If it at all possible, try to procure a liter measuring container to provide the best learning experience for the students.

During April, students will use the date to form the denominator of a fraction representing a portion of a liter. The numerator will always be 1. Each day that you use this element, select a student to determine the number of milliliters represented by the fraction for the day. The student will calculate the resulting fractional amount of a liter in terms of milliliters and either pour this amount of water into the liter measuring container or color the amount on the Liter (TR15). Then the student will determine the percentage of the liter that remains empty and record the percentage on the chart. For example, on the 2nd day the student will determine how many milliliters are in 1/2 of a liter, pour or color 500 milliliters and then record that 50% of the container is empty.

In addition to providing experience using liters and milliliters, this activity also reinforces the concept of multiplication by a fraction as a shrinking or expanding operation, and provides practice in the conversion of thousandths into percents. Be sure to let students discover their own strategies for solving these problems.

For purposes of the discussions during the month, it is assumed that a liter measuring container will be used. If you choose to use the Liter (TR15), you will need to make some changes to this material.

50% empty

50% full

SAMPLE DISCUSSION FOR THE FOURTH DAY OF THE MONTH

Teacher: Last month, we used metric units to measure lengths. This month, we will use metric units to measure the amount held by a container. The metric unit used to measure the capacity of a container is called a liter. Can anyone think of something familiar that uses a liter as a measurement?

Student: Our math book had them.

Teacher: Let's try to think of something other than your math book.

Student: My soda bottle says 2 liters on it.

Teacher: Next time you are in the supermarket, look at some of the bottles to see how much liquid they contain. I think you will find quite a few that refer to the number of liters in them. (Display the liter measuring container.) This is a one-liter container. When it is filled to the top line, it holds one liter. The small lines indicate the number of milliliters. There are 1000 milliliters in a liter. Each of these bigger lines indicates 100 milliliters. The abbreviation for milliliters is ml. Let's make a fraction each day this month using the date as the denominator. The numerator will always be 1. Today is the 4th of April, so we'll use the fraction $\frac{1}{4}$. How much liquid is $\frac{1}{4}$ of a liter?

Student: What do you mean?

Teacher: Well our container doesn't indicate where $\frac{1}{4}$ is. It indicates milliliters. So we need to know how many milliliters there are in $\frac{1}{4}$ of a liter.

Student: $\frac{1}{4}$ of a liter would be 250 milliliters, because 1000 divided into 4 equal parts is 250.

Teacher: How do we write this with symbols?

Student: (Writes on chalkboard) $\frac{1}{4} \times 1000 = 250$

Teacher: When we want to know what $\frac{1}{4}$ of a quantity is, we multiply the quantity by $\frac{1}{4}$, which means we are shrinking it by dividing it into four equal parts and taking only one of those parts. How can we tell how much 250 milliliters is using the marks on the container?

Student: It's right in the middle between the 200 and 300 milliliter marks.

Teacher: (Pouring 250 milliliters of water into the container) What percentage of the container is empty?

Student: $\frac{3}{4}$.

Teacher: What percentage is that?

Student: 75%.

Teacher: Yes. 3 out of 4 is the same as 75 out of 100, or 75%. When we use the container again, we'll use the date as the denominator of a fraction, figure out how many milliliters that fraction represents, pour that amount of water into the container, and determine what percent of the liter is empty.

75% empty

250 ml

SAMPLE DISCUSSION FOR THE TENTH DAY OF THE MONTH

Teacher: Today is the 10th, so we want to find $\frac{1}{10}$ of a liter. That is the same as shrinking it by a factor of 10. What is $\frac{1}{10}$ of a liter?

Student: 100 milliliters.

Teacher: How did you do that?

Student: One liter is 1000 milliliters, and 1000 divided by 10 is 100. So we need to put 100 milliliters into the container.

Teacher: How do we write this?

Student: (Writes on chalkboard) $\frac{1}{10} \times 1000 = 100$

Teacher: How do we say that?
Student: One tenth of 1000 is 100.
Teacher: What percentage of the container is empty?
Student: 90%.
Teacher: How do you know?
Student: If $\frac{1}{10}$ is filled, $\frac{9}{10}$ is empty, and $\frac{9}{10}$ is the same as 90%.
Teacher: Can anyone tell us another strategy to do this?
Student: $\frac{900}{1000}$ is 90%.
Teacher: How do you know?
Student: 900 out of 1000 is the same as 90 out of 100.
Teacher: That's interesting. Is there any general rule we can use for changing thousandths to percents? For example, what percent is $\frac{250}{1000}$?
Student: 25%. Change the fraction to a decimal and you can see how easy it is to figure out.
Teacher: (Writes *0.250* on the chalkboard) So 0.250 is what percent?
Student: 25%.
Teacher: (Writes *0.900* on the chalkboard) And .900 is 90%. (Writes *0.125* on the chalkboard) What percent do you think 0.125 will be?
Student: 12.5%.
Teacher: I would like you to think about why that is true, and think about how you would explain converting thousandths into percents to someone who doesn't know how to do it.

90% empty

100 ml

DISCUSSION FOR THE REMAINDER OF THE MONTH

Use these questions and others like them to reinforce the concepts covered in this element.

▶ What is $\frac{1}{16}$ of a liter? (62.5 milliliters.) How did you figure that out? (1000 milliliters divided by 16 is 62.5.)

▶ Can you describe a way to do that without using a calculator or pencil and paper? (Figure out $\frac{1}{8}$ of a liter, or 125 milliliters, and then take half of that, or realize that 1000 divided by 16 is the same as 500 divided by 8, and 250 divided by 4, and 125 divided by 2.) If we have 62.5 milliliters in the container, how many milliliters are empty? (937.5 milliliters.) What percent is empty? (93.75%.)

▶ As the date increases, our fraction gets smaller. How can we measure these small amounts? (Get a more precise measure, such as a container showing divisions to 10 milliliters.)

▶ What fraction of a liter is 50 milliliters? ($\frac{1}{20}$ of a liter.)

▶ What fraction of a liter is 10 milliliters? ($\frac{1}{100}$ of a liter.)

HELPFUL HINTS

▶ Allowing students to use the liter measuring container and to measure the amount of water poured into it are good ways to increase their ability to use metric units of capacity and to develop benchmarks for understanding metric amounts.

▶ Encourage students to bring in containers or labels that are marked in milliliters or liters. Play a guessing game in which students make reasonable estimates for the capacity of the container brought in.

Day	Fraction	Milliliters	% Empty
2	$\frac{1}{2}$	500	50%
3	$\frac{1}{3}$	333.3	66.7%
4	$\frac{1}{4}$	250	75%
5	$\frac{1}{5}$	200	80%
8	$\frac{1}{8}$	125	87.5%
10	$\frac{1}{10}$	100	90%
15	$\frac{1}{15}$	66.6	93.3%
16	$\frac{1}{16}$	62.5	93.75%
20	$\frac{1}{20}$	50	95%
23	$\frac{1}{23}$	43.5	95.65%
25	$\frac{1}{25}$	40	96%
27	$\frac{1}{27}$	37	96.3%
30	$\frac{1}{30}$	33.3	96.67%

MAY/JUNE

FINISHING UP

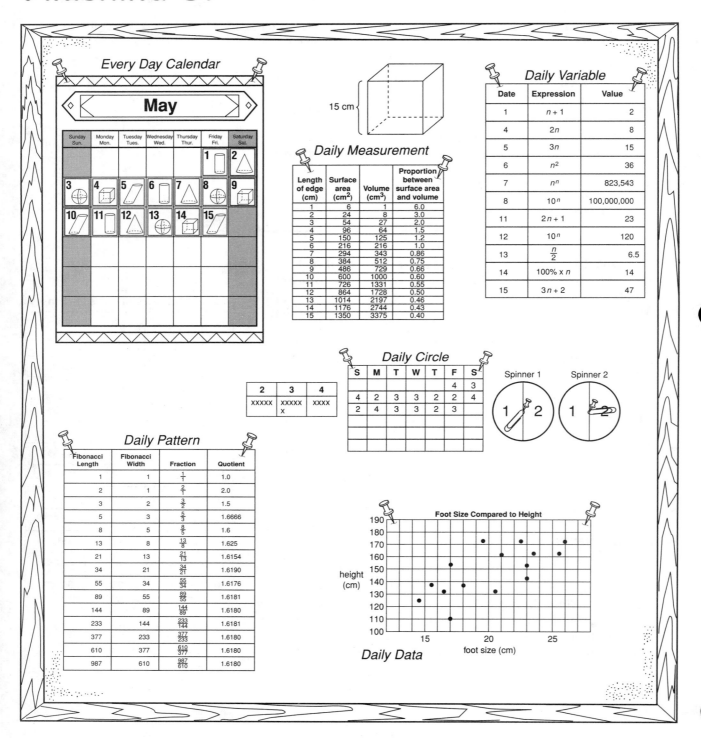

Every Day Calendar

May

Sunday Sun.	Monday Mon.	Tuesday Tues.	Wednesday Wed.	Thursday Thur.	Friday Fri.	Saturday Sat.
					1	2
3	4	5	6	7	8	9
10	11	12	13	14	15	

15 cm

Daily Measurement

Length of edge (cm)	Surface area (cm²)	Volume (cm³)	Proportion between surface area and volume
1	6	1	6.0
2	24	8	3.0
3	54	27	2.0
4	96	64	1.5
5	150	125	1.2
6	216	216	1.0
7	294	343	0.86
8	384	512	0.75
9	486	729	0.66
10	600	1000	0.60
11	726	1331	0.55
12	864	1728	0.50
13	1014	2197	0.46
14	1176	2744	0.43
15	1350	3375	0.40

Daily Variable

Date	Expression	Value
1	$n+1$	2
4	$2n$	8
5	$3n$	15
6	n^2	36
7	n^n	823,543
8	10^n	100,000,000
11	$2n+1$	23
12	$10n$	120
13	$\frac{n}{2}$	6.5
14	$100\% \times n$	14
15	$3n+2$	47

Daily Circle

S	M	T	W	T	F	S
					4	3
4	2	3	3	2	2	4
2	4	3	3	2	3	

2	3	4
xxxxx	xxxxx x	xxxx

Spinner 1 — 1 | 2

Spinner 2 — 1 | 2

Daily Pattern

Fibonacci Length	Fibonacci Width	Fraction	Quotient
1	1	$\frac{1}{1}$	1.0
2	1	$\frac{2}{1}$	2.0
3	2	$\frac{3}{2}$	1.5
5	3	$\frac{5}{3}$	1.6666
8	5	$\frac{8}{5}$	1.6
13	8	$\frac{13}{8}$	1.625
21	13	$\frac{21}{13}$	1.6154
34	21	$\frac{34}{21}$	1.6190
55	34	$\frac{55}{34}$	1.6176
89	55	$\frac{89}{55}$	1.6181
144	89	$\frac{144}{89}$	1.6180
233	144	$\frac{233}{144}$	1.6181
377	233	$\frac{377}{233}$	1.6180
610	377	$\frac{610}{377}$	1.6180
987	610	$\frac{987}{610}$	1.6180

Daily Data

Foot Size Compared to Height

height (cm) — vertical axis: 100, 110, 120, 130, 140, 150, 160, 170, 180, 190

foot size (cm) — horizontal axis: 15, 20, 25

As the weather warms up and the school year draws to a conclusion, the various Calendar Math elements will be used to review the concepts developed throughout the year and to anticipate next year's curriculum. The Every Day Calendar features three-dimensional round solids this month. The Daily Circle is used to continue the discussion of probability. The Daily Pattern extends the discussion of Fibonacci numbers to the Golden Proportion, another famous mathematical relationship. The Daily Variable asks students to evaluate a variety of expressions and they will use the Daily Data element to construct a scatter plot comparing foot size to height. The Daily Measurement will be used to investigate the surface area and volume of cubes.

The Counting Tape and Percent Circle, the Daily Array, and the Daily Depositor elements were concluded in previous months. Hopefully, this will make time available in May and June for including some elements that you had to skip earlier in the year. June is also a good time to review and extend work on any elements that were especially challenging for the students. If time allows, you may also want to revisit the elements that were most enjoyed by the students.

EVERY DAY ELEMENT

CALENDAR

FOCUS
▶ Recognizing cylinders, cones, and spheres
▶ Recognizing and describing nets of solid figures
▶ Describing attributes of solids and cross-sections of solids
▶ Comparing volumes of solid figures
▶ Developing informal deductive reasoning

MATERIALS
Every Day Calendar, May Month Strip, May Calendar Pieces, or Solid Figures Cutouts (TR19) and marker

SUGGESTED PATTERN FOR MAY
Circular three-dimensional figures will be featured in the Calendar pattern during May. It is a simple five-day repeating pattern using four circular three-dimensional figures and a cube. The pattern is a right cylinder, a cone, a sphere, a cube, and an oblique cylinder. The pattern has been kept simple so that students can compare and contrast the different solids, consider what shapes result when they are flattened, and compare their volumes. As in previous months, the emphasis will be on informal assumptions and reasoning rather than on formulas or proofs.

FREQUENCY
Update daily. Discuss at the end of each week.

right cylinder   cone   sphere   cube   oblique cylinder

UPDATE PROCEDURE

Each day, post the Calendar Piece for the date. Remember to update the weekend dates every Monday. If you choose to use the Solid Figures Cutouts (TR19), write the date on each piece with a marker before posting. Ask the students to consider the properties of the shapes as well as the pattern.

SAMPLE DISCUSSION FOR THE END OF THE FIRST WEEK

Teacher: What do these shapes have in common?

Student: They are all solids, three-dimensional, or space figures.

Teacher: Do you notice anything else?

Student: They all are round figures, except the cube .

Teacher: So can we say all the shapes are round?

Student: No.

Teacher: I want to be sure that we all know the names of these shapes. What is the first figure called?

Student: It's a cylinder. So is the fifth figure, but it's a different kind.

Teacher: Yes, and we'll come back to that one later. What are the other two round solids called?

Student: There's a cone followed by a sphere.

Teacher: Yes, and then a cube. Maybe it would be easier to find some of the differences between these figures. You've already mentioned that the cube is different. How is it different?

Student: Well it has flat faces and straight edges, and the others are all round.

Teacher: Yes, the cube is made up of polygons. Are there polygons in the other figures?

Student: No.

Teacher: That's right. What are some other differences?

Student: The cylinders have two circles, the cone has one circle, and the cube has none. But I'm not sure about the sphere. There's no flat circle anywhere on the sphere, but it looks like there are circles everywhere.

Teacher: Yes. If you look at a circumference of the sphere you see a circle, but when you look at the whole sphere there aren't any circles. Let's go back and look again at the figure on the fifth day. How is it the same as the cylinder on the first day?

Student: Well, they both have circular bases, but they look like ovals.

Teacher: Remember that we are looking at pictorial representations of three-dimensional figures. If we were looking at the actual cylinders, we would see that all the bases are really circular. They are drawn this way to look three dimensional. Is there anything else the same between these two cylinders?

Student: The bases are parallel and equal or congruent.

Student: Both have curved surfaces connecting the bases.

Teacher: Yes. How are these two figures different?

Student: The second one is leaning.

Teacher: How can we describe this mathematically? Think about the angles.

Student: The bases of the first one are perpendicular to the curved sides, but they aren't in the fifth one.

Teacher: That's why we call the first one a right cylinder and the second one an oblique cylinder, meaning that it is not perpendicular.

DISCUSSION THROUGHOUT THE MONTH

▶ Imagine that we can unroll the right cylinder to create the flat surfaces that are part of it. What would those flat surfaces look like? (There would be two circles and a rectangle. You might want to cut a paper towel tube up to demonstrate this. These flat shapes are called the nets of the solids.)

▶ What would the net of a cone look like? (There would be one circle and a "curved" triangle.)

▶ Can a sphere be cut open and laid flat? (No, but students might enjoy trying by using a whole orange peel or by cutting open a tennis ball. Map makers have tried many different solutions to create flat maps of a spherical world. It is mathematically impossible to depict a sphere on a flat surface accurately.)

▶ If you make a straight cut perpendicular to the base of a right cylinder, what shape will you see? (A rectangle.)

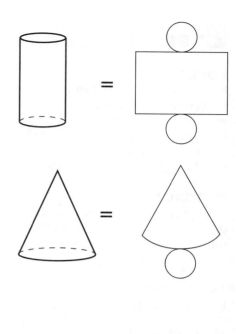

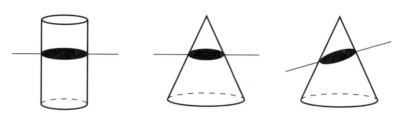

▶ If you make a straight cut parallel to the base of a right cylinder, what shape will result? (A circle.)

▶ If you make a straight cut parallel to the base of the cone, what shape will you get? (A circle.) How does this circle compare to the circle of the base? (It's a smaller circle.)

▶ If you make a cut through the cone that is not parallel to the base, what shape will you see? (An ellipse, or an oval.)

▶ If you cut through the center of the sphere, what shape will result? (A circle.) What shape results if you cut through the sphere somewhere other than the center? (An ellipse.)

▶ If we had a cube and a sphere of the same height and width, which would have the greatest volume? (The cube. This can be demonstrated by drawing a sphere inside a cube with an edge length equal to the diameter of the sphere.) Compare a cube and a cylinder with the same height and width. Which has the greater volume? What about a cube and a cone of the same height and width? (In both cases, the cube has the greater volume. Drawing the figures will make this easy to see.)

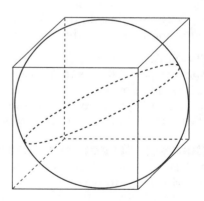

▶ If we had a cone and a cylinder of the same height and with equal bases, which would have the greater volume? (The cylinder. Even though they are the same height, the cone narrows as you go toward the top.)

▶ If a cube has a height of one foot, what is its volume? (One cubic foot.) Why? (The volume is the area of its base times its height. Think of the cube as layers of the base, with enough layers to reach the top of the cube.)

▶ What is the volume of a cylinder that is one foot high and one foot wide? (Think of the cylinder as layers of the base one foot high, or the height times the area of the base. The area of the base is the radius squared times pi, or $0.5^2\pi$, or 0.25π, which is 0.785 cubic feet.)

Spinner 1

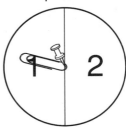

Spinner 2

FOCUS

▶ Recognizing probability based on the circumferences of two circular spinners

▶ Analyzing probability with more than one variable

▶ Recognizing the difference between theoretical and experimental probability

▶ Identifying the role of sample size in experimental probability

MATERIALS

Two cardstock copies of the May Circle Spinner, or two copies of the May Circle Spinner (TR20); two paper clips or bobby pins for the spinners, pencils or pins to hold the spinners in place, paper for two charts

FREQUENCY

Update daily. Discuss once a week.

UPDATE PROCEDURE

This month, students will perform another experiment to compare the theoretical likelihood of an event and the actual occurrence of the event. In May, the students will use two circular spinners. Use both copies of the May Circle Spinner and label them Spinner 1 and Spinner 2. You may choose to color them in different colors. You may also choose to copy them onto acetate and use them as overhead transparencies, using pencils to hold the spinners in place. As in April, be sure that the spinners lie as flat as possible when spinning. Each day, a student will spin both spinners and record the results on two charts. The first chart will list the numbers as they appear on the spinners each day and the second chart will tally the results of the spins. Students will be asked to predict the most likely sum of the two spins and to notice when the actual results come close to the predicted results. On Mondays, the students should update the charts for the weekend days.

This activity can easily be extended to include three spinners. Another possibility is to use two copies of the April Circle Spinner (TR17) to allow time for additional interesting predictions and results. It is probably best to start with the two spinners, perhaps saving the addition of the third one for June.

DISCUSSION FOR THE BEGINNING OF THE MONTH

▶ Display one of the May Circle Spinners. This spinner is evenly divided into two halves, one labeled 1 and the other 2. What is the likelihood that 1 will occur when it is spun? (It will probably occur half the time, or 0.5.) Can you explain why you think so? (If the spinner is "fair," the chances are equal to spin either number. Half the circumference is 1 and half is 2. You may want to demonstrate an "unfair" spinner by holding the spinner at a steep angle to throw off the results.)

▶ If 1 comes up on the first spin, what is the likelihood that it will come up again on the next spin? (It will still probably occur half the time. The spinner has no memory of the previous spin.)

▶ Which of these sequences is more likely to occur if we spin five times: 1, 1, 1, 2, 2, or 2, 1, 1, 2, 1, or 1, 2, 1, 2, 1? (They are all equally likely, but students may think that the one that looks more random is more likely.)

▶ This month, we are going to spin two identical spinners like this one each day. What are the possible sums that could result? (Sums of 2, 3, or 4.) Which is most likely to occur? (A sum of 3. When we use two spinners, it is possible that Spinner 1 will come up with a 1 and Spinner 2 with a 2. It is also possible that Spinner 1 will come up with a 2 and Spinner 2 with a 1. These are not the same results, although both give a sum of 3. Allow some time to discuss this question. Encourage students to express their thinking about this in as many ways as possible. For example, they may say that 1 plus 2 can occur in two different ways, or that there is only one way to spin a sum of 2 or 4, or they may suggest making a chart of all the possible ways to arrive at a sum and notice that the 3 shows up in the chart twice.)

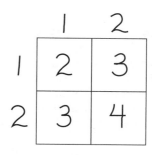

▶ How often do you expect a sum of 3 to occur? (Half the time. Don't explain this to the students if they are unable to see it yet. Simply allow more time for this to become clear.)

▶ When we spin both spinners, how often will 1 occur? (Never.) How often will 2 occur? (It will probably occur one quarter of the time.) Can you explain why this is so? (Again, allow plenty of time for discussion. There are only four possible results, one of which is the sum of 2. Come back to this discussion later in the month if it is not clear to the students.)

▶ After four days of spinning, what sum will occur most often? (A sum of 3 is more likely, but the sample size is very small. A different sum could easily occur.)

▶ Is there a way to predict the order of the sums for the first week? (No, not the exact order. We can only predict the chance of an event happening.)

DISCUSSION FOR THE MIDDLE AND END OF THE MONTH

▶ What is the order of the sums so far this month?

▶ What fraction of the spins resulted in a sum of 2? Of 3? Of 4?

▶ How does this compare to what we predicted?

▶ Why might it be different than what we expected? (The sample size might not be large enough.)

▶ How many more times did 3 occur than either 2 or 4?

▶ Why does 3 occur more often?

▶ Looking at our charts, was there a time in the month when a sum of 3 had occurred half the time?

▶ Did 4 occur as many times as 2? Do you think it should occur as often? (In theory, yes. However, it probably won't occur exactly that way in the experiments.)

▶ On any one turn, how many different results are possible? (Four. Make a chart of the possible results to help students understand this point.)

▶ Of the four possible results, how many produce a sum of 2? (One.) Of 4? (One.) Of 3? (Two.)

Possible Results using the May Circle Spinners

2	3	4
xxxxx xxxx	xxxxx xxxxx xxxxx	xxxxx xx

S	M	T	W	T	F	S
					4	3
4	2	3	3	2	2	4
2	4	3	3	2	3	3
3	2	3	4	2	3	3
2	3	2	4	3	3	4
3						

- ▶ If we took one hundred turns spinning both spinners, how many times would you expect a sum of 3 to occur? (Fifty.) Will it occur fifty times? (No, it is just more likely that it will.)
- ▶ If we tossed two coins, what is the likelihood that both a head and a tail would result? (It would probably happen half the time, the same as getting a 1 and a 2 on the spinners.)

HELPFUL HINTS

- ▶ Near the end of the month, you may want to experiment with using three copies of the May Circle Spinner (TR20). What are the possible sums? (3, 4, 5, and 6.) Which sums are least likely to occur? (3 and 6.) Try the experiment and analyze why sums of 4 and 5 occur so often. Did a sum of 4 occur as many times as a sum of 5? Encourage the students to explain in their own words why these results are likely.
- ▶ In June, you may want to try the experiment using two copies of the April Circle Spinner (TR17). Take between forty and fifty turns spinning both spinners and recording the results. Students may be surprised to see that a sum of 4 is most likely to occur. The theoretical probabilities are that a sum of six would occur $\frac{1}{16}$ of the time, a sum of five $\frac{1}{8}$ of the time, sums of two and three each $\frac{1}{4}$ of the time, and a sum of four $\frac{5}{16}$ of the time.
- ▶ If you have examined the patterns in Pascal's Triangle, this may be a wonderful opportunity to revisit it. Each line in the Triangle shows the distribution of possible events when there is an even chance of each occurring, like flipping a coin or spinning our spinner.
- ▶ The more experience students have with experimental probability, the deeper their understanding of probability will be. If students learn only how to compute the chance of an event, they can become confused when the actual events don't occur as predicted. Conducting experiments and analyzing the results is more likely to produce understanding.

Possible Results using the April Circle Spinner

	1	1	2	3
1	2	2	3	4
1	2	2	3	4
2	3	3	4	5
3	4	4	5	6

Pascal's Triangle

				1					
			1		1				1 spin
		1		2		1			2 spins
	1		3		3		1		3 spins
1		4		6		4		1	4 spins

EVERY DAY ELEMENT

DAILY PATTERN

FOCUS

- ▶ Recognizing aspects of numbers in the Fibonacci series
- ▶ Discovering the Golden Proportion
- ▶ Discovering number patterns in nature and the arts
- ▶ Connecting mathematical patterns to the real world

MATERIALS

List of Fibonacci numbers created in April, a 3 × 5 index card, a 5 × 8 index card, paper for a chart, calculators

FREQUENCY

Update daily, including the weekend days on Monday. Discuss once a week.

UPDATE PROCEDURE

The Fibonacci series has an unexpected connection to a famous proportion called the Golden Proportion. It is also called the Golden Ratio or the Golden Section. The Golden Proportion occurs in a line that can be divided into two unequal segments such that the ratio between the lengths of the longer segment and the shorter segment is the same as the ratio between the length of the whole line and the length of the longer segment. A Golden Rectangle is a rectangle in which the ratio between the lengths of the longer side and the shorter side is the same as the ratio between the sum of the length of both of those sides to the length of the longer side. This ratio is about 1.6180. Legend has it that the Greeks used this proportion to design buildings such as the Parthenon because they believed it to be the most aesthetically pleasing proportion. In Michaelangelo's painting depicting the proportions of the human body, he repeatedly uses this Golden Section. One example is the thumb, in which the distance from the tip to the knuckle and from the knuckle to the joint with the hand forms a Golden Section in relation to the length of the whole thumb. While there is some dispute about the importance of the Golden Ratio in Greek architecture, the ratio appears often in nature and throughout the history of art and design.

The Golden Ratio has a remarkable connection to the Fibonacci series. If you start with the first pair of numbers in the sequence and divide the larger by the smaller number, and continue doing this with every consecutive pair of numbers, the successive quotients result in a closer and closer approximation of the Golden Ratio, or 1.6180. This month's Daily Pattern will allow students to discover the convergence of this division toward the Golden Ratio.

This month, students will imagine a rectangle each day with a width of a Fibonacci number and a length of the next highest Fibonacci number in the series. They will then divide the length by the width for each rectangle. Thus, they will be dividing a pair of consecutive numbers from the Fibonacci series each day. During the first twelve days of the month, the division should be done with pencil and paper to provide practice with division and rounding skills. For the remainder of the month, calculators should be used for the division. Students should round all numbers to four places throughout the month. They will be asked to speculate on which number the successive quotients appear to converge.

Begin the month by creating a chart with four columns labeled *Fibonacci Length*, *Fibonacci Width*, *Fraction*, and *Quotient*. On the first day of the month, post the list of Fibonacci numbers created in April and select a student to describe the rectangle created when the first two Fibonacci numbers are used as the length and width. On the first day of the month, this results in a square. The student should then divide the second Fibonacci number by the first one. Record the length (1) in the first column, the width (1) in the second column, the fraction ($\frac{1}{1}$) in the third column, and the resulting quotient (1.0) in the fourth column. The next day, select a student to follow the same procedure using the third number in the series as the length and the second as the width of an imagined rectangle. The student should do the division and record all the information on the chart. Continue using each consecutive number pair throughout the month.

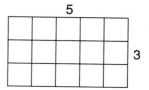

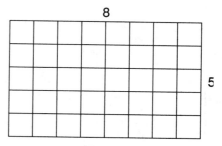

Golden Rectangles

Fraction	Quotient
$\frac{1}{1}$	1.0
$\frac{2}{1}$	2.0
$\frac{3}{2}$	1.5
$\frac{5}{3}$	1.6666
$\frac{8}{5}$	1.6
$\frac{13}{8}$	1.625
$\frac{21}{13}$	1.6154
$\frac{34}{21}$	1.6190

Teacher: Last month, we discovered the numbers in the Fibonacci series. We talked about many examples of these numbers that occur in art and nature. This month, we will consider these same numbers as they define a rectangle. Using consecutive pairs of numbers from the series, we will consider rectangles where the larger of the two Fibonacci numbers is the length and the smaller number is the width. On the first day, our rectangle is a square since the first pair of Fibonacci numbers is 1 and 1. The rectangle for the second day will have a length of 2 and width of 1. By the fourth day, the rectangle will have a length of 5 and a width of 3. (Displaying a 3 × 5 index card.) Here's an interesting connection. This index card is five inches long and three inches wide. (Displaying a 5 × 8 index card.) And this card is eight inches long and five inches wide. 3 and 5 and 5 and 8 are numbers in consecutive pairs of Fibonacci numbers. I wonder why these numbers were chosen for these cards. Do you have any ideas?

Student: They wanted to use Fibonacci numbers?

Teacher: Actually, I doubt that the makers of these cards cared about Fibonacci numbers. So why were these numbers chosen?

Student: Maybe it's easy to cut rectangles into those lengths.

Teacher: Would it be any easier than using other dimensions?

Student: Probably not.

Teacher: As you can see, there is something special about rectangles whose sides are consecutive Fibonacci numbers in length. We'll be analyzing many such rectangles this month. Think about these shapes, and see if you can discover other places where they show up. You may want to look at boxes in the grocery store. What I can tell you now is that if we compare the lengths of these rectangles to their widths, we will discover an amazing relationship called the Golden Proportion. Sometimes it is called the Golden Ratio or the Golden Section. Some people think that shapes having this Golden Proportion are especially pleasing to look at. As we consider the Fibonacci rectangles each day, we will try to discover the relationship between their lengths and widths. Each day, one of you will be responsible for using consecutive pairs of Fibonacci numbers from our April Pattern chart to construct an imaginary rectangle. The larger of the two numbers will be the length of the rectangle and the smaller number will be the width. An easy way to remember which pair of numbers we are working with each day is to remember that today's length becomes the width of the rectangle we will think about tomorrow. The length of tomorrow's rectangle will be the next number in the Fibonacci series. We will fill in the chart each day by recording the Fibonacci numbers we are using, creating a fraction with those numbers showing the larger number divided by the smaller one, and then do the division. For the first few days, I think you can probably do the division mentally. Use pencil and paper when the numbers get larger. You can ask a friend for help if you're not sure how to do the division. Later in the month, we will use calculators to do the division. As we go along, the quotients will have a lot of numbers to the right of the decimal point. We will round all of the quotients to the fourth decimal place. Remember to record your answer on the chart.

After two weeks, continue the discussion of the Golden Proportion by mentioning several examples of this ratio found in the real world. The Egyptian pyramid at Giza, the Greek Parthenon, the shapes of index cards and cereal boxes are good examples to use. Explain the Golden Proportion to the students. A Golden Rectangle is defined as one in which the proportion between the lengths of the larger and smaller sides is the same as the proportion between the sum of those two sides and the longer side. Demonstrate this using the rectangle from the seventh day, having a length of 21 and a width of 13. The proportion between those lengths, $\frac{21}{13}$ or 1.6154, is close to the proportion between the sum of the lengths of those sides to the length of the longer side, $\frac{34}{21}$ or 1.6190.

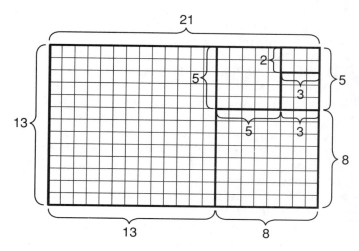

The 21 × 13 Golden Rectangle is also intriguing because if you draw a 13 × 13 square in it, you are left with an 8 × 13 rectangle, which is also a Golden Rectangle. If you then draw an 8 × 8 square in that rectangle, you are left with a 5 × 8 rectangle, which is also a Golden Rectangle, and so on. Taking a square out of any Golden Rectangle always leaves another Golden Rectangle. A good way to think of this is to remember that the sides of these rectangles are in the proportion of a Golden Rectangle, and that removing a square leaves a rectangle with the same proportion.

Ask students to notice any pattern they may have discovered about the division of successive terms in the Fibonacci sequence.

DISCUSSION FOR THE MIDDLE AND END OF THE MONTH

▶ What is a strategy for dividing 8 by 5 mentally? (It is the same as $1\frac{3}{5}$, which is 1.6.)

▶ What about for dividing 13 by 8? (It is the same as $1\frac{5}{8}$. You may want to refer to the Counting Tape to remind students of the discussion for determining the decimal equivalent of $\frac{5}{8}$. $1\frac{5}{8}$ is the same as 1.625.)

▶ Divide 21 by 13 with pencil and paper to three decimal places. What decimal place do you need to know in order to round to the third decimal place? (The fourth decimal place.)

▶ Can you explain how to divide 55 by 34 and round to the fourth decimal place? (Divide to the fifth decimal place and then round.)

▶ When you use the calculator to divide 610 by 377, the result is 1.6180371353, if your calculator can show results to that many places. How do you round that number to the fourth decimal place? (Look at the fifth decimal place, the hundred thousandths place. If that number is less than 5 then round to the number in the fourth decimal place, or the ten thousandths place. It becomes 1.6180.) How do we say that number? (One and six thousand one hundred eighty ten thousandths.)

- Look at the *Quotient* column on our chart. Do the results of our division seem to be getting close to any certain number? (After two weeks, the number 1.6180 will be the result three times, rounding to the fourth decimal place. After that, 1.6180 shows up every time.)
- How would you describe how our quotients have become close to this number? (Some quotients are a little less, and some are a little more than 1.6180. The quotients seem to be converging on that number.)
- Do you have any guesses as to why this proportion is called the Golden Proportion? (Golden may mean that is close to perfection, or ideal.)
- Do you think all box makers, window designers and architects use this proportion for everything they build or design? (No, but some do.)
- Which rectangle do you prefer, a 13 × 8, or a 13 × 4? (Allow some time for discussion and a variety of answers.)
- What are some common occurrences of the Golden Rectangle? (Index cards, cereal boxes, window frames, and so on. There are many common rectangles that are not Golden Rectangles, such as a sheet of notebook paper. It will be helpful to work with the students to discover what the ratios of these rectangles are.)
- If the quotients are rounded to the fourth decimal place, on which day does the proportion begin to remain constant? (On the thirteenth day.) What pair of Fibonacci numbers did we use that day? (377 and 233.) Are the ratios really constant from that day on? (No, but rounding to the fourth decimal place makes them all the same. The differences in succeeding ratios occur at many more decimal places.)
- (Write 1.61803 on the chalkboard.) How do we say this number? (one and sixty-one thousand eight hundred three hundred thousandths.)

Fibonacci Length	Fibonacci Width	Fraction	Quotient
1	1	$\frac{1}{1}$	1.0
2	1	$\frac{2}{1}$	2.0
3	2	$\frac{3}{2}$	1.5
5	3	$\frac{5}{3}$	1.6666
8	5	$\frac{8}{5}$	1.6
13	8	$\frac{13}{8}$	1.625
21	13	$\frac{21}{13}$	1.6154
34	21	$\frac{34}{21}$	1.6190
55	34	$\frac{55}{34}$	1.6176
89	55	$\frac{89}{55}$	1.6181
144	89	$\frac{144}{89}$	1.6180
233	144	$\frac{233}{144}$	1.6181
377	233	$\frac{377}{233}$	1.6180
610	377	$\frac{610}{377}$	1.6180
987	610	$\frac{987}{610}$	1.6180
1597	987	$\frac{1597}{987}$	1.6180
2584	1597	$\frac{2584}{1597}$	1.6180
4181	2584	$\frac{4181}{2584}$	1.6180
6765	4181	$\frac{6765}{4181}$	1.6180
10,946	6765	$\frac{10,946}{6765}$	1.6180
17,711	10,946	$\frac{17,711}{10,946}$	1.6180
28,657	17,711	$\frac{28,657}{17,711}$	1.6180
46,368	28,657	$\frac{46,368}{28,657}$	1.6180
75,025	46,368	$\frac{75,025}{46,368}$	1.6180
121,393	75,025	$\frac{121,393}{75,025}$	1.6180
196,418	121,393	$\frac{196,418}{121,393}$	1.6180
317,811	196,418	$\frac{317,911}{196,418}$	1.6180
514,229	317,811	$\frac{514,229}{317,811}$	1.6180
832,040	514,229	$\frac{832,040}{514,229}$	1.6180
1,346,269	832,040	$\frac{1,346,269}{832,040}$	1.6180
2,178,309	1,346,269	$\frac{2,178,309}{1,346,269}$	1.6180

HELPFUL HINTS

▶ Look up the Golden Proportion or the Golden Mean in the library or on the World Wide Web. On the World Wide Web, someone has listed the first 10,000 decimals of the Golden Ratio. There are many intriguing examples of the Golden Ratio in nature and in art. From the spirals of stars in the Milky Way to the spiral sections in the shell of the chambered nautilus, the sequence of Fibonacci numbers appears. In the growth patterns of plants and the behavior patterns of atoms we encounter the numbers of the Fibonacci series. They are also to be found in Indonesian gamelan music and in the music of Johann Sebastian Bach, Claude Debussy, and Bela Bartok.

▶ This activity can be used as a review for long division and rounding. However, tell students that when numbers become cumbersome we use the capabilities of the calculator.

▶ Some ratios, such as $\frac{21}{13}$, have repeating decimals. Students may not be aware of this because the calculator shows only a certain number of decimal places. Students may be interested in exploring these fractions.

EVERY DAY ELEMENT

DAILY VARIABLE

FOCUS

▶ Using variables to describe mathematical relationships
▶ Solving expressions using variables
▶ Comparing expressions with variables

MATERIALS

Paper for a chart

FREQUENCY

Allow a student to update the chart daily. Weekend days need not be included. Discuss once a week.

UPDATE PROCEDURE

In May, students will be asked to write and evaluate a mathematical expression tied to the date, using n or x as the variable. The expression will be different each day. Create a chart with three columns labeled *Date*, *Expression*, and *Value*. This chart should be updated each school day during May. Each day, state the expression verbally and allow a student volunteer to write the expression on the chart, using a variable. The student should then evaluate the expression and record the result on the chart. You may also choose to write the expression on the chart and let the student evaluate it and record the result. Discussing the expressions and comparing the values once each week is probably sufficient.

Making this a challenging and fun activity is our goal for this month. By the end of the month, students should be asking to make up expressions of their own, and challenging the class to evaluate them. Enough expressions are included here to cover most of the month, but this activity can be continued into June by encouraging the students to create their own expressions, always tied to the date. Students should use calculators whenever necessary. A list of twenty-one suggested expressions follows.

EXPRESSIONS FOR MAY

Day 1	The date plus 1, or $n + 1$
Day 2	Two times the date, or $2n$
Day 3	Three times the date, or $3n$
Day 4	The date squared, or n^2
Day 5	The date raised to the power of the date, or n^n
Day 6	Ten raised to the power of the date, or 10^n
Day 7	One more than two times the date, or $2n + 1$. If the student writes $2(n+1)$, discuss why these two mathematical expressions are quite different.
Day 8	Ten times the date, or $10n$
Day 9	One half of the date, or $\frac{n}{2}$
Day 10	One hundred percent of the date, or n
Day 11	Two more than three times the date, or $3n + 2$
Day 12	One third of the date, or $\frac{n}{3}$
Day 13	One more than half the date, or $1 + \frac{n}{2}$
Day 14	Two times the date plus one, or $2(n + 1)$
Day 15	Five more than ten times the date, or $10n + 5$
Day 16	The date cubed, or n^3
Day 17	One thousand times the date, or $1000n$
Day 18	Five more than the date squared, or $n^2 + 5$
Day 19	Two raised to the power of the date, or 2^n
Day 20	Ten percent of the date, or $0.1n$
Day 21	The date squared plus the date, or $n^2 + n$

HELPFUL HINT

► Students will enjoy creating their own mathematical expressions. Later in the month, and in June, assign a student to create a new expression as homework that will be shared with the class the next day. You may choose to let the whole class evaluate these student expressions.

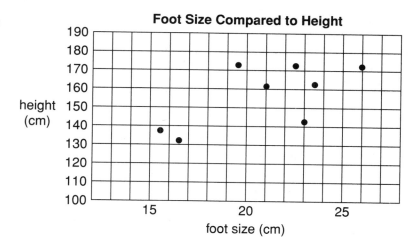

Foot Size Compared to Height

FOCUS
▶ Relating two variables to each other
▶ Interpreting relationships from real data
▶ Using a scatter plot to display data
▶ Using lines of best fit to interpret data

MATERIALS
A large piece of graph paper, metric rulers

FREQUENCY
Update daily. Discuss once a week for the first three weeks.
Discuss more frequently during the last week.

UPDATE PROCEDURE
The daily newspaper is full of reports connecting events. Headlines
proclaim "Taking Vitamin C Prevents the Common Cold," or
"Juvenile Crime Rate Declines With Curfews," or "Knee Injuries
Increase With Size of Football Players." In science, medicine, politics,
and many other fields there are daily advances in finding these connections. To make these conclusions, researchers must make connections between two measures or variables and must show that there is
a close connection between them. This month, students will collect
data, create a scatter plot, and analyze the results to make a connection between two variables. They will practice finding a line of best fit
for the data on the scatter plot. As with any real world measurement,
the data does not always behave as we hope. However, we can still
attempt to discover relationships between two measures.

In May, students will collect data comparing their foot size to their
height to see if any relationship can be discovered between these
two variables. On a piece of graph paper, label the x-axis *Foot size*
and the y-axis *Height*. All measurements will be made in centimeters. Select a pair of students each day to update the graph. One
student will measure the length of a shoe and the height of the
other student and record the data on the scatter plot. As the month
proceeds, students will make predictions about the connection
between shoe length and height. At the end of the month, students
will attempt to make a line of best fit to describe the relationship
between shoe length and height.

DISCUSSION FOR THE FIRST DAY OF THE MONTH

▶ Do you think there is any connection between how old you are and how tall you are? Do you think there might be a connection between how much you study and how well you do on a test? (Allow time for discussion of these questions. Accept a variety of responses. You might want to point out that while there may seem to be a clear connection between age and height to students in the sixth grade who are still growing, this connection does not continue into adulthood.)

▶ This month, we are going to measure how long our feet are and also how tall we are. I want you to think about whether or not there is any connection between the two measurements. What would be a good way to measure your height? (Stand against a wall, use a string, attach a tape measure to the wall, and so on.) How about your shoe size? We don't want to measure the size of your shoes the way they do in a store when you go to buy shoes. In other words, we don't want to know that you wear size seven shoes. We want to know how many centimeters long your shoes are. How can we measure this? (Trace the outline on paper, mark the front and back on paper, and so on.)

▶ On our graph, we will keep track of foot size on the x-axis and height on the y-axis. Let's say that one of you has a shoe length of 20 centimeters and is 150 centimeters tall. Who can show me how we would indicate this on the graph paper? (Make a point above the 20 centimeter mark on the x-axis where that line intersects the 150 centimeter line on the y-axis. This can be thought of as going over to 20 and then up to 150. Notice that we don't mark whose foot and height it is.)

▶ We'll start by measuring one person today and record the information on the graph. This type of graph is called a scatter plot. For the rest of the month, two of you will work together to update the scatter plot each day. One person will measure the shoe length and the height of the other and record the data on the scatter plot. Each student will have a mark on the scatter plot showing that person's height and foot size.

DISCUSSION FOR THE MIDDLE OF THE MONTH

▶ Let's pretend that everyone in our class was the same height, but that we all had different shoe lengths. What would the scatter plot look like? (It would be a horizontal row of dots along one line of the y-axis.) If we all wore the same size shoes but were all different heights, what would it look like? (It would be a vertical row of dots along a line of the x-axis.) Do the points on our scatter plot look like either of these? (No.)

▶ Why do you think this is called a scatter plot? (The points seem to be scattered. They are not in a row or line.)

▶ Is there any pattern to these scattered points? (Hopefully, the points begin to define a diagonal line slanting upward from the lower left. This may not be clear yet because not enough data has been collected.)

▶ Which point represents the smallest shoe length? Which the largest?

▶ Which point represents the shortest height? Which the tallest?

▶ Does the tallest person have the largest shoe length? (Not necessarily.)

- ▶ Are there any people of the same height who have different shoe sizes?
- ▶ How can we record two people whose height and shoe size are the same? (The points would be in the same place on the scatter plot. Perhaps two different colors could be used.)

DISCUSSION FOR THE END OF THE MONTH

- ▶ Are the points on the scatter plot completely random or does a pattern seem to be showing up? If there is a pattern, it means there is a relationship between shoe size and height. How would you describe this pattern? (It appears that height increases as shoe size increases.)
- ▶ Does everyone with a certain shoe size have the same height? (No.) Does everyone with the same height have the same shoe size? (No.)
- ▶ How does the scatter plot show us that there is a relationship between shoe size and height? (The points seem to form a line running diagonally from the lower left corner, where the smallest shoe sizes and heights are, to the upper right corner, where the largest shoe sizes and heights are.)
- ▶ If the shape made by the points moved from the upper left diagonally down to the lower right, what would that tell us about the relationship between shoe size and height? (It would mean that height decreases as shoe size increases.)
- ▶ Sometimes it helps to draw a line that almost fits these points. Even though the points are not in a straight line, it does appear that these points almost make a line. This line is called a line of best fit, and we can use it to make predictions about foot size and height. How can the line of best fit be drawn through these scattered points? (Ideas may include using a ruler to draw a line that passes through as many points as possible or close to the largest number of points, or to use a length of string and move it on the scatter plot until it passes through or close to as many points as possible, or to draw a line so that there are as many points under the line as above it, and so on.)

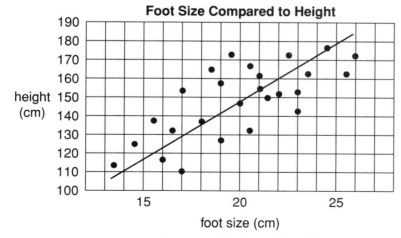

One possible line of best fit

► Let's try several different ways to draw a line of best fit for these points. Are several different lines possible? (Yes.) Which one seems best? (Allow for a variety of answers, and be sure to allow time for discussion.)

► Each line that we have drawn shows a different relationship between shoe size and height. Do they all show a similar relationship? (Probably.)

► Make a decision with the students about which line of best fit seems most accurate. Then ask, Using this line of best fit, can we make a prediction about the height of a person with a shoe length of 20 centimeters? How does this compare to the actual points on the scatter plot? Using this line of best fit, what can we predict about the height of a person with a shoe size of 30 centimeters? How can we test this prediction? (Find some adults with large shoe sizes and measure their heights.)

► How good is our line of best fit at predicting the height and shoe size of a person? (Responses will vary depending on the data and how well the line represents that data.)

► Are there any points that lie very far from the line of best fit? What does this mean? (The line may not be a good rule or pattern for the data.)

HELPFUL HINTS

► Two other strategies are often used to draw a line of best fit.
1. Determine the average shoe size and the average height and make a point at this location on the scatter plot with a red marker. This point is the mean of both the heights and the shoe sizes. Then draw a line that passes through or near as many points as possible, making sure that it passes through this red point.

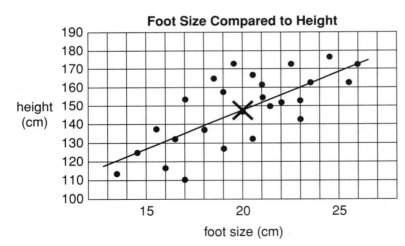

average height – 148 cm
average foot size – 20 cm

2. Divide the points on the scatter plot into three equal groups, except that the lower and upper groups need to contain an odd number of points. Determine the median height and shoe size in both the upper and lower groups and mark these two points with a red marker. The line drawn through these two points should also result in a good line of best fit.

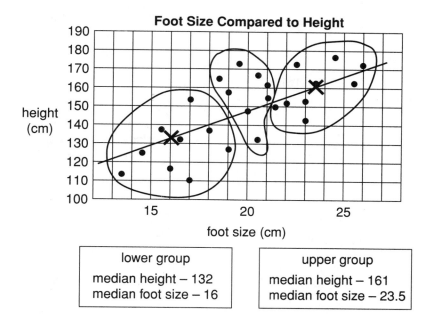

Foot Size Compared to Height

lower group	upper group
median height – 132	median height – 161
median foot size – 16	median foot size – 23.5

▶ The actual data may not lend itself to drawing a line of best fit. The points may be too scattered either because there is no relationship between shoe size and height among the students in the class or because of inaccuracies in the measurements. In this case, the activity will still have the value of demonstrating the difficulty of discovering relationships between two different measures. This may be the first time the students have tried to discover connections between two variables. Even if all you do is to measure the students and plot the data, students will profit from the experience.

▶ Avoid too much formal discussion of lines of best fit. Invite the students to speculate and reason with the data. Encourage them to explain their thinking, rather than imposing rules.

EVERY DAY ELEMENT

DAILY MEASUREMENT

FOCUS

▶ Using concepts of surface area and volume of cubes

▶ Visualizing flat versions, or nets, of three-dimensional shapes

▶ Discovering relationships between edges, surface areas, and volumes of cubes

▶ Identifying the importance of the relationship between surface area and volume in nature

MATERIALS

Centimeter Squared Paper (TR10), Isometric Dot Paper (TR18), paper for a chart, graph paper for two graphs

FREQUENCY

Build or draw the cubes daily for the first two weeks. Later in the month, draw them only when time allows for discussion. Discuss once or twice a week.

UPDATE PROCEDURE

Shape, form, design, and structure are very important parts of our natural world and of the world of things created by human beings. This month, students will explore the concept of surface area and volume of the cube as an introduction to the subject of the volume of solid figures. Before students can use formulas for volume, they need to understand the concept of unit cubes, and how they fill a container. To thoroughly understand surface area, students should practice and visualize wrapping solid figures by using flat versions, or nets, of those figures. Making flat patterns that can be folded into three-dimensional shapes will help students develop strategies for calculating surface area. By examining the relationships between the edges, volumes, and surface areas of cubes that increase in size daily, students can develop important scientific and design insights.

Each day, students will examine a cube with the length of each edge equal to the date in centimeters. The first cube will be the unit cube. In this case, the unit cube is a cube with an edge length of one centimeter. You can use a centimeter cube from a set of base ten blocks or make the unit cube using Centimeter Squared Paper (TR10). Keep it nearby for reference through the month. It is a good visual aid for students who are learning how to understand the volume of cubes. Students will calculate the surface area and volume of each cube and record the values on a chart. For the first few days, students will actually construct the cube, calculating how many squares of the Centimeter Squared Paper (TR10) will be necessary to wrap or cover the cube. As the cubes grow and it becomes impractical to build each one, students can draw the cubes on the Isometric Dot Paper (TR18) in order to visualize the dimensions. At the end of the month, students will study the chart, comparing the length of the edge of each cube with its surface area and volume. Finally, students will consider what happens to the relationship between the surface area and the volume as the cubes grow larger. They will discover that the ratio of surface area to volume decreases as the cubes increase in size.

Unit Cube

Cube 1

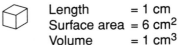

Length = 1 cm
Surface area = 6 cm^2
Volume = 1 cm^3

Cube 2

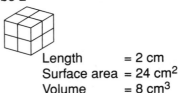

Length = 2 cm
Surface area = 24 cm^2
Volume = 8 cm^3

Cube 3

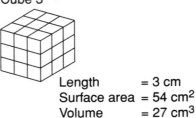

Length = 3 cm
Surface area = 54 cm^2
Volume = 27 cm^3

Cube 4

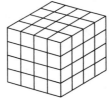

Length = 4 cm
Surface area = 96 cm^2
Volume = 64 cm^3

SAMPLE DISCUSSION FOR THE FIRST DAY OF THE MONTH

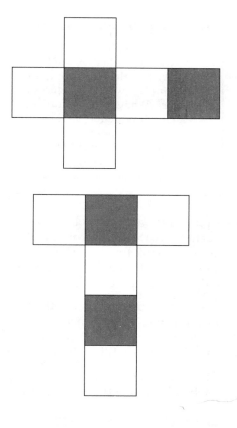

Teacher: (Displaying the unit cube.) Let's look at this single cube. Each edge is one centimeter long. What is the area of one face?

Student: One square centimeter.

Teacher: How many faces does it have?

Student: Six.

Teacher: If I want to wrap this cube with Centimeter Squared Paper, how many square centimeters will it take?

Student: Six.

Teacher: Yes. When manufacturers build boxes, they usually start with flat pieces and then fold them to make the boxes. When you recycle cardboard, you usually undo the folds of the boxes to make them flat again. Sometimes these flat versions of the solids are called nets. Here is a piece of Centimeter Squared Paper. Do you think I could cut out a flat shape that could be folded to make a cube?

Student: Oh, we've done that before. I'll show you how to do it. (Cuts and folds the paper to form a cube.)

Teacher: All right. Can anyone show me a different way to cut and fold a piece of paper to make a cube?

Student: You can move the two side squares next to the top square, like this. (Cuts and folds a differently shaped piece of paper to form a cube.)

Teacher: I'll leave some of this paper out and challenge you to find all the ways that six squares can be arranged so they fold up to make a cube. There may be more ways than you think. How many one-centimeter-long cubes will fit into the cube we have made from the paper?

Student: One.

Teacher: That's right. The volume of this cube is one cubic centimeter. We need 6 square centimeters of paper to cover the cube. That is called the surface area of the cube. Think of it as the amount of paper necessary to cover all the surfaces of the cube, including the bottom. Let's make a chart. What is the length of one edge of this cube?

Student: One centimeter.

Teacher: What is the surface area?

Student: Six square centimeters.

Teacher: What is the volume of this cube?

Student: 1 cubic centimeter.

Teacher: Yes. Tomorrow is the 2nd day of May. We'll build a cube with an edge of 2 centimeters. What will the surface area of that cube be?

Student: Four square centimeters?

Teacher: How did you get that?

Student: Well, there are four square centimeters on each face.

Teacher: True, and how many faces are there?

Student: Oh, six. So there are 6 times 4 squares, or 24 square centimeters.

Teacher: How many cubic centimeters will we need to build this cube?

Student: Eight.

Teacher: How did you get that?

Student: There are four cubic centimeters on the bottom row and four on the top.

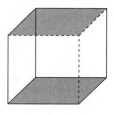

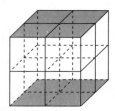

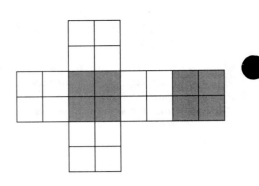

SAMPLE DISCUSSION CONTINUED

Teacher: I would like you to think about what square paper shapes can be made that will fold into a cube that looks like this. What is the height of this cube?

Student: It's two centimeters high.

Teacher: What are the width and length of the cube?

Student: It is a cube, so they are all two centimeters long.

Teacher: If we increase the length of the edge each day by one centimeter, I wonder how many cubic centimeters it will take to fill the cube on the last day of the month. What will the dimensions of that cube be?

Create a four-column chart to show the length of the edge, the surface area, and the volume of each cube. Leave the fourth column blank for now. Have the students calculate and record the values daily for each cube, even if you don't take time to build the cubes or discuss them every day.

Create a graph comparing the length of an edge to the surface area of each cube. Label the x-axis *Length of edge* and label the y-axis *Surface area*. Points on the graph can be plotted at the same time the students are filling in the chart each day.

Create a graph comparing the length of an edge to the volume of each cube. Label the x-axis *Length of edge* and the y-axis *Volume*.

Length of edge (cm)	Surface area (cm²)	Volume (cm³)	
1	6	1	
2	24	8	
3	54	27	
4	96	64	
5	150	125	
6	216	216	
7	294	343	
8	384	512	
9	486	729	
10	600	1000	
11	726	1331	
12	864	1728	
13	1014	2197	
14	1176	2744	
15	1350	3375	
16	1536	4096	
17	1734	4913	
18	1944	5832	
19	2166	6859	
20	2400	8000	

DISCUSSION FOR THE MIDDLE OF THE MONTH

Refer often to the chart and the graphs to help the students understand the mathematical relationships being discussed.

▶ What scale do you think we will need to record the surface area and volume of the cubes? We know that the largest edge length we'll record is 31 centimeters, because the length is always the same as the date. But how high do you think the numbers for the surface area will go? (There will be 5766 square centimeters of surface area.) Should we label the y-axis in increments of 10, 100, or 200 centimeters? (Using the larger increment will make the size of the graph reasonable, but the first few points will be difficult to plot.) What range of numbers will we need to record the volume on the other graph? (From 1 to 29,791 cubic centimeters. Again, using a larger increment will help to make the graph manageable but will also make it hard to plot the points. Wrestling with these issues of graphing and scale will help students as they advance in mathematics.)

▶ Do the points on these graphs give us a straight line? (No, because they are graphs showing exponential growth.)

▶ Which increases more, the surface area or the volume, as the length of each edge increases? (The volume, because it is the length cubed.)

▶ As the cube grows, what happens to the relationship between the surface area and the volume? (This proportion decreases. On the 5th day, the proportion is 150 square centimeters to 125 cubic centimeters. On the 20th day, it is 2400 square centimeters to 8000 cubic centimeters.)

DISCUSSION FOR THE END OF THE MONTH

Label the fourth column of the chart *Proportion between surface area and volume.* Explain that to determine the proportion between the surface area of an object and its volume, we need to discover how many times larger one is than the other. We do this by dividing the surface area by the volume. The column should then be filled in from the beginning of the month. Calculators should be used for the calculations once the numbers get too large for easy mental computing.

▶ What happens to the proportion between the surface area and the volume of the cubes as the length increases? (It decreases.)

▶ When does it equal 1? (On the 6th day, when the edge is six centimeters long.) Can you explain why that is true? (Because the surface area and the volume are both 6 × 6 × 6.)

▶ What other patterns do you see on this chart? (If you multiply the length of the edge times the surface area and divide that number by the volume, you always get six.) How can we explain why that is true? (The volume of a cube is the edge times the edge times the edge. The surface area of a cube is 6 times the edge times the edge. When you multiply the surface area by the edge, you get 6 times the edge times the edge times the edge, which is the same expression as the one we used to describe the volume, except for the 6. In other words, you have this mathematical expression:

$$\frac{\text{length of edge times surface area}}{\text{volume}} = \frac{6\,(\text{edge} \times \text{edge} \times \text{edge})}{(\text{edge} \times \text{edge} \times \text{edge})} = 6$$

Students may be intrigued by this relationship, but it may be very difficult to understand. Be sure to use block models or drawings to demonstrate it. This should not be considered an essential part of the discussion, but rather as an incentive for further understanding of the relationship between the surface area and volume of three-dimensional figures.)

▶ The relationship between surface area and volume plays a critical role in the natural world. Small plants and animals have more surface area compared to their volume. They easily lose moisture or heat. Large plants and animals have smaller surface areas compared to their volume, generating lots of heat or retaining more water. They don't lose as much water or heat to evaporation. This relationship also helps to see why it is more expensive to gift wrap many small packages than it is to wrap one large package made up of several smaller ones. We can say that it is cheaper to wrap one large cube made up of many small cubes than it is to wrap lots of individual small cubes.

▶ Encourage the students to find examples of the relationship between surface area and volume in the natural world. For example, they might examine desert animals and plants and compare them to cold climate animals and plants.

Length of edge (cm)	Surface area (cm²)	Volume (cm³)	Proportion between surface area and volume
1	6	1	6.0
2	24	8	3.0
3	54	27	2.0
4	96	64	1.5
5	150	125	1.2
6	216	216	1.0
7	294	343	0.86
8	384	512	0.75
9	486	729	0.66
10	600	1000	0.60
11	726	1331	0.55
12	864	1728	0.50
13	1014	2197	0.46
14	1176	2744	0.43
15	1350	3375	0.40
16	1536	4096	0.38
17	1734	4913	0.35
18	1944	5832	0.33
19	2166	6859	0.32
20	2400	8000	0.30
21	2646	9261	0.29
22	2904	10,648	0.27
23	3174	12,167	0.26
24	3456	13,824	0.25
25	3750	15,625	0.24
26	4056	17,576	0.23
27	4374	19,683	0.22
28	4704	21,952	0.21
29	5046	24,389	0.21
30	5400	27,000	0.20
31	5766	29,791	0.19

HELPFUL HINTS

▶ You may want to make models of all eleven nets of a cube and display them for the students. Be sure to show them how each one folds to create the cube.

▶ Ask the students to find ways to put six small cubes together in such a way that they do not form a cube. There are, of course, many ways to do this, but it will be interesting for the students to see how many different and unusual three-dimensional shapes can be created.

▶ Some students may enjoy building nets of the cubes on different days. This is best done early in the month, when the size of the paper needed is manageable.

▶ Beginning around the 7th day, have the students draw the cubes on Isometric Dot Paper (TR18) instead of having them build actual models. Students enjoy the three-dimensional quality of this paper and, with some practice, can use it effectively.

▶ It is not necessary to update this element every day after the first ten or eleven cubes. When you do update, be sure to build or draw the cubes whenever you have discussion days.

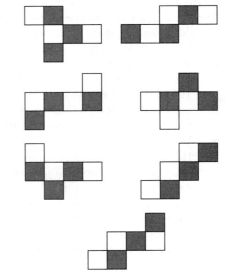

Every day element   CODA

As you can tell, this book emphasizes strategies for helping mathematics make sense to students. It attempts to highlight the underlying patterns of mathematics and to enable students to appreciate the usefulness of these patterns, as well as their beauty and intricacy. If we can capture the imagination and sense of wonder of the students, as well as their reasoning ability, we provide them the means to pursue and enjoy mathematics throughout their school careers and long after.

In music, a coda is a section at the end of a composition that restates or reuses some of the themes from the main body of the work and draws it to a conclusion. It is as if the composer is reluctant to let go of the material that has been developed throughout the piece. In that same way, as a celebration of the incredible beauty of patterns in mathematics, this final pattern is offered to be studied and enjoyed by both teacher and students.

1	X	1	=	1
11	X	11	=	121
111	X	111	=	12321
1111	X	1111	=	1234321
11111	X	11111	=	123454321
111111	X	111111	=	12345654321
1111111	X	1111111	=	1234567654321
11111111	X	11111111	=	123456787654321
111111111	X	111111111	=	12345678987654321

Baratta-Lorton, Mary. "The Opening," *Math Their Way Newsletter 1977–78*. Saratoga, CA: The Center for Innovation in Education.

Blocksma, Mary. *Reading the Numbers*. New York, NY: Viking, 1989.

Burns, Marilyn. *About Teaching Mathematics*. Sausalito, CA: Math Solutions Publications, 1992.

Burns, Marilyn, and Cathy Humphreys. *A Collection of Math Lessons From Grades 6 Through 8*. Sausalito, CA: Math Solutions Publications, 1990.

Curcio, Frances R., Nadine S. Bezuk, and others. *Understanding Rational Numbers and Proportions: Addenda Series, Grades 5–8*. Reston, VA: National Council of Teachers of Mathematics, 1991.

Friel, Susan, Janice Mokros, and Susan Jo Russell. *Middles, Means, and In-Betweens*, a unit of study from *Used Numbers: Real Data in the Classroom*. Palo Alto, CA: Dale Seymour Publications, 1992.

Garland, Trudi Hammel. *Fascinating Fibonaccis: Mystery and Magic in Numbers*. Palo Alto, CA: Dale Seymour Publications, 1987.

Green, Thomas, and Charles L. Hamberg. *Pascal's Triangle*. Palo Alto, CA: Dale Seymour Publications, 1986.

Hyde, Arthur A., and Pamela R. Hyde. *Mathwise: Teaching Mathematical Thinking and Problem Solving*. Portsmouth, NH: Heinemann Educational Books, Inc., 1991.

Mathematical Sciences Education Board. *Measuring Up: Prototypes for Mathematics Assessment*. Washington, DC: National Academy Press, 1993.

Pappas, Theoni. *The Magic of Mathematics*. San Carlos, CA: Wide World Publishing/Tetra, 1994.

Pappas, Theoni. *More Joy of Mathematics*. San Carlos, CA: Wide World Publishing/Tetra, 1991.

Phillips, Elizabeth, with Theodore Gardella, Constance Kelly, and Jacqueline Stewart. *Patterns and Functions: Addenda Series, Grades 5–8*. Reston, VA: National Council of Teachers of Mathematics, 1991.

Rowan, Thomas E., and Lorna J. Morrow. *Implementing the K–8 Curriculum and Evaluation Standards: Readings from the Arithmetic Teacher*. Reston, VA: National Council of Teachers of Mathematics, 1992.

Wirtz, Robert. *Drill and Practice at a Problem-Solving Level*. Monterey, CA: Curriculum Development Assoc., Inc., 1980.

Zawojewski, Judith S., and others. *Dealing with Data and Chance: Addenda Series Grades 5–8*. Reston, VA: National Council of Teachers of Mathematics, 1991.

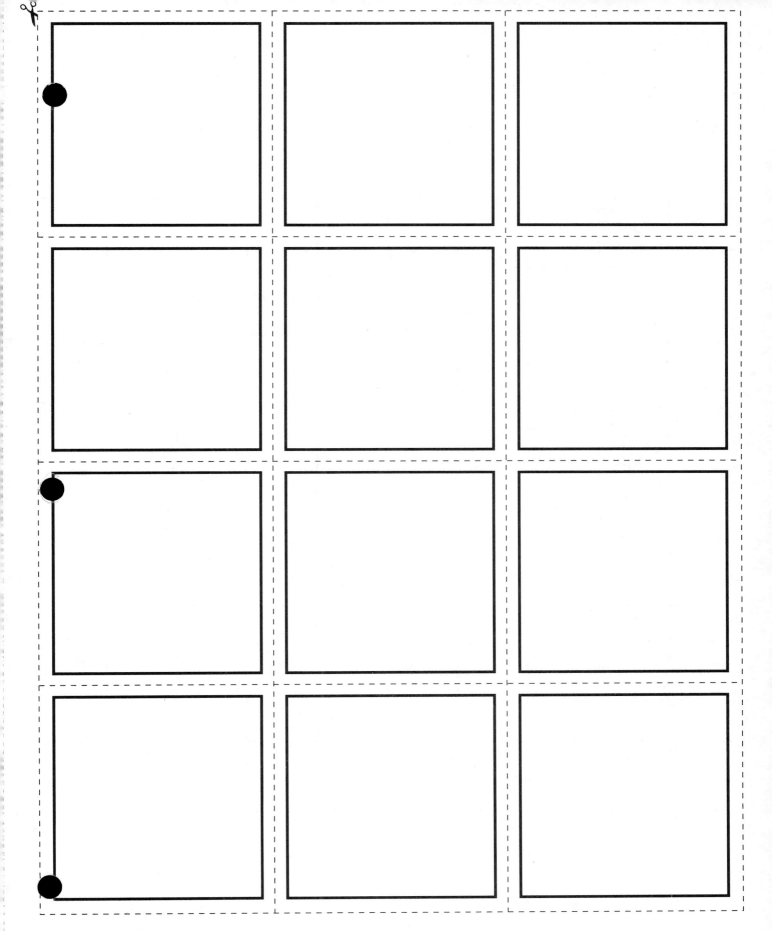

TR1 Square Cutouts

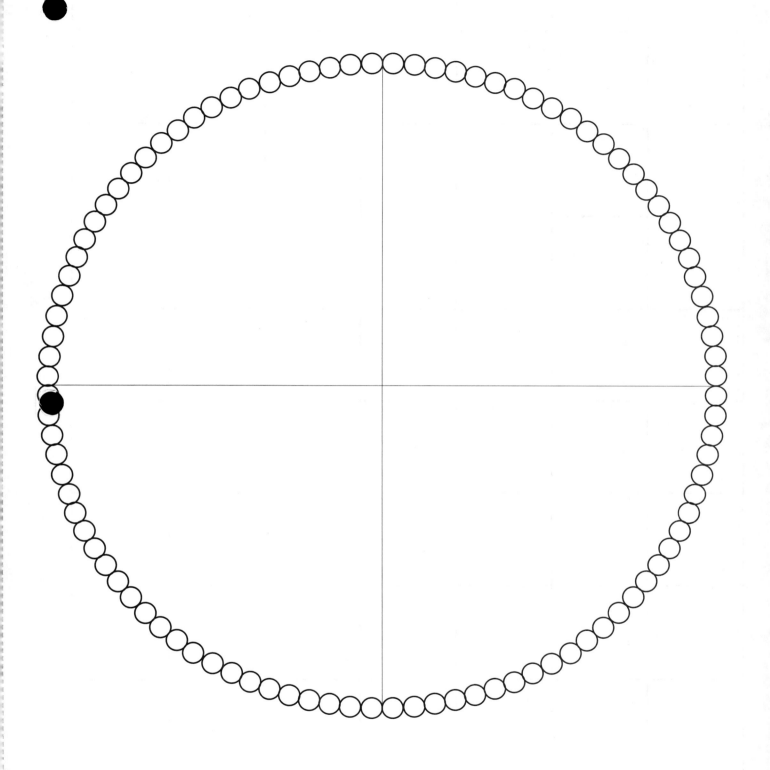

TR3 Percent Circle

TR4 Inch Squared Paper

TR5 **Play Money: Small Bills**

TR6   Play Money: Large Bills

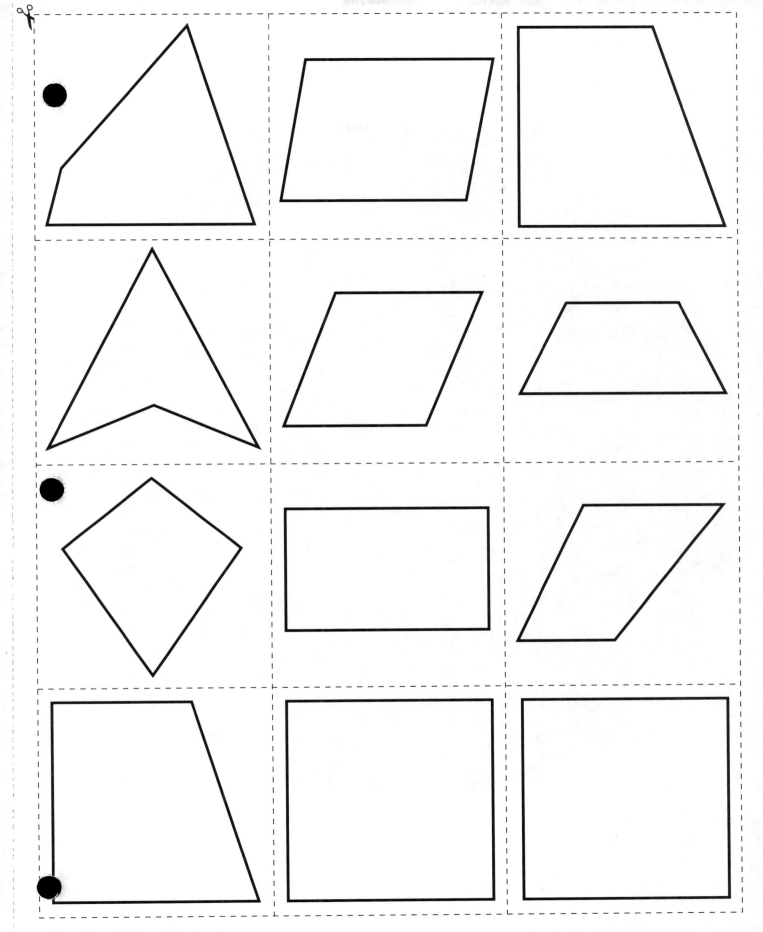

TR7 Quadrilateral Cutouts

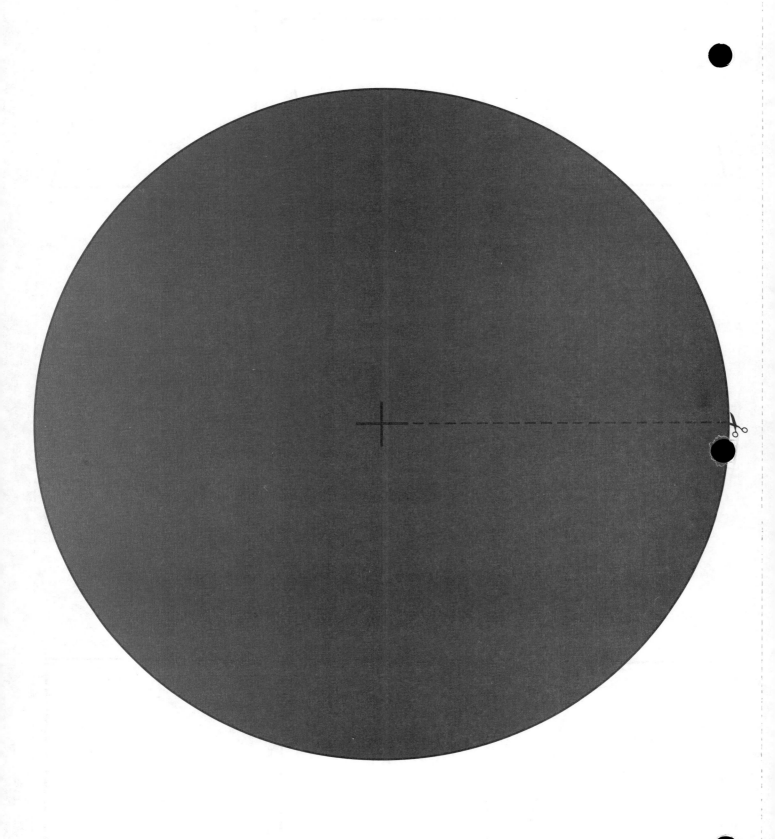

TR8   November Circle (Gray)

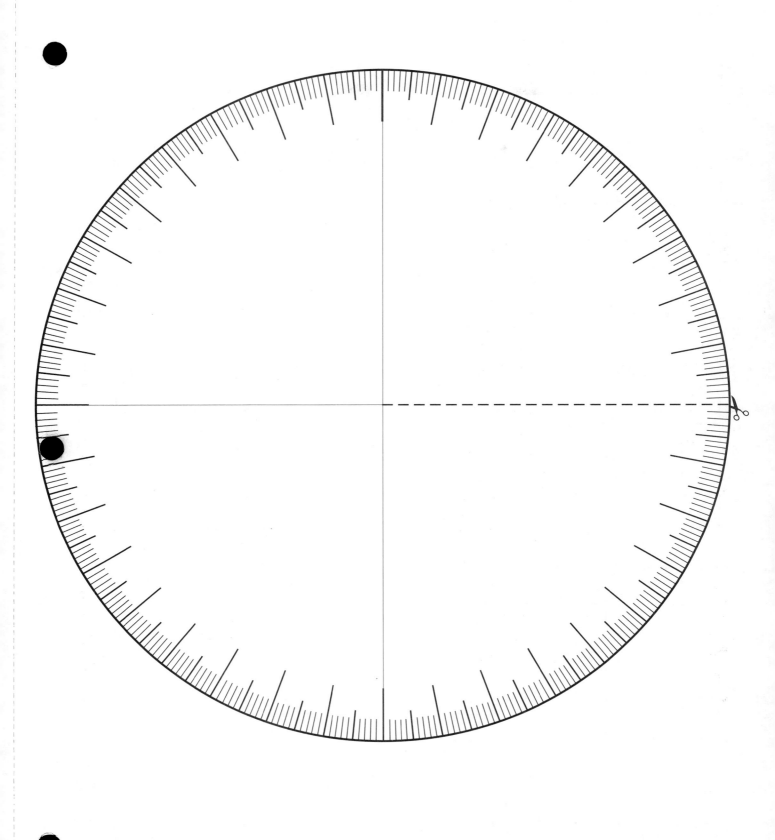

TR9 **November Circle (White)**

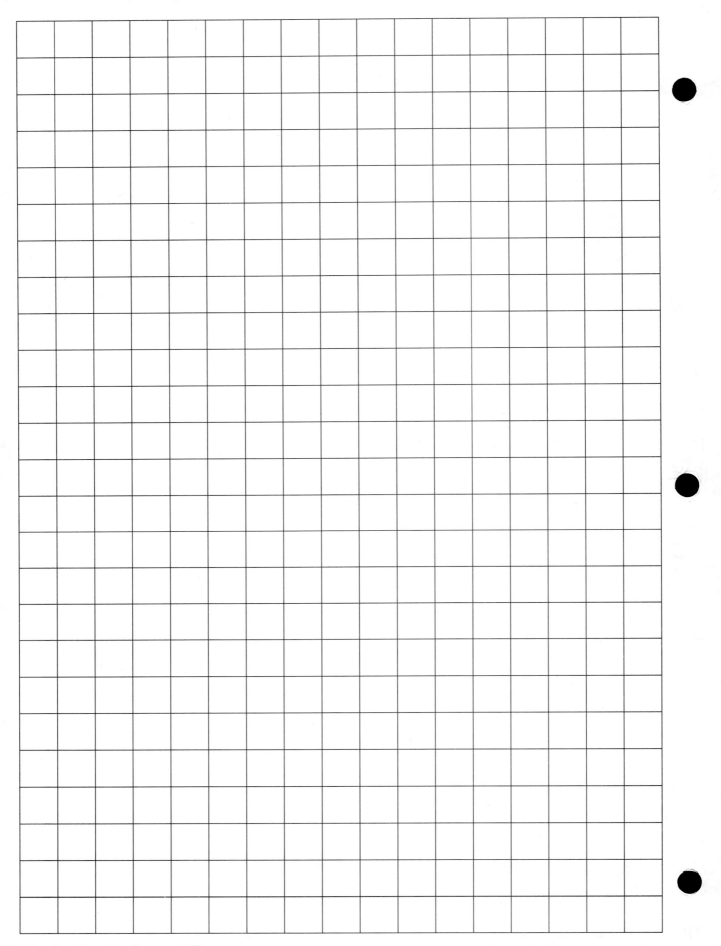

TR10 **Centimeter Squared Paper**

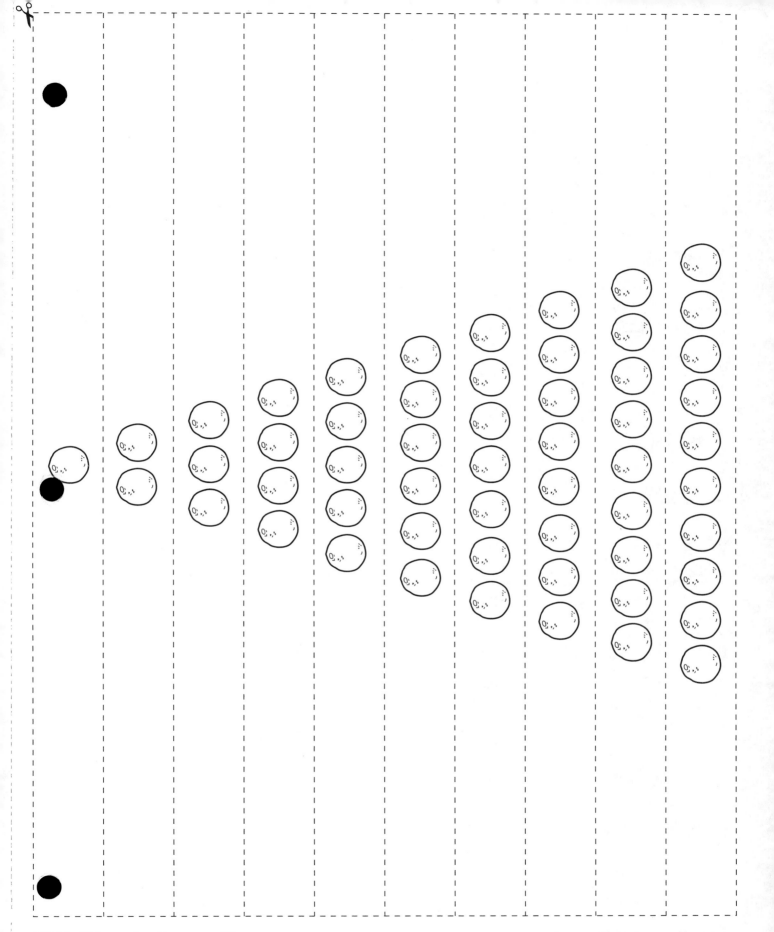

TR11   Triangular Oranges (1)

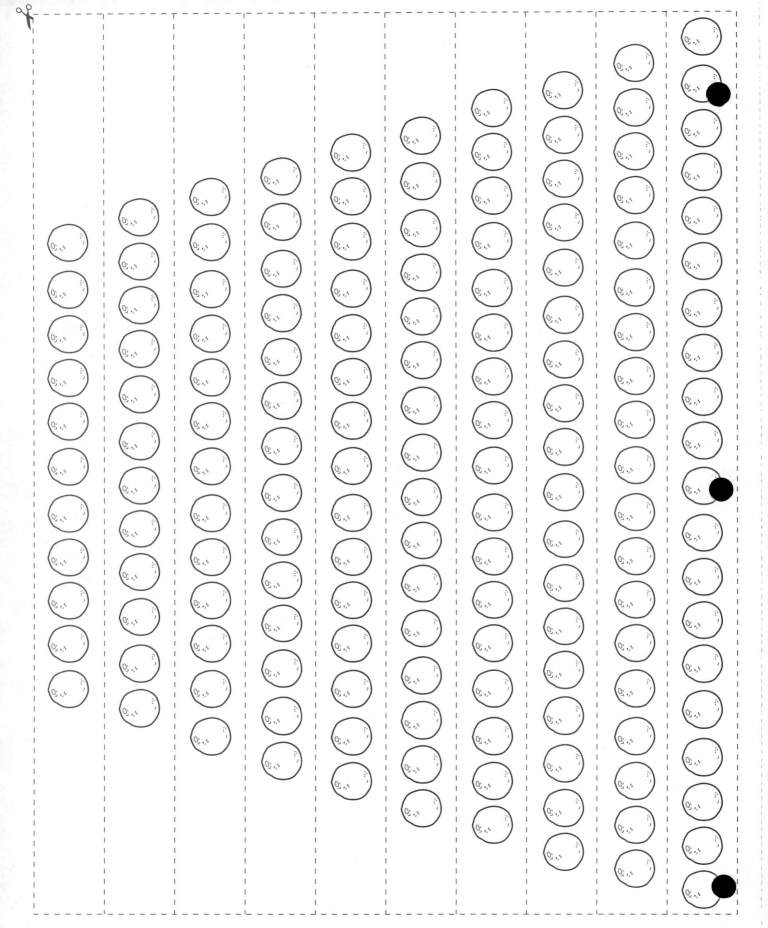

TR12 **Triangular Oranges (2)**

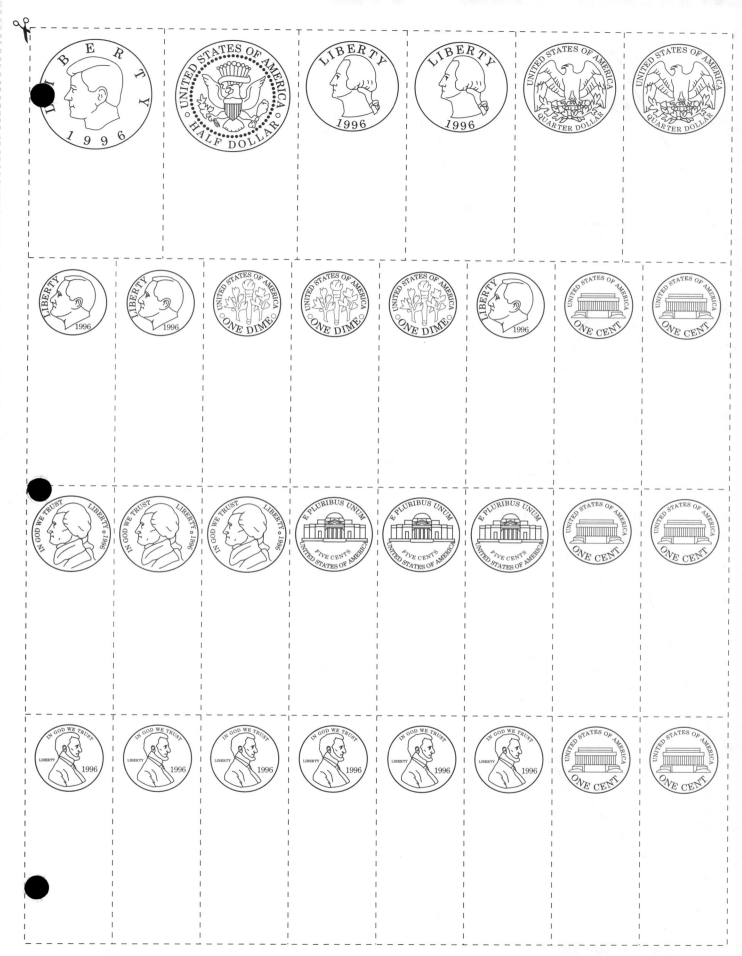

TR13 Play Money—Coins

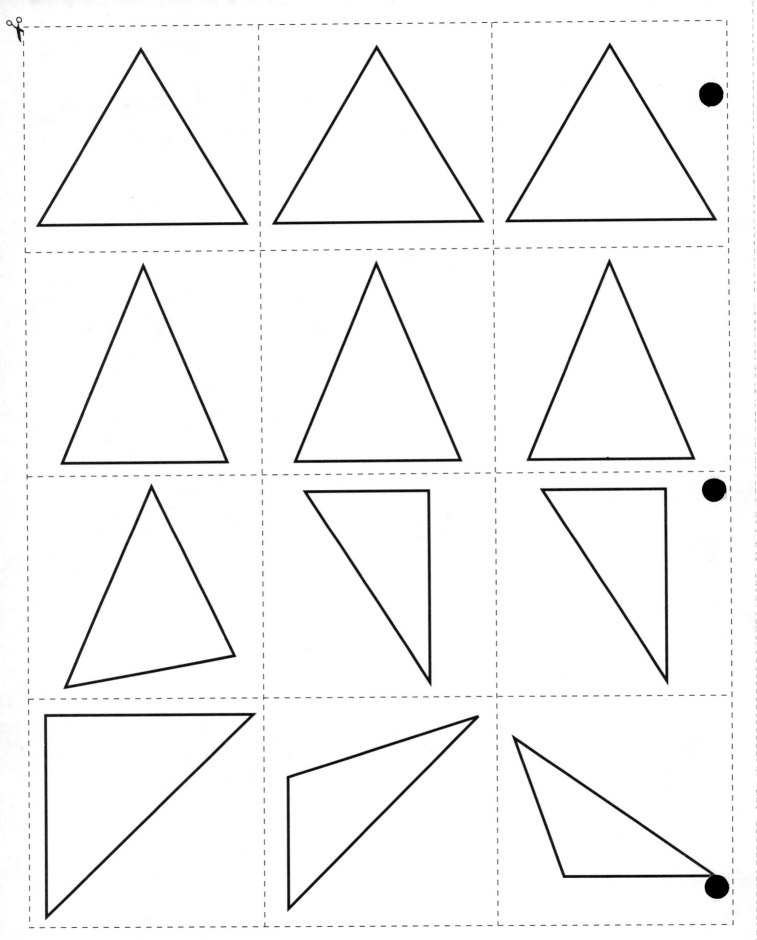

TR14 Triangle Cutouts

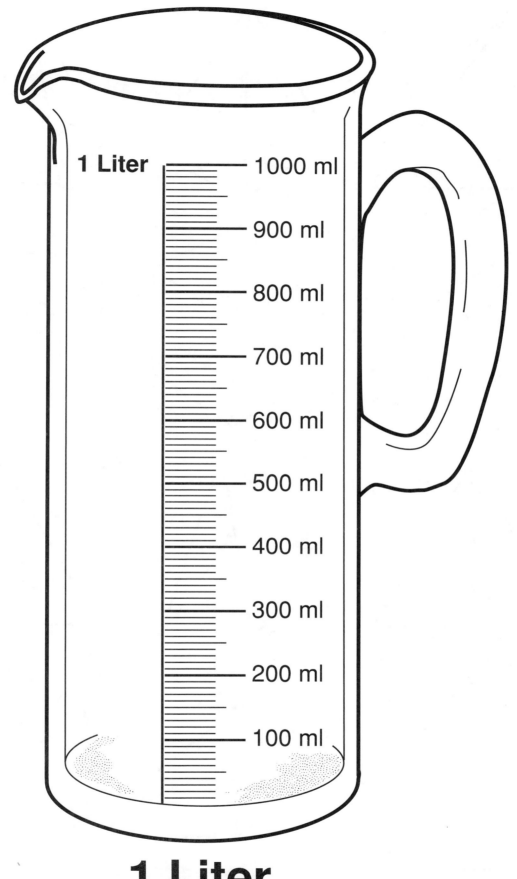

1 Liter

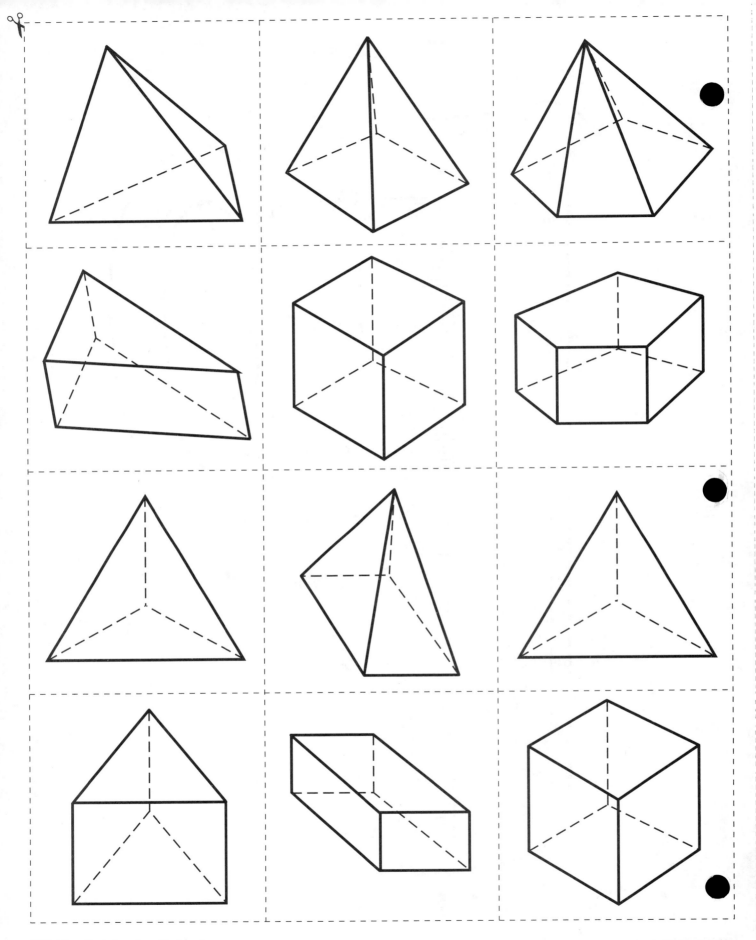

TR16   Polyhedra Cutouts

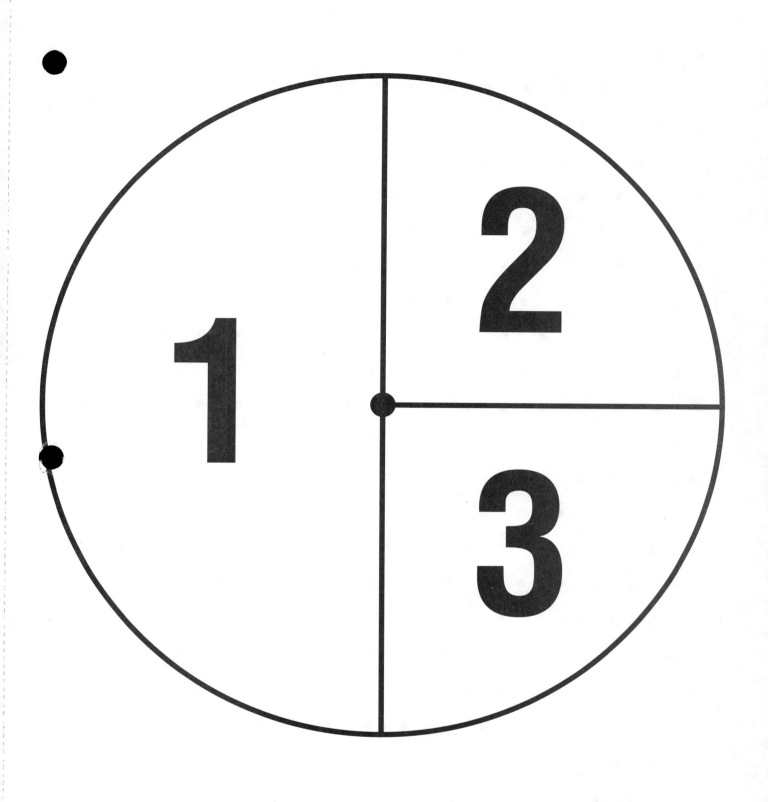

TR17 **April Circle Spinner**

TR18 **Isometric Dot Paper**

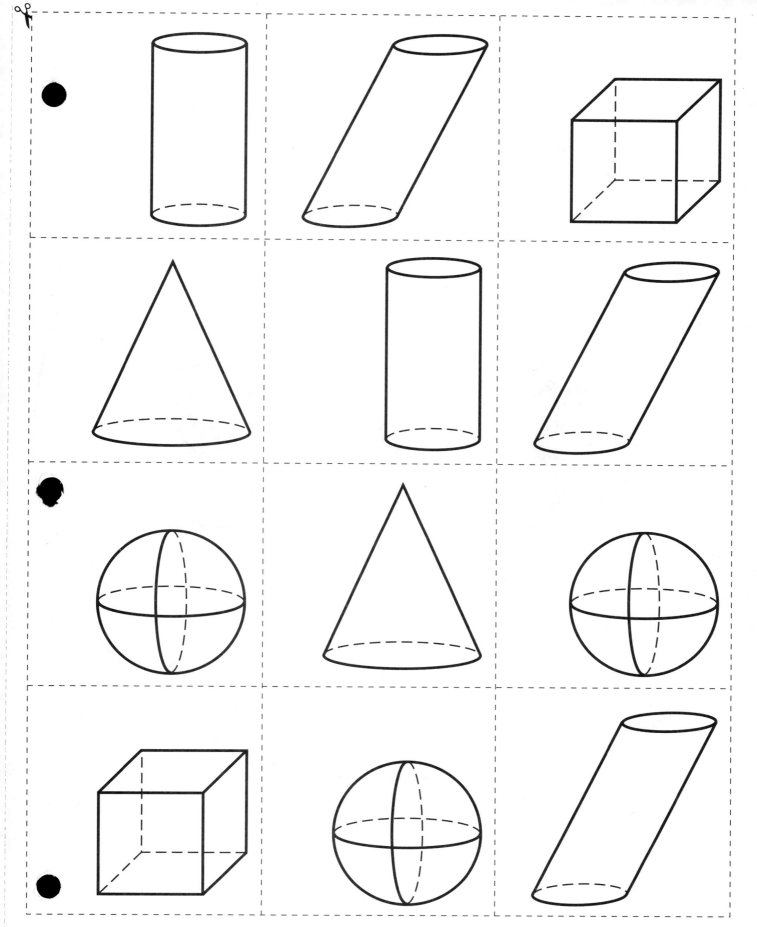

TR19 **Solid Figures Cutouts**

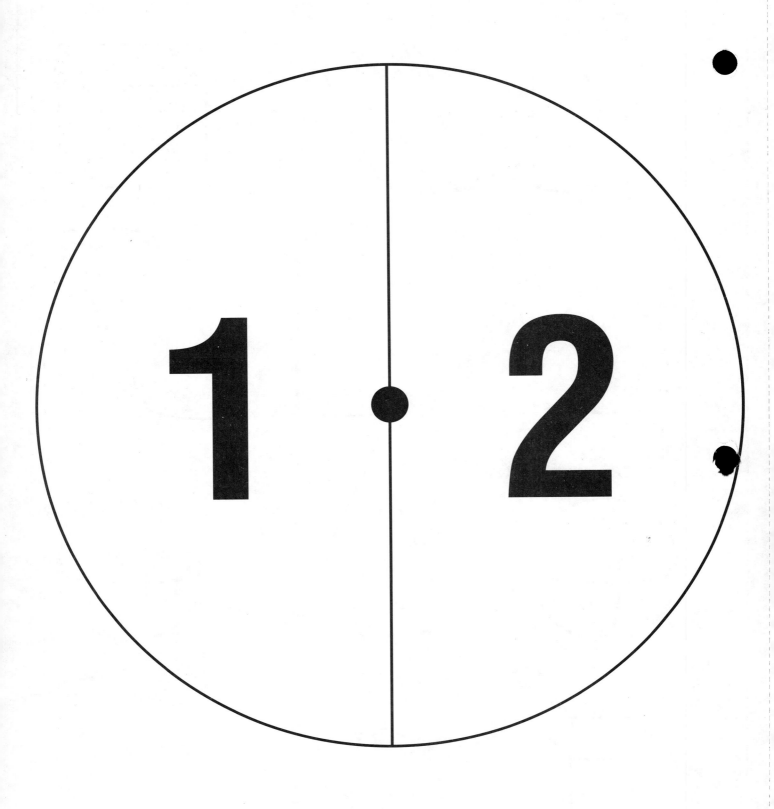

TR20 May Circle Spinner